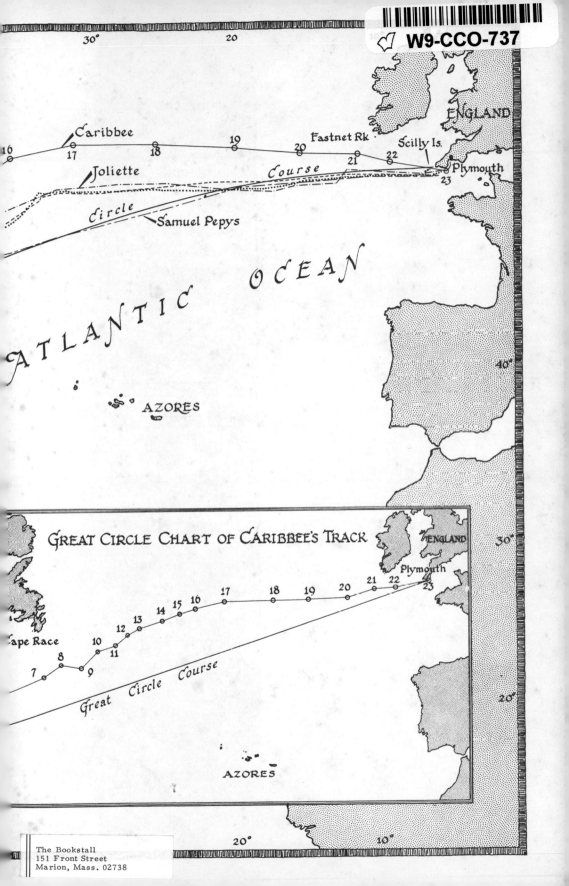

30°   20

Caribbee
16   17   18   19   20   Fastnet Rk   Scilly Is.
                                            21   22   Plymouth
Joliette   Course   23
Circle
Samuel Pepys

ATLANTIC   OCEAN

AZORES

40°

GREAT CIRCLE CHART OF CARIBBEE'S TRACK

ENGLAND
Plymouth
                                        21   22
                    17   18   19   20   23
              15 16
           14
        13
     12
Cape Race   10   30°
  8   11
7   9

Great Circle Course

20°

AZORES

20°   10°

Passage East

Books by Carleton Mitchell

ISLANDS TO WINDWARD

YACHTSMAN'S CAMERA

BEYOND HORIZONS

PASSAGE EAST

Passage East

BY CARLETON MITCHELL

W · W · NORTON & COMPANY · INC · New York

Copyright © 1953 by Carleton Mitchell. All rights reserved. Published simultaneously
in Canada by George J. McLeod Limited, Toronto. Printed in the United States of
America.

Library of Congress Cataloging in Publication Data
Mitchell, Carleton, 1910–
    Passage east.

    1. Caribee (Yawl).   2. North Atlantic Ocean.
I. Title.
GV822.C3M5   1977   910'.45   77–14491
ISBN 0–393–03208–6

1 2 3 4 5 6 7 8 9 0

To My Shipmates

Contents

Illustrations

Preface

THIS BOOK has two purposes: to give anyone interested in the sea, even those not "sailors" in the usual sense of the word, an understanding of a long ocean race under sail; and to explain some of the concepts which divide the seaman's world from the landsman's—a three-deck world: the surface of the sea, the ocean of atmosphere above, the hidden depths beneath.

Modern man has almost forgotten the feeling of dependence upon the elements, of moving only at the will of wind and current. But the ocean in 1952 was as in 1492: despite comforts, equipment, and food not available to the old voyagers, the basic problems are unchanged.

Racing a small yacht across the North Atlantic is not entirely a technical feat nor even an adventure in the classic sense; but it is a great emotional and physical experience for those involved— moments of exhaustion and exultation, of cold fog and blazing sunshine, of hard driving and maddening drifting. And always watch after watch the routine of living and shipkeeping goes on, day and night, with never a sense of monotony.

Admittedly those whose knowledge of sailing and the sea is limited will fail to follow certain terms, yet the author has especially tried to communicate some of the moments he has been fortunate enough to experience to those whose voyaging is done from that chair by the fire.

This then is essentially the story of nine people aboard a 57-foot yawl for 21 days 3 hours 19 minutes 40 seconds, intent on sailing as quickly as possible a course of 2870 miles across the most varied of waters, the North Atlantic Ocean between Bermuda and England. It is a record of the good moments and the bad, of hopes and fears, triumphs and disappointments, put down as close as possible to the moment of action.

I hope you will come aboard as the tenth shipmate.

Christmas Day, 1952
On board *The Boatel*
Annapolis, Maryland.

Preface to the 1977 Edition

In the span of years since *Passage East* was written, yachting has undergone many changes. Yet as I noted in the Preface to the original edition, "the ocean in 1952 was as in 1492," and the same is true today. New measurement rules have radically altered design, traditional materials have been replaced by technological miracles, the proliferation of fleets and composition of crews reflect a whole new way of life ashore. But waiting beyond the last buoy are the timeless elements of what I think of as the Sailor's Three-Deck World: the surface of the sea, the atmosphere above, and the hidden depths below. Together they have influenced every voyage since man first ventured onto wide waters. A Bahamian fisherman squinting at the sky as norther clouds gathered once observed, "You eats what the cook serves," and here is a watch by watch chronicle of how it is, set down while it is happening—moments of fatigue, discomfort, frustration, and apprehension, intermingled with elation, laughter, and just plain joy in the way of a boat with wind and wave. Such memories are timeless, and I hope this new edition of *Passage East* will share them with those who sail in *Caribbee's* wake, including those whose distant voyaging is done from that chair by the fire.

Aboard *Coyaba*
Gorda Sound,
British Virgin Islands

After Bermuda comes the Royal Ocean Racing Club's Trans-Atlantic Race. . . . With a course of 2870 miles to Plymouth, it is more of a steeplechase, the "Grand National" of sailing, the fences being the heat of the Sargasso Sea, a slice of Gulf Stream, Grand Banks fog combined with drift ice, the mid-ocean "area of maximum gale probabilities," a landfall on the Scillies after a long sea passage, and finally the chance of a calm with a foul tide at the Lizard.

Royal Naval Sailing Association Journal
May 1952

It is 7:15 Bermuda time: 7:15 P.M. of Wednesday, July 2, 1952. The wind is northeast by east at 22 miles an hour, and the sky is overcast—a most un-Bermudalike day and extremely careless of the Royal Bermuda Yacht Club, to say nothing of the Trade Development Board.

We are now on the starboard tack. Clear of the backwash along the reefs the sea is longer and more regular. *Caribbee* is driving through, rather than plunging. Sheets of spray rifle back along the weather deck, wetting the lower part of the mainsail and us in the cockpit. Along the lee deck there is a millrace, a solid mass of rushing water. When we tacked Bobby was swept to his knees as he took the backstay forward. But this is Sargasso Sea water, pleasant from the stored heat of the tropical sun. No one minds a dunking. It will be different in a few days.

We go well. I can feel it in the seat of my pants, and see it by the way we are dropping the other boats and by the needle of the Kenyon speed indicator in the cockpit—we never slow below 7 knots, and most of the time are touching eight. We carry the double head rig combination of large jibtopsail, forestaysail, main, and mizzen, best for this amount of wind and sea. We sail *Caribbee* full, getting maximum drive to smash through crests which would otherwise stop her. Wet, but effective. Once again I am reminded that in other than calm water you don't sail a boat to windward—you force her. Delicacy of touch on the helm and the trim of the sails and knowledge of all the factors involved is necessary, but real headway is a matter of brute force, of sheer power, the drive of the wind pitted against the resistance of the sea, an elemental struggle.

15

Our course is nowhere near the most direct line to England, the great-circle route. Somehow it doesn't seem fair to start a race of 2870 miles with a dead muzzler on a gray chill day. We have to expect a little of everything on the way across, but at least we should have some encouragement as long as land is in sight. This is rubbing it in.

Already the fleet has scattered. We started at 6:00 off St. David's Head, just where we had finished the race from Newport a week ago. Although we have spent 4 days 7 hours 23 minutes racing over a course of 635 nautical miles to reach this point in our passage east, we still have nearly as far to go as when we lost sight of Block Island at dusk on June 21. So we're actually crossing the North Atlantic on what a golfer would call a "dogleg" course.

At the start *Janabel*, the French entry, and *Caribbee*, which might be called the American entry, crossed the line on the port tack. The committee boat was rolling and plunging heavily, being anchored on a lee shore, but we came close enough to exchange insults with Commodore "Shorty" Trimingham and the other representatives of the Royal Bermuda Yacht Club, which with the Royal Ocean Racing Club is jointly sponsoring this Trans-Atlantic Race. We boiled down on the committee boat as we broke out the topsail, somebody yelled "The first 3000 miles are the toughest!" and we were off—dead in *Janabel's* wake and backwind. But it was still a good start, all five boats crossing within a few seconds, and *Caribee* soon walked out to weather of *Janabel*.

The English boats—*Marabu, Joliette*, and *Samuel Pepys*—chose the other end of the line and a starboard tack start. They are sailing parallel to the reefs, and it does not appear they can clear without tacking. They may figure on smoother water in close, or perhaps a favoring current, but earlier we decided to stand right out into deep water before coming about. We tacked at 6:45—half an hour ago—and *Janabel* followed immediately. At this moment she is dead in our wake and nearly a half-mile back, seeming to be slowed by hobbyhorsing in this particular condition

Hoisting sails before the start:

"It is a most un-Bermudalike day, extremely careless of the Royal Bermuda Yacht Club...somehow it doesn't seem fair to start a race of 2870 miles with a dead muzzler on a gray chill day."

"There is no sensation in the world to equal driving to windward in the open sea with just the right amount of breeze . . . . This is it; this is what we came for."

of sea. It is still too soon to tell whether playing the reefs paid off for the English boats, but it doesn't look as though it did.

11:15 p.m.—My last log entry was rudely interrupted by a thumping sound from the bow at every plunge. On going forward I found the port spinnaker pole adrift and in great danger of going overboard. It was secured in a teak chock forward and a teak cup aft; the force of water had split the chock and the pole was loose except for the heel resting in the cup. If it jumped out there wasn't anything to keep it from washing aft in the millrace along the lee deck and right out under the life lines. So I scrambled down and wrapped arms and legs around everything in range, and yelled like hell. Bobby Symonette and Frank MacLear immediately came to help, and we got it lashed. This new system of chocking was put on before sailing to eliminate lashing. But now both poles are lashed—at the cost of a thorough wetting. It was like being dunked clear under in those dear dead bowsprit days. Streams jetted up oilskin pant legs and down sleeves, meeting a major river through the neck. All met at the navel. I was wrong about this water not being cold. But think of it another 15 or 20 degrees farther north, somewhere up in the area of the Labrador Current, with a few freshly melted icebergs mixed in!

This is being written sitting on the top step of the companionway, sheltered by the canvas hood; the notebook is on my knees and a flashlight is wedged against the centerboard trunk. Months ago, when I decided to enter *Caribbee* in the Trans-Atlantic Race and began planning, I made up my mind to keep a personal log all the way, and to set down thoughts and feelings as close as possible to the moment of action. Since I am lazy about such things, and rarely keep good resolutions, that entry made right after the start is almost a surprise. If I could settle down enough to do it then, the rest should be easy.

It has been a hard day. For that matter, it has been a hard five months, ever since St. Petersburg, a few hours before the race to Havana. I had spoken to Frank MacLear in Nassau about coming along as navigator, if *Caribbee* went to England; I had spoken to others, too, and talked it over with Zib, but somehow couldn't really decide. Then Frank came walking down the dock and I heard my voice saying: "Glad to see you, Frank. Wanted to let you know *Caribbee* definitely will race to England." So that was that. From then until the gun went off this afternoon it has been a grind to be ready for that gun—details, details, details. Now the tension is ebbing and a sense of enjoyment—maybe even a sense of humor—is reasserting itself. After all, everything possible has been done to make the boat fast and fully ready for sea, and stocked against every possible need and emergency, and we have aboard as good a group of sailors as could be found anywhere— so from now on to hell with everything except making the boat go, and having fun doing it.

Maybe a sense of humor is reasserting itself already because suddenly today seems funny. My depression began with a first look from the window of our rented cottage: the morning was gray and overcast and a chill northeast wind whipped up white-caps all across Hamilton Harbor. Being sensitive to weather, I don't like nor'easters, not even this far south—not even at what Erroll Bruce last night called "the capital of the Sargasso Sea." Or maybe they seem particularly disagreeable in a part of the world where you don't expect them. Anyway, after one look at the toss-ing fleet I felt lower than a barnacle on a submarine cable—with maybe a bit of backlash from our "last supper" wine contributing to the very gray grayness of the day. I dressed dolefully, packed my duffle bag with all the impatient haste of a man catching a tumbrel, and kissed Zib goodbye with a sensation of finality.

On arriving at *Caribbee* I found the dinghy had vanished—no one knew where, when, or why—and a spare genoa jib, flown down from New York to replace one lost in the Bermuda Race, had not come aboard. In the first case, a dinghy was required not only by the racing rules but by common sense; in the second, the previous afternoon a dusky gentleman had declared, "That sail been put aboard by me pusson-ally." So the yacht club launch departed on a search for the former, half of the race committee began telephoning about the latter, and Shorty Trimingham led me off to have a festering splinter cut from my right hand.

But finally Jerry Trimingham flew over the harbor and spotted the dinghy sunk on a lee shore, and it was duly retrieved; the sail arrived and was deposited in the forecastle; my splinter reposed on a bit of sterile gauze; and *Caribbee's* crew was assembled. This last was perhaps the final shock; with me as skipper a critical observer would not have chosen us as a group to cross Central Park lagoon in a rowboat, especially with a nor'easter blowing. To borrow an appropriate English phrase, we looked as though "we'd 'ad it."

Anyway, we got the anchor aboard and the motor going and fell in behind the committee boat, which towed out the English entries, and got the stops off and the sails up and hit the line within a few seconds of the gun, as noted. And we still drive along at better than 7 knots. The wind is now east by north ½ north at around twenty, and the night utterly dark except for one pale shaft of moonlight astern.

Nothing breaks the dim line of the horizon. For an hour or so after dark we saw the loom of St. David's Head, but now it is probably hidden by clouds. Nor can we see the lights of our competitors, although they cannot be far away. By dusk *Janabel* had dropped back considerably, and the English boats were strung out so far to leeward it was hard to identify them, especially as all are sloop rigged. At 8:30 Frank noted in the ship's log: "*Marabu* 3 miles to leeward and abeam." She is the only English boat in our class; in fact, she sails at scratch and gives us time under the Royal Ocean Racing Club rule. So we go well.

Spray rattles against the hood over my head. It sounds like handfuls of pebbles being tossed against a drum in a regular cadence. To windward there is nothing but sheets of spray driving aft, briefly tinted pale green in passing the starboard running light. But it is different to leeward: each time *Caribbee* slams into one of these steep crests a solid mass of white comes rushing back to cover the bulwarks and at times bury the life rail stanchions. There is a feeling of lift as she rises to each successive sea—up, up . . . then slam! as she shoulders through, and the spray flies to windward and the lee deck buries; then she lifts again and the lee scuppers jet and she is ready for the next.

This is almost perfect going. There is no sensation in the world to equal driving to windward in the open sea with just the right amount of breeze. Too much wind builds too big a sea and the boat labors and plunges and is stopped; too little breeze lacks the feeling of power and the exhilaration of speed. . . . This is it; this is what we came for. It all won't be as good as this. But as Sherman Hoyt once said after a miserable session off Cape Fear: "You've got to take the bad nights to get the good days." Still, no night at sea could be as bad as a night in New York when I awoke in a blue funk after having dreamed every disaster that could form a sailor's nightmare. That's behind, part of life ashore. This is life at sea—reality, tangible problems to meet as they arise. All my doubts about hazards and expense and the rest are gone now we are underway, and they won't return.

I'm in a very sentimental mood. Down below my shipmates of the off watch are asleep, confident of us on deck. I look down and see the oil lamp swinging in its gimbals on the bookcase over the fireplace. By its light the cabin is very snug and cozy, completely disassociated from the noise and rushing water on deck. Every detail of that cabin is familiar, every corner and even every blemish on the paneling. It is my true home. Sitting at the table I have eaten conch in the Bahamas, soft-shell crab on the Chesapeake, and herring in the Baltic. Leaning back against the cushions I have laughed and sung and swapped lies with a wonderful succession of shipmates. At that spot just abaft the mainmast my closest friend was married. At that chart table I have known uncertainty and indecision, yet have ticked off thousands of miles

from the tropics to just short of the polar circle; in those bunks I
have slept the deep relaxed sleep so impossible ashore. No other
place means so much to me. In fact, as Rat said to Mole of "mess-
ing about in boats"—"Nice? It's the *only* thing."

Time to relieve the wheel.

1st Day

34° 25′ N.
64° 05′ W.
Run: 1800 to noon: 125 miles
Average speed: 6.95 knots

Thursday, July 3. 12:10 p.m.: From across the cabin I must look like a three-toed sloth, or whatever it is that hangs upside-down from trees. My knees are wedged against the deck beams and my toes curled over a tie-rod, while this notebook balances on my stomach. Staying in the windward bunk in a rail breeze is a somewhat acrobatic maneuver, but nothing to getting in and out. For this passage we installed aluminum pipe berths in place of the regular mattresses. They not only save weight but give us an enormous storage space for extra clothes; also, as they are hinged on the outboard side they can be raised or lowered considerably to compensate for the angle of heel. Right now mine is triced up as far as it will go.

I have not yet figured quite the best way to get in. When using the "head-first" method of standing on the bureau and squeezing head and shoulders through the gap, and sliding nose first toward the far side, all goes well until my fanny jams under the deck. Then there is nothing to grab to pull myself the rest of the way, and my feet beat futilely around in the air. But if I try to get in feet first, I have a terrible time hoisting up my fanny. Getting out is even worse. There is the "back-arch" method of putting the feet out first and hunching along on the shoulders while feeling for the bureau top with the toes; this has the great disadvantage of skinning the forehead and nose against the overhead when

22

the back will bend no more. But somehow this seems more practical than the "forward jackknife," where I slide the feet out, as in the previous method, but pivot on my stomach while groping for a toe hold below. It is a problem which must be solved before the first urgent "all hands." Perhaps Dick, who sleeps in this same bunk when the other watch is below, has the answer.

We are still close-hauled with conditions little changed from yesterday, except it is sunny. At dawn we swept the ocean with binoculars but could not see any sails. So we are alone. The others are somewhere over the curve of the horizon, each little ship an entity unto itself. It is somehow a wonderful thing to imagine: five white sails against the blue vastness of the Atlantic, five crews completely cut off from all other men on this planet, accepting a certain amount of risk and hardship simply for the love of an intangible. There is nothing comparable except possibly the compulsion that drives men to climb remote mountains.

The lee porthole across the cabin is like a tiny but brilliant movie screen: when we rise on a sea there is a brief glimpse of the blue backs of passing seas; then we roll down and foam patterns go rushing past, very white against the blue; then we heel further and a torrent of solid water boils against the glass as the lee deck buries.

It is cool here in the after stateroom and the sunshine makes it gay and colorful. Orange lifejackets are lashed with marline to the mahogany bulkheads between the portholes; a scarlet Hudson Bay blanket is spread over the opposite bunk; and there is a loose pile of green and yellow oilskins—my own mostly, I am afraid—on the deck. The oil lamps at either side of the mirror over the bureau oscillate to the general rhythm, as do the neckties hanging from them—my own again, I think! It is time to get up and get busy.

Something smells good. Lunch must be nearly ready. We are standing a system of watches suggested by Dick Bertram. Beginning last night at 7:00 my watch was on deck for 4 hours. Then we changed at 11:00 P.M., at 3:00 A.M., and again at 7:00 A.M. So far, normal 4-hour watches, except we began at the unusual hour of 7:00. But the daylight period of 7:00 A.M. to 7:00 P.M. is divided into two 6-hour watches, shifting at 1:00 P.M. This eliminates the usual 2-hour "dog watch" in the afternoon, yet rotates the night watches. Thus each watch has a solid 6 hours of rest each 24 hours: time enough to get "slept out" and catch up on little jobs of laundry, keeping notes, fussing over gear, and the rest. The 2 hours of a dog watch are usually wasted, anyway. For a period which will run into weeks this arrangement seems ideal.

In addition, meals are scheduled at logical times. There is nothing worse, when standing the morning watch, than waiting until after 8 o'clock for breakfast. Our meal times now are 6:30 and 7:00 for breakfast, 12:30 and 1:00 for lunch, and 6:30 and 7:00 for dinner. In each case the watch below eats before relieving the deck, and the watch coming off before turning in.

We are nine aboard, two watches of four and Henry, the cook, who stands no watches, enjoying what someone called "banker's hours"—in the sack from 10:00 at night until 5:00 in the morning. The rest of us will rotate on the above schedule, crawling into a "hot bunk" as our opposite number crawls out—which it is time for me to do right now.

1:50 p.m.: It is a most brilliant sunny day. Everything sparkles. Each wave reflects a thousand little points of sunshine. The sky is very blue but the sea is bluer. Overhead drift the fat little cumulus clouds of fair weather. For this latitude the breeze is cool, but we wear only shorts. As Jack Littlefield said when we came on watch, "This should be a nor'wester day." And so it should: the air has exactly that same crisp freshness. Yet the wind holds in the east; slightly more to the south than yesterday, but we continue close-hauled and well north of the desired great-circle course of 066° magnetic. The track of the barograph shows a slow steady climb; there is so little sea we think this may be a fairly local condition and by pulling out ahead on this windward work—which might be all we will have, as we will soon be in the area of westerlies—we may get the jump on the others.

There are five boats fanning out across this trackless expanse, each intent on getting to the far shore as quickly as possible. The race committee certainly cannot be accused of limiting us in our choice of routes. "Start between the committee boat and the fairway buoy off St. David's Head, and finish at the Breakwater Lighthouse, Plymouth," say the instructions in essence. Thus the whole vast North Atlantic Ocean is our playing field, and it is up to each of us to find the way with the most favorable wind and current.

From the viewpoint of grand strategy there are three general routes available: first, and most obvious, is the direct great circle from Bermuda to Bishop Rock, a lighthouse on one of the Scilly Isles, riding in the open ocean off the southwestern tip of England. This is shortest, keeps a boat in the helping current of the Gulf Stream a fair percentage of the distance, and extends far enough into higher latitudes to come well within the strong westerlies normally prevailing over the northern wastes.

The second route is the rhumb-line course between the same two points. It would carry a competitor to the south of the great circle, and thus is longer. The only possible advantage might be increased crew efficiency through less exhaustion from gales and cold, and perhaps the ability to carry on if boats to the north encountered conditions which forced them to heave to during a really severe storm. On this southern route there would be less fog, with consequent less danger from shipping, and virtually no danger whatever from drifting ice. But it would almost guarantee lighter winds and long spells of calm—a pleasanter but slower way to reach England: fine for cruising but not for racing.

And finally there is the northern route, curving up into the strong cold westerlies of the high latitudes. Longer than the direct great-circle course, it offers the chance of wind constant and fresh enough to more than compensate for the extra distance sailed. And this cold wind, because of greater density, exerts more drive against canvas for a given velocity than the warmer winds of the south. Yet the northern route is not without drawbacks and even dangers: on the Grand Banks of Newfoundland there is the probability of almost constant fog during the month of July, and this fog can shroud large fishing trawlers, steamers converging on Cape Race, and icebergs brought down from the Arctic by the Labrador Current. Beyond the Banks it leads across the Atlantic in latitudes the British Admiralty sailing directions term "the mid-ocean area of maximum gale probabilities," where the frequency of "winds of Force 8 and above" is appreciably higher than to the south. It does fail to make maximum use of the Gulf Stream drift, but this is relatively unimportant if the winds encountered are strong enough. Thus if boat and crew can take it the northern route is theoretically fastest, provided it is carefully planned and successfully executed, so the distance sailed does not become too much greater than the great-circle track.

Our decision must be made on the basis of past Trans-Atlantic races, and our estimate of the competition. We cannot change our minds once we are fully committed; up to now neither we nor the others have been able to decide for ourselves, the wind forcing us to do its will, but soon we should be able to steer almost as we please. Then we must be ready for the final decision: it is something I have discussed with Frank and Dick often enough in the past, and I believe we are in agreement. If we guess wrong and another part of the ocean is more favored, our other efforts will be in vain. There can be no greater gamble in sport.

According to *Ocean Racing,* by Alfred F. Loomis, this is the eleventh race across the North Atlantic Ocean. The first, held just after the Civil War, is probably the most famous: the race from Sandy Hook to the Isle of Wight, sailed in December of 1866 for a winner-take-all pool of ninety thousand dollars, no small sum even today but enough then to sound like a king's ransom—the "Great Race of '66" between the *Vesta,* the *Fleetwing,* and the

Henrietta. Bookmakers along Broadway posted odds and covered bets, crowds lined the waterfront to see the contestants, and until the last moment frantic mothers and wives used every subterfuge to keep their menfolk from participating. By modern standards the yachts were large—all over 100 feet on deck—and they were captained and sailed by professionals. The famous Dick Brown strode the quarter-deck of *Fleetwing;* he was renowned for having campaigned *America* to victory over the English fleet in '51. The equally famous Bully Samuels of the clipper *Dreadnought* roared orders and defiance from *Henrietta.* On the latter sailed the only owner to even participate, James Gordon Bennett, Junior, son of the founder of the New York *Herald.* Most interesting to me, the race came about as the result of a discussion and wager on the relative speed and seaworthiness of keel boats versus centerboarders, an argument I still carry on.

It was a rugged and brutal race, as might be expected of midwinter on the North Atlantic, a severe test of men and boats. *Henrietta* won, despite having hove-to in a mid-ocean gale for 13 hours while the centerboard *Vesta* drove on past to establish and maintain a lead which she held until the landfall, sighting the Scilly Isles nearly an hour before *Henrietta* but then losing in the last few miles because of poor pilotage. Surely one of the great heartbreaks of racing! But *Fleetwing* suffered more than a disappointment; on December 19 a sea burst aboard to sweep eight men from the cockpit, six of whom were never seen again, while the ship lay over until her upper shrouds were in the water and only high hatch coamings and tight skylights kept her from following the drowning men to the bottom.

Between 1870 and 1905 there were three other races, and in the final one the noble schooner *Atlantic*—185 feet on deck, spreading 18,500 square feet of working canvas—established a record probably destined to hold for all time: 12 days 4 hours 1 minute 19 seconds from Sandy Hook to the Lizard, including one fabulous day of 341 miles for an average speed of 14.2 knots.

The first Trans-Atlantic event in the modern sense—relatively small boats captained and crewed by amateurs—was the "small class" in the race from New York to Santander, Spain in 1928. In it there were three finishers of around 60 feet over-all, all schooners, and it was won in the final stages by a boat still a threat in any race, the redoubtable *Niña*.

Yet none of these races, although interesting enough to consider historically, had any real lessons for us in *Caribbee* in our strategic planning. But in 1931 and 1935 occurred races of particular interest. The first was sailed from Newport to Plymouth, the second from Newport to Bergen, Norway. Both were won by yawls— *Dorade* and *Stormy Weather* respectively—which braved the northern route while competitors proceeded comfortably in the more southerly reaches of the Gulf Stream. In both cases the track across the higher latitudes paid off handsomely—so much so in the case of *Dorade* that when the much larger *Landfall* and *Highland Light* reached Plymouth Breakwater after a neck-and-neck battle for the supposed honor of being first to finish, they had the horrible shock of sighting *Dorade* cruising around on an afternoon sail. She had come in two days earlier! And virtually the same thing happened again in 1935, when *Stormy Weather* skinned by Cape Sable, hugged the Nova Scotia shore, and drove through an open lane reported to extend across the Grand Banks close to Cape Race. Ice and fog were both heavy that year. As Alf Loomis writes: "They admit it was pretty bad. The strain (was) still showing in the faces of some of *Stormy's* crew when they got to Bergen . . ." But again the gamble paid, and the 54-foot *Stormy* after a 3050-mile course arrived only 5 hours behind the 72-foot *Vamarie*, which had also sailed a northerly route, but not an extreme one, having kept south of the Grand Banks. This race has other lessons for yachtsmen sailing hard offshore in small boats: the need for life rails around a deck, and personal life lines fast to the waist of every man aboard in bad weather. For in the '35 race men went overboard from two contestants: on *Vamarie* a rescue was effected due to skillful helmsmanship, but on *Hamrah* a father was swept into the sea by a boarding wave, and his two sons were lost with him attempting a rescue.

In 1951 a race was sailed from Havana, Cuba, to San Sebastian, Spain. It was won by *Malabar XIII*. Dick and Frank sailed aboard. However, although they followed a great-circle course across fairly high latitudes after leaving the North American coast, their starting and finishing points were well southward of ours, so it has fewer lessons for us than the previous races sailed from Bermuda. The first of these was in 1936. It was won by the German yawl *Roland von Bremen*, very similar to *Caribbee* in all dimensions except beam and draft. This race finished at Cuxhaven, but as most contestants made a landfall on the Scilly Isles and entered the North Sea from the English Channel the open ocean leg was similar. The *Roland* stayed to the south of the great circle, and even there found plenty of wind—almost too much for gear and crew. Sherman Hoyt's account is a somewhat harrowing recital of blown sails, strained rigging, difficult steering, and emergency repairs. Those who went farther north encountered roughly similar conditions but made no better passages, perhaps —if I may put it delicately—because they did not sail quite so hard as they might. But unquestionably in '36 there was wind everywhere, and winning was more a question of relative speed potential and driving than choice of course.

But of all past events, the Bermuda to Plymouth race of 1950 holds the greatest interest for us. It was sailed over this same course, even beginning on the same date, and included one of our present competitors, *Samuel Pepys*. All the boats were English, and the fleet then—as now—was divided into two classes, large and small. But while in '50 there were three small yachts in Class III, there was only one in Class I; this time there are two in Class III, and three of us in Class I. Because of the great difference in size and resultant speed between the classes, it was originally planned to sail this year's event as two separate races, without an over-all winner, it being argued by some that after a few hundred miles there would be so much distance between leader and tail-ender, and therefore such a difference in weather conditions, it would not really be the same race. But when we arrived in Bermuda we found that Commodore Robert Somerset of the Royal Ocean Racing Club had put up an over-all trophy, so we sail against the whole fleet. Which is as it should be and no complaints win or lose, but it gives us a very special problem because of the size and nature of one competitor, that same *Samuel Pepys*.

Caribbee is 57.5 feet on deck and 42.6 feet on the waterline; the *Pepys* is 31.1 feet on deck and 24.0 feet on the waterline—quite a difference in length, but comparisons do not end there. We are nearly twice as wide, having a beam of 14 feet against her 7.4 feet, yet draw only a few inches more with our centerboard up, 6.3 against 5.8 feet. In sail area there is an even more apparent difference, 1585 square feet against 445, but it is in a somewhat intangible realm that the difference is greatest of all. For the two boats are farther apart in type—in underlying philosophy—than in physical dimensions. *Samuel Pepys* represents a radical departure in yachting design, the "light-displacement" boat. In practice, the weight of construction and wetted surface is kept as scant as possible, resulting in a hull easily driven by a minimum of sail; in theory, such a boat is not only cheaper to build but enjoys certain advantages in racing, the principal one being an ability to "plane" off before a strong wind at speeds much higher than the theoretical limitation of normal ocean-racing hulls, which is usually considered as 1.4 times the square root of the waterline, or approximately 8.4 knots on a length of 36 feet. Exponents of light-displacement types claim almost double this speed for their creations, given ideal conditions. Naturally, all excess weight must be kept out of such hulls, as even an extra pair of false teeth can make a difference—which a light-displacement man would answer by saying anyone in need of such articles should stay at home, and a critic would supplement by saying on hulls which pound so badly in a head sea one spare pair wouldn't be enough. But I do not want to rehash the arguments. I only want to put down that *Caribbee* is about as different as possible, being the heaviest of heavy-displacement boats: beamy, ruggedly constructed, with all the comforts of home—wide bunks, big galley, bookcases, fireplace—the works. Plus two banks of storage batteries and a diesel engine. Yet neither now nor later do I intend to write into these notes an assumption of which type is best, whether we beat her badly or vice versa, as this one race won't tell the whole story.

But, as I said before, we have a very special problem. All races between boats of different size and type are sailed on a handicap basis, and on this course of 2870 miles we will have to give that little red devil the *Pepys* over 4 days. If this turns out to be a slow race, her time allowance might even go to 5 days or more, because we are sailing under the Royal Ocean Racing Club rule where allowances are figured on a "time on time" basis. By this system each yacht is measured and given a rating based on the usual things—length, beam, depth of hull, sail area, and the rest. But then that rating is used to calculate a "Time Correction Factor," by which a yacht's elapsed time is multiplied to find her corrected time. So you never know exactly how much time you are getting or giving until all other boats have finished; and when a large boat and a small boat are both moving at well below potential hull speed, the little boat is gaining because her handicap is constantly increasing.

In *Ocean Racing* Alf Loomis wrote of the 1931 Newport to Plymouth Race: "The limit boat was *Amberjack,* and she received from *Landfall* no less than 76 hours 55 minutes. I am sure that if I had sailed in this race aboard *Landfall* I'd have been mortally afraid of *Amberjack.* . . . There would have been hours of soft weather in which I pictured her streaking around my particular hell with a bone in her teeth. . . . I was spared the torture, but it's a safe bet that every contestant suffered it when his boat's speed dropped below six knots." Yet on this slightly shorter course we will give the *Pepys* a minimum of 96 hours, and probably more, due to that RORC "time on time" system. Thus we can sail 1½ knots faster than the *Pepys* every hour for 18 days and work out a lead of 648 miles—nearly one-fourth of the course, a distance greater than the entire Bermuda Race—and she still will be within her time allowance if she has four perfect days at the finish. Which makes our job pretty tough.

To go back to the 1950 race: the most important lesson for us lies in the fate of *Gulvain,* a boat of approximately the same size and speed potential as *Caribbee.* Although after light winds at the start the race was sailed in a succession of gales and near-gales, and she had rigging trouble, *Gulvain* finished in 18 days 3 hours— good time for the distance. Yet on corrected time she was beaten by all three Class III boats by over a day, despite crossing the line 3 days 6 hours ahead of the winner. For us, the major lesson was this: *Gulvain* had followed the great-circle route as closely as possible and so had the others. All had encountered approximately similar conditions. But the result seemed to prove what Commodore Somerset of the RORC said to me at a cocktail party last week in Bermuda: "Under our rule you can't save your time on a small boat in a downwind race." So gambling becomes conservative policy.

Our Class I competitors we worry less about, perhaps because we are almost even on a time basis, and in the Bermuda race *Caribbee* seemed to go well against them when we were in the same breeze. But both are definite threats: *Janabel,* the French entry, is a lovely sloop, only a year old, and closely resembles *Gesture,* the '46 Bermuda winner and a boat for which we have the greatest respect. *Janabel* is 57.7 feet over-all, 40.0 feet on the waterline, has a beam of 12.6 and a draft of 8.2 feet. She is beautifully built and well kept, and is being sailed by a French and American crew. Her owner is M. Jacques Barbou of Paris, and

"Mitch"   Carleton Mitchell   *"Frank"*   Frank MacLear

"Jack"   John B. Littlefield   *"Bobby"*   Robert H. Symonette

STARBOARD WATCH

"Basil"   Basil McKinney   *"Dick"*   Richard H. Bertram

"Bill"   J. W. Sherar   *"Cap'n Nick"*   A. E. Nichol

PORT WATCH

Mme. Barbou and another lady are aboard—a fine display of the feminine spirit of La Belle France.

The other competitor in the large class is *Marabu,* an ex-German 100-square-meter seized by the British Admiralty as a prize of war and assigned to "H. M. S. *Hornet,*" a motor-torpedo-boat based on the English Channel. Her crew are all Royal Navy, hard drivers who are giving up leave and pay for the privilege of this passage. Lieutenant Commander Sam Brooks is their skipper, and aboard is the indomitable Chief Shipwright D. Flux, R.N.—the "Fluxey" of *Samuel Pepys's* 1950 crossing. *Marabu* is not a type which would be considered the ideal offshore racer by American standards, but in continuous hard going could do well. She is 57.7 feet over-all, 39.0 feet on the waterline, has a beam of 11.2 and a draft of 7.6 feet.

In Class III also is the sloop *Joliette,* built in 1950. She is skippered by her owner, F. W. Morgan, and her designer, Robert Clark, is on board. Next to the *Pepys* she is the smallest boat in the race: 37.6 feet on deck, 28.6 feet on the water, a beam of 9.0 feet, and a draft of 6.6 feet. She is not of the light displacement type, but is a conventional and attractive little cruiser racer, which could save her time if this turns into a light reaching race.

So here we are, five against the gods in a very literal sense. Ahead lies the whole North Atlantic Ocean, and anything can happen—that too in a very literal sense. A small boat alone on the ocean is a vulnerable thing. Many are the ways disaster can strike, yet I am willing to bet that aboard every boat thoughts are only on getting to England as fast as possible, and the only worries concern the other fellow's getting a better slant of breeze. This then is the eleventh time in a little less than a century boats and men have sailed forth for the ultimate test of yacht racing, and may the best win—a phrase that has become a cliché through meaningless repetition, but which is sincerely meant.

As I think back over what I have written, it might seem that my concern about *Samuel Pepys* as a competitor constitutes a great personal indorsement of the light displacement type. Actually it is more a matter of admiration for her crew and distrust of the boys with the slide rule—the men who frame the rules. Aboard the *Pepys* as skipper is Lieutenant Commander Erroll Bruce, R.N., who also commanded her for the Royal Naval Sailing Association in 1950; he was second then, and is back with much greater knowledge and a real determination to win. His probably will be the most scientific approach to all problems encountered, just as I believe the *Pepys* is the most carefully prepared of our competitors. His crew is experienced and well drilled. Sailing anything they would be a threat. But that is where the slide-rule boys come in, on the matter of handicap allowances; not that I don't think the *Pepys* a good boat despite not particularly liking the type, but when corrected time is figured with a calendar rather than a clock I worry about anything carrying a mast and a sail if the crew is willing to keep the sail up blow high or blow low. And the gang aboard *Pepys* is willing and ready to do just that.

6:00 p.m.: Our perfect afternoon is softening into an appropriate sunset, with every indication of a night ahead as beautiful in its way as the day has been. Although the sun is still well above the horizon, sky and water have darkened and the clouds are taking on delicate tints. The radio brings us reports of unprecedented heat along the eastern seaboard and describes people sweltering in cities far north of our present position. But I just went down for a wool shirt, and when the sun is an hour lower a good heavy jacket will be in order.

While below, I was reminded how difficult the most simple chore can become when the going gets bad. This is no more than a pleasant rail breeze in a relatively smooth sea, yet getting around even now requires a bit of that automatic sense of balance called "sea legs."

Henry in his galley was cooking dinner on a stove sloping at about the angle of a barn roof. Anything he let go skidded away as merrily as a skier starting down a slope; he was wedged in one corner trying to hold two pots and a frying pan in place, get the top off a can, slice bread, lay out dishes and tableware, and achieve other assorted details. He was having a tough time. Unfortunately the only creature nature has properly fashioned as a seagoing cook is the octopus, but it cannot survive on the amount of oxygen found in a battened-down galley and, besides, is reputed to prefer eating guests to cooking for them.

In the main cabin two members of the port watch clung to windward and leeward bunks with every external appearance and sound of blissful slumber. Bill Sherar, to windward, had his bunk swung up as high as it would go and still had to be held inside by broad canvas "bunk boards" that tie to rings in the deck overhead. Cap'n Nick, to leeward, had his bunk fully dropped, yet lay more on the wooden side of the hull than on the mattress.

Frank MacLear at the navigator's desk was fairly comfortable, being to leeward, but at the same angle of heel on the other tack he has to be held in place by a canvas strap—a flier's safety belt I picked up at an army surplus store—screwed into the bulkheads at each side. But even now if he leans forward over a chart, kneeling on the seat below, he has to be careful a lurch does not pitch him head first into the radiotelephone.

In the after stateroom I found the saddest spectacle in this round of the eternal battle of men against the sea. Dick Bertram, still nine-tenths asleep, was trying to get into his pants. He began on the windward settee, feet braced against the bureau aft and the bulkhead forward, but each time he arched his back and lifted his fanny to slide the pants under, *Caribbee* would dive and he would have to grab the edge of the bunk to keep from being catapulted to leeward. Finally he surrendered and slid across to the other settee.

Meanwhile I progressed from handhold to handhold, caroming off table and chart desk, and struggled to keep myself in place with one hand while fumbling through the locker with the other.

And putting on the shirt required its own scheming and artful balance.

Such minor tribulations are hard to convey to a landsman, and especially the cumulative effect of them. Everything becomes an effort: dressing and undressing, preparing and eating meals, getting into or out of a bunk, even brushing the teeth or going to the toilet. As the weather worsens during a gale and the seas get bigger and more irregular, every job for self or ship becomes progressively more difficult and tiring. And always there is the chance that a sudden unexpected lurch can bring tragedy: broken ribs or arms from being canted across cabin or deck, or painful and incapacitating bruises. In a bad gale dressing—or perhaps I should say putting on oilskins and seaboots, as no one is likely to be further undressed—may take 15 minutes. With a bunk gyrating violently, even sleep is not an escape for most until utter exhaustion sets in. Thus the old saying that "the ship will take more than the crew." Long before a boat is overpowered the men aboard can become too fatigued to handle her. It is something a skipper must always remember.

While we were below Dick, Frank, and I held a chart-table conference on strategy. As I thought, we are in general agreement on chancing the northern route. We will use this unexpected gift of wind to get out of the area the pilot chart shows as generally having light variables and drive for the band of prevailing westerlies. After all, we are still on the edge of the calm belt between trade winds and westerlies that frustrated sailing ships in the old days; in these latitudes cargos of horses consigned to West Indian and Gulf ports were jettisoned so frequently when water ran low that even modern weather charts use the sailor's term "horse latitudes" when describing them.

Our plan is to get north at maximum speed even if it means sagging off. When the wind shifts enough to let us sail any course we choose, we will still go somewhat north of the great circle, the amount to be determined by the conditions we find.

Our analysis of the strategy of the other boats is all, with the possible exception of *Samuel Pepys*, will hold as close as possible to the great-circle track. We believe the *Pepys* will too, sailing the shortest possible distance and therefore capitalizing on her time allowance, but we also realize that Erroll Bruce might anticipate our strategy and come north to cover us. But it is a gamble we have to take.

According to the pilot chart and generations of sailing-ship skippers, the farther north you go the more wind you get. We'll see. It is almost the only chance to save our time. It is also a tough choice. No sailor in his right mind casually takes a vessel into an "area of maximum gale probabilities" any more than a hunter deliberately crawls into a lion's den. Cruising, I would do much to avoid a gale. Yet the human mind is a curious thing. Thus, to put it bluntly—and admittedly somewhat frighteningly—we go gale-hunting.

So we had better enjoy this lovely going while we may. Our average speed remains better than 7 knots although the wind softened a hair as it backed. We are steering about a point higher than we did yesterday, now heading 028° by compass. The lee deck buries less often, but spray continues to blow back to the cockpit, as the smears on this page show.

I was just thinking this was like a day in the Bahamas—one of those perfect late spring days after the last norther of the winter has swung 'round into the east—when Bobby Symonette suddenly said: this is like going up for Hole-in-the-Wall; and I said yes, but so long as we're only cruising and in no hurry let's anchor for the night behind Great Stirrup Cay and get a mess of conch and crawfish, and he said fine, but crawfish are out of season. So we decided to keep on.

☆　☆
☆

THE sea is older than the land, and incomparably more vast. Its deepest depths are deeper than any valleys seen by man, and its mountains higher. It is the mother of all life on this planet and its components form the basic necessities for all things living— animal and vegetable—of the land, of the sky, of fresh water, of the sea itself.

For countless ages it has hammered and whittled at the land, shaping and altering continents, swallowing and disgorging islands. It has known the advance and retreat of vast blankets of ice, and the lash of incessant winds during eons of utter darkness, and the stirrings of strange and terrible creatures whose bones now lie forever hidden in the rock of its depths.

Since the dawn of time, as it can be conceived on this minute point in the universe, the sea has remained visibly unchanged, while all else has altered: the continents took their shapes and the evolutionary miracle progressed through myriad forms. Man appeared—man, that complex development capable of conquering the land, and the air, and even himself as a biological phase. Yet the sea remains unconquered and unconquerable, a vast mystery of Stygian depths, of intolerable pressures, of silence and cold, and slow wellings of life.

Man through the centuries of his development has felt the challenge of wide waters. From the day a coastal Neolithic tribe launched the first crude hull the lore of the sailor has been part of the advance of civilization. As frontiers expanded on land, so did horizons at sea. Generations of men sailed out beyond successive headlands. Some returned, others did not.

But gradually knowledge of the sea and its fringing dangers accumulated. Ships grew larger and voyages longer; men learned the secrets of the heavens, and devised instruments and tables to tell them where they were, and reduced to precise charts the crude outlines of distant lands. There came a comprehension of the systems of winds, and the laws of storms; of the vast ocean currents and the action of water of different temperatures, or chemical composition; of the effect of the sun and the moon on the tides, and the seasonal changes of the equinoctial procession. Slowly there accumulated a mass of lore, an enormous and complex knowledge not shared or even suspected by landsmen.

For the sailor's world is a different world. It is a concept of this planet as a vast pattern of land and water, seven-tenths navigable and three-tenths obstruction—the latter admittedly highly necessary and sometimes even desirable. At sea it is easy to remember the earth is globular in shape. The sailor watches ships and headlands lift above or sink below the horizon, foot by foot. He consults tables which take into consideration the curvature of the surface, or the distance objects will be visible from a given height of eye.

The sailor can choose his own path across the sea, with due regard for dangers. Unless forced to detour by land or unfavorable conditions—areas of calm, or ice, or seasonal storm—he can sail directly from one point to another in a straight line. Which brings us to one of those concepts unfamiliar to the landsman, or even those who ply coastal waters—the concept of "great-circle" sailing.

Over long distances, a great-circle course is the shortest distance between two points. This should be a straight line. But on analysis a great circle proves not actually straight. Viewed from the side it is a curve, a curve following the contour of this globular earth. It is as though pins were stuck in two places in the skin of an orange, and connected by thread. Looking down from above, the thread would appear straight; from the side, it would be a segment of a circle. Now if a knife is passed along the line of the thread and through the center to divide the orange into two equal halves, the rim of each would be a great circle. The distance between any two points along the rim would be the shortest distance possible on a spherical surface.

What complicates great-circle sailing is that all navigational *charts*—and *maps* of land areas, to use the customary distinction

—must be drawn on a flat surface. There is no way to project the surface of a sphere onto a flat piece of paper without distortion. The most generally satisfactory rendering is the system devised by the Flemish geographer Gerhard Mercator in 1569. Now, although some twenty-five other projections are employed for special purposes, Mercator's is the one so universally used that to most people the rendering of others appears incorrect; we are so accustomed to world maps showing Greenland as large as South America we are likely to be surprised if we make a comparison on a globe, or look in an atlas, and find Greenland one-tenth the size.

This distortion is due to the properties of Mercator's method. Without going into the complexities involved, segments of the globe—like triangles cut from the skin of our orange—are expanded into rectangles. While on the chart parallels of latitude always parallel the equator, and meridians of longitude are always at right angles to them, the scale is constantly increasing as the distance away from the equator increases and the triangle nears the polar apex. In fact, it becomes so great near the poles that Mercator charts do not reach beyond 80 degrees. Thus Greenland, well to the north, appears as large as South America astride the equator.

All short voyages are plotted on Mercator charts because "rhumb lines"—compass courses to steer—can be read directly by laying down a straight line between any two points. But on a long voyage crossing each meridian at the same angle—except close to the equator—would mean that due to the curvature of the earth the course sailed would actually be an arc. In our case, sailing from Bermuda to England, the rhumb-line distance would have been over 60 miles greater, a distance which would translate into many hours of time and mean certain defeat.

To plot the great-circle course navigators use a chart constructed as though a section of the surface of the earth, as viewed from the center of the earth, were projected on a tangent plane. In this *gnomonic* projection neither meridians nor parallels of latitude show as parallel lines, and neither courses nor distances can be taken off directly. But this projection is so constructed that a straight line between any two points represents the great-circle track. The points at which the track crosses the parallels of latitude and the meridians of longitude—say at each 5 degrees of longitude—can be noted and transferred to a Mercator chart in order to get compass courses. Thus a great-circle course in practice is actually a series of rhumb lines. Yet curiously enough when a great-circle course is laid down on a Mercator chart, it becomes an arc.

It is not a new concept. John Purdy wrote in his *Memoir, Descriptive and Explanatory, of the Northern Atlantic Ocean:* "Great-circle sailing was known and acted on very early in the history of navigation. It is more than probable that Cabot, Columbus, Magalhaens, and all the first great navigators, were acquainted with the subject. . . ." And in the edition of 1853 he continued with a footnote: "It is alluded to, directly, in a work by Pedro Nunez, in 1537; again, by Pedro de Medina, in 1545; but his system was erroneous, and was corrected by Martine Cortes, whose 'Arte of Navigation' was soon after, in 1561, translated out of the Spanish into English. . . . John Davis in August 1594 published a work called 'The Seaman's Secrets; where is Taught the *Three* Kinds of Sayling—Horizontall, Paradoxall, and *Sayling upon a Great Circle.*' It is also described in Richard Polter's 'Pathway to Perfect Sayling' about the same time. After this it is found in most of the old works on navigation."

But recently the great circle has been brought into new prominence through the development of long-range aircraft. So many drawings have been published showing "short cuts" over the polar regions and across oceans many people think the great circle a modern discovery, an outgrowth of the air age. But *Caribbee* and the most advanced jet plane are only following in the wake of those ghostly men and ships who went before, pushing back the horizons of knowledge and passing from generation to generation the accumulated lore. For there is nothing new save that which has been forgotten.

2nd Day

36° 41′ N.
61° 57′ W.
Run: noon to noon: 170 miles
Average speed: 7.08 knots
Total run to date: 295 miles

Friday, July 4. 2:00 a.m.: Writing this by lamplight in the galley, half-standing, half-sitting on the sink drainboard while waiting for water to boil. My turn to get the middle-of-the-watch mug-up. Henry leaves things ready every night: instant cocoa, powdered coffee, tea bags, and bouillon cubes, plus the makings for sandwiches. Quite a contrast to the skillagolee of the old timers! One of the miracles of modern cruising is the assortment of food available. We carry no ice on this race—in Bermuda we filled the box with some of the 3750 pounds of stores that came aboard —but lack nothing, nor will we unless we eat ourselves out. And judging from the ferocity of the first onslaught there might be some danger!

It is almost a shame to be below, even for a few minutes. There was never a more beautiful night. We came on deck at 11:00 to find brilliant moonlight, the horizon so clearly defined it looked like the glow of coming dawn. The few puffy clouds drifting overhead seemed to be lighted from within and the path of moonlight across the water was almost blinding. Is there anything more fascinating to watch than the play of moonlight at sea? Anything more infinitely varied than the patterns of light and shadow? And especially when the track lies directly astern, so it lights the wake, emphasizing in tumbling disturbed water the sensation of speed.

We roll, we boil. Gradually the wind has been veering. Between 2:00 and 4:00 this afternoon it let us head up from 028 to 050 degrees. Through the early evening it continued on around to the south of east, so now for the first time we can steer our compromise great-circle course of 063°. The sheets are slightly started but we continue under double head rig. There is still enough sea to endanger a genoa by scooping the bow wave.

Everyone is settling down into sea routine. Already watches rotate smoothly and naturally and seem perfectly balanced. I am in charge of the starboard watch, Dick Bertram of the port. Some skippers prefer not to stand a regular watch, but I like to pick a man in whom I have complete confidence and turn over to him full responsibility for half the time. It is part of my feeling that racing a boat is a completely co-operative venture, and that ownership confers only the right of ultimate decision, not constant supervision and regulation. Part of my own pleasure in sailing comes from shipmates who are sailors in the true sense of the word—and this group now on *Caribbee* teethed on a jib sheet.

Dick Bertram has raced everything from dinghies on up, winning the Intercollegiate Dinghy Championship while still in Cornell, the Lightning Class International Championship in 1948 and 1949, and serving as watch officer in ocean races too numerous to list but including the 1951 race from Cuba to Spain in *Malabar XIII*. He is as fine an all-around seaman as has ever come aboard, with a sound judgment of conditions and a positive genius for making a boat go her best.

Our other Trans-Atlantic veteran is Frank MacLear, navigator and mate of my watch. Frank not only sailed to Spain last year in *Malabar*, but during the winter came back via the Trades to Miami in *Sunbeam*, so this is his third ocean crossing in a year. As the ultimate in versatility he is our masthead man, going aloft with the ease of the daring young man; a naval architect; and our interpreter—as a result of Continental schooling he speaks French with so flawless an accent that in Bermuda M. Barbou of the

Janabel said he could not believe our "Mess'u MacLear" was not a Frenchman.

Mate of the port watch is Basil McKinney ("known from coast to coast as Hard-Luck McKinney"), eminent legislator representing Fresh Creek, Pure Gold, Love Hill, Bitch Cay, Conch Sound, Small Hope, Moxey Town, and other Andros Island constituencies in the Bahamas House of Assembly. Basil is a *Caribbee* regular; although he has had much experience on other ocean racers, including sailing two previous Bermuda Races, he has been aboard for the last two Southern Ocean Racing Circuit campaigns, the New York Yacht Club cruise of '51, the Newport-to-Annapolis Race of the same year, and many others.

Our second Bahamian is Bobby Symonette, also a member of the House of Assembly, representing Exuma, that cruising paradise. He is a member of a sailing family, his father being the perennial commodore of the Nassau Yacht Club and co-founder of the Miami-Nassau Race. Bobby has sailed all his life and has raced everything from Stars to *Ticonderoga*. He and Basil are somewhat in a hurry to get to Plymouth as both are members of the Bahamas Olympic Team, scheduled to sail five-point-five-meter boats at Helsinki later this month.

Divided between the two watches are two juniors, Jack Littlefield and Bill Sherar, thoroughly competent sailors yet retaining that elasticity of leg which permits uncomplaining execution of minor assignments. Jack's offshore experience began aboard his father's schooner *Blackfish;* Bill's as a midshipman on the Naval Academy's *Highland Light*. Bill is using his graduation leave to sail across the ocean, making this a real postman's holiday.

And we have two professionals, Gene Nichols and Henry Davis, both seasoned veterans of wide experience. Cap'n Nick is a ship's husband second to none, a repository of much lore of sail and the sea now nearly forgotten. There is no job of maintenance or repair he is not capable of tackling and no type of vessel he has not been aboard during his career.

Last but not least is Henry Davis, recently renamed *"Henri du Caribbee"* by his grateful flock. "Never has so much been consumed by so few" was his epitaph on the Bermuda Race, and we daily rise to new heights of gastronomic endeavor. Henry will need his strength and disposition at this rate, but he has only himself to blame: he is too good a cook. And his galley skill is matched by his ability on deck.

Caribbee won't suffer so far as her crew are concerned, and her crew won't suffer so far as Henry is concerned—so all should go well, especially as I am equally sure the crew will not suffer so far as *Caribbee* herself is conce ned.

10:15 a.m.: We are tearing along under genoa, the port watch having made the first sail change of the race before daylight when the wind moderated. Now it has freshened again to a rail breeze but the genoa seems safe enough, although occasionally the bow wave spurts in a dollop that sends spray up to the miter. In the Bermuda Race we lost a genoa when the weight of a scooped sea burst it along the luff from deck to masthead. But now we take nothing solid.

Dick came on deck after breakfast to toss firecrackers over the stern in honor of the grand and glorious Fourth, and *Caribbee* took off. Maybe this fresh breeze is the result of all the oratory going on back home. Anyway, we now make nearly eight right on course.

It is another warm sparkling day of blue water and blue sky, although a towering thunderhead which we call "Uncle Joe" has been stalking us from the south-southwest since dawn. He must have been there even earlier as the port watch noted "lightning to SSW" at 0430. Uncle Joe has not changed bearing, although he is changing shape as he gets bigger, spreading out over more of the sky. Now he is a perfect textbook diagram of an approaching front: before him there extends a long cirrus veil, at first filmy but thickening at his feet to small dark clouds, above which Uncle Joe towers turret on turret to the classic anvil headdress, a mighty crest bowed only by the winds of the stratosphere. Still the barograph shows a slight rise, so we hope Uncle Joe intends no harm.

1:50 p.m.: The day continues fair and the breeze fairer— both in a literal sense. Although Uncle Joe has spread himself across the horizon from southeast through southwest, he has lost the look of getting ready to pounce. He is becoming flatter and fatter, a good sign; also we seem to be outfooting him. For a long while it was hard to decide whether he might be the forerunner of a front or just a bit of Gulf Stream dirt. Now it looks like the latter, as the barometer remains steady and he is hanging almost stationary.

The breeze has also become fairer in respect to our course, having gone into the east-southeast at between 22 and 25 knots. We steer 063 degrees with sheets well started and show nine on the Kenyon. For the first time a sea builds, but on the quarter.

The water around us is that unmistakable Gulf Stream blue, the purest and deepest blue in the world. Its temperature at noon was 76 degrees. Occasionally pieces of driftwood or bits of broken crates slide past, and we sail through streaks and patches of brown Sargasso weed. But not all the flotsam is so innocent: shortly after coming on watch I spotted an odd shape ahead and a hair to leeward of our course. As we surged down a sea broke over it to expose a rusty steel cylinder, thickly encrusted with barnacles. It was floating very deep, rising and falling sluggishly. From the cockpit we could have touched it with a spinnaker pole; we could not tell how deep it went, but it was about a foot and a half in diameter. Frank logged it as a floating mine. We'll never know. But from the way it lay in the water it was heavy enough to crush through our planking, sinking us just as surely as if it went boom. Add hazards of the deep. Strange how you never really think about such things, or worry about them, yet sometimes during a night watch, driving along into a black void, you will suddenly become afraid; you shiver and hunch your shoulders against an imagined impact, and then the feeling completely vanishes, and you may not have it again for years. This is the third time I have passed a floating danger at close range by daylight. Wonder how many at night—and could some deep instinct cause that surge of fear, as you visualize in your mind something the eye cannot see?

7:20 p.m.: Heavy clouds are banking up to windward, killing the breeze. For the first time since leaving Bermuda we log it at less than 15 knots, but have been freed enough to be able to carry the mizzen staysail. A little more and a spinnaker will draw.

At this moment all of us of the starboard watch sit in the cockpit, waiting to see what will happen. The sea is smoothing out very fast, so this is probably only another local squall. Bobby just said something about the course for England, and Frank pointed down diagonally through the bottom of the cockpit and said: "England's there." A good reminder of the facts of great-circle sailing, and Bobby answered: "All right, but let's not take any short cuts."

"It is a most brilliant sunny day. Everything sparkles. Each wave reflects a thousand little points of sunshine. The sky is very blue but the sea is bluer. Overhead drift the fat little cumulus clouds of fair weather."

"*Is there anything more fascinating to watch than the play of moonlight at sea? Anything more infinitely varied than the patterns of light and shadow? And especially when the track lies directly astern, so it lights the wake, emphasizing in tumbling disturbed water the sensation of speed.*"

3rd Day

39° 00′ N.
58° 41′ W.
Run: noon to noon: 208 miles
Average speed: 8.67 knots
Total run to date: 503 miles

Saturday, July 5. 8:45 a.m.: For long periods the needle of the Kenyon hangs at nine and better. Since the squall moved ahead last night and the wind came back we have not dropped below eight, carrying the same combination of sail: genoa, main, mizzen staysail, and mizzen. The sea remains small. Both watches continue to note in the log "sea smooth" with an air of amazement, for it stays as flat as Long Island Sound or the Chesapeake. Now the wind is south-southeast at nearly twenty-five. And it is still smooth.

We steer 070 degrees magnetic, slightly above the great circle. This course should take us across the southeastern tip of the Grand Banks. We are soon due for a weather and sea change; on the Banks the Gulf Stream encounters the cold waters of the Labrador Current, flowing south from the Arctic wastes. The result is almost constant fog at this time of year, a lumpy tumbling sea, and much colder air and water. It is a bad spot to be caught in a blow, especially as the relatively shallow water adds to the confusion of the sea. But with any luck we should be clear within a couple of days, riding the westerlies promised by the pilot chart and now overdue.

On the Banks there is some danger from drifting icebergs, but all available reports show them fairly far north this year. Depends somewhat on how far up we go ourselves and, of course, on conditions still farther up along the Labrador and Newfoundland coasts. Beyond the Banks our course should follow the middle of the 55- and 60-degree temperature curves most of the way to England, and once we are a few degrees east of the Banks there should not be even an outside chance of encountering a berg.

But as I write this ice seems very remote. It is warm and getting warmer as the overcast opens up. At morning twilight Frank clung to the mizzen rigging for half an hour with sextant ready and got nothing, but soon he should be able to shoot the sun. Earlier the water was very dark; it is regaining that Gulf Stream color as the day brightens. We pass many Portuguese men-of-war, and flying fish skitter under the bow.

For the first time in my sailing experience we use degrees rather than points for compass courses. I admit loving to roll out the old steering instructions: "nor'east," or "nor'west by west one-half west," but I must also admit "45" and "298" are a lot simpler and less liable to confusion. Being the most incurable of romantics about the traditions of the sea I find this hard to concede, but even we anachronistic fellows who by choice potter like senile snails might as well embrace certain developments. And the modern spherical compass certainly destroys the validity of the argument against degrees: they can be read and steered to as closely and comfortably as points. You can't steer to a degree in rough going—but can you steer to a quarter-point, either? And the navigator's job becomes simpler. Offshore all celestial observations and plots are laid down in degrees true, and great-circle courses calculated on the same basis. Therefore thinking of the compass course in degrees magnetic acts as a constant reminder of variation and other factors that could induce error. I'm sold, but still think of wind direction in the old way.

9:30 a.m.: This fever! Here I write instead of sleep. From various sounds on deck and through the hull I could tell *Caribbee* was traveling around nine, but now I am back in the bunk after going on deck to suggest setting the balloon forestaysail. It now draws inside the genoa and gives us another two-tenths of a knot.

I don't know when in my sailing career it happened to me, this craving for speed. I was just a-settin' and a-dozin' and not a-botherin' nobody when the old go-fast bug came a-sashayin' up and bit me hard. And it took. From a lazy character who would just as soon loll in the cockpit watching Portuguese men-of-war sail through his lee I became the wild-eyed type who laughs demoniacally as the lee rail disappears and looks around for something else to set. So long as the boat is moving I'm happy; when she slows, I die. A terrible thing to confess. Yet now I pity the cruising man I used to be: you get more real sailing—more of the real feel of wind, and sea, and a boat—in a week of racing than in a year of cruising.

When I came below Dick said his watch would set a spinnaker if the wind steadied. At the moment it is about abeam, but occasionally it draws ahead. So long as we average close to nine we will carry the genoa and maintain course; but if wind and speed drop we will set a 'chute even if it means sailing a point below course. We continue to believe getting north is putting money in the bank. If this strong breeze holds right up to the westerlies we may get a real jump on the fleet—meaning *Samuel Pepys*—as the absence of sea makes us believe this condition may be local in character.

11:35 a.m.: The spinnaker work has started. After the last entry I fell asleep, awakening to noises on deck. Suddenly there was a twang like the lowest string on a bass viol. Then another. Immediately *Caribbee* surged in response to a new force; foam rushes past the lee port even faster, and a voice just called: "She's touching ten." So maybe we're in those westerlies and away.

For the first time there are complaints below. Bulkheads creak and groan, and the sound of water rushing past the hull at my ear has a new note. Parachute spinnakers are efficient brutes, but the strains they set up are incredible. Often I wonder how wood and metal can be engineered to withstand the strains imposed. Despite my prayers for strong fair winds here endeth the period of relaxed calm. Beating to windward at sea can be wet and uncomfortable, but things are always under control; forces can be accurately judged and strains evaluated. But running off before it is something else, the most difficult and delicate test of seamanship. But seamanship, as Uffa Fox once pointed out, is only another name for common sense—the latter commodity not entirely compatible with ocean racing.

5:45 p.m.: "A clean ship is a happy ship." If our Southern Circuit motto still holds we're happier than ever. All hands bathed in the lee scuppers this afternoon. Every modern convenience aboard *Caribbee,* even running water—in fact, if you weren't careful it would run you right over the side. A glorious sensation to lie on deck abaft the main shrouds, the spinnaker overhead bellied out against the blue sky, the water singing past below. Then the bow would slice through a sea and a mass of frothing white would surge back, breaking against your body and almost tearing loose your grip. You would come up gasping and blowing, a little chilled, dab at yourself with the Lava soap while watching ahead, and suddenly toss the soap under the dinghy and grab the shrouds again. If not absolutely cleansing at least wholly satisfying.

A half-hour on the wheel is a workout. My only complaint against *Caribbee* is hard steering with a strong wind on the quarter, a fault common to all centerboarders. Our rotation system on watch has evolved into a half-hour trick at the helm, a half-hour relaxing period—standing by, but no definite job, allowing a bath, writing notes, making a sandwich, or what have you—a half-hour on the spinnaker sheet jerking line, and a half-hour forward calling the spinnaker. For the wind is barely abaft the beam, and occasionally we surge up despite everything the helmsman can do.

So far the only casualty has been the mizzen staysail halyard chafing through aloft. It came down twice, in fact, and the rope has been replaced with wire. The only sail-sewing has been along the luff of that same mizzen staysail.

Down below we have in reserve four other spinnakers, two nylon parachutes, a small cotton parachute roped all around, and an old genoa with the hanks removed cut down to RORC overlap limitations, which we will set flying to balance the helm in gale conditions. We will replace the hanks for racing in England.

This morning I was thinking the gent who first said "The wind is free" lived before the days of hand-sewn Egyptian mainsails, Fibre-V genoas, and nylon parachutes. Nowadays the wind becomes one of the more precious commodities!

4th Day

~~~~~~

41° 13′ N.
55° 07′ W.
Run: noon to noon: 214 miles
Average speed: 8.92 knots
Total run to date: 717 miles

Sunday, July 6. 1:50 p.m.: This is the most memorable day of my life. First, it is as beautiful as any I recall: brilliantly sunny, water sparkling, tiny whitecaps, fleecy clouds, balmy. Never was sailing more perfect.

Second, it has not been without excitement—sometimes nearly too much. At noon we completed a run of 214 miles, the best ever for *Caribbee* and for me. Our average speed for the 24 hours—not actually 24 hours, since in sun time we lose the amount of our easting—was 8.92 knots, good going for a 42-foot waterline. Most of the time we were lugging sail—decks awash, steering hard, man forward calling constantly: "curling," "too high," "breaking." Seas bursting over counter—shooting down crests, pausing, shooting again; and sometimes taking wild sheers, spinnaker collapsing and filling with crashes that shook the whole boat.

Now, within the last hour, it has moderated. Less than an hour from our most difficult moments, it has become easy. The sea is dropping and the threat of imminent disaster gone, as the sky, overcast all night and morning, has suddenly cleared to this perfect day.

The first half-hour trick at the wheel this morning was almost too much; I took over wearing oilskins and within a few minutes my body was hotter under them than in any Finnish bath. Some workout! Yet *Caribbee* was going faster than ever before and I hated to quit even to strip down; for minutes at a time the Kenyon needle would hold above ten, and repeatedly when shooting waves would climb above eleven, once touching and going beyond 11.5 knots. No time to stop! So I kept my teeth clenched to hold down the breakfast pancakes and got through, but afterwards had to change from skin out, being just as wet as that day the spinnaker pole got adrift.

Toward the end of the ordeal my wristwatch stopped, and in the midst of grinding and pumping away—giving my all, sweat running out of my hair to almost blind me—I remembered a clerk in a New York store just before I left for Newport. He had listened to my complaint, wound and listened to the watch I had handed him, and said in a reproachful tone: "Perhaps you live too sedentary a life for a self-winding watch, sir."

Last night was the best of the passage, an experience I'll never forget. And neither will anyone else who shared it. Our watch came on at eleven; it was black dark, a heavy overcast blanketing even a glimmer from the moon. After our eyes became adjusted Jack sighted the range lights of a steamer well astern. She slowly overtook us; her running lights became visible, then ports along her side. The bearing hung unchanged. We flashed a spotlight on our sails. For several minutes nothing happened, then we were suddenly blinded by her searchlight. *Caribbee* was as sharply etched as the carving on a cameo, each sail standing out against the black background of the night, each drop of the bow wave sparkling like a diamond. We were carrying parachute spinnaker, balloon forestaysail, main, mizzen staysail, and mizzen. The wind was slightly abaft the beam at a logged 22 knots. From bow to stern we were a smother of breaking water, while overhead a literal cloud of sail soared. The steamer made no signal—just that unwinking glare for perhaps 15 minutes, then suddenly it was black again, leaving us blinded, and the steamer drew ahead, traveling barely faster than *Caribbee*.

What must the men on her bridge have thought? What were their nationalities, their backgrounds? Was one an old man who may have remembered the days of his youth, when vanished and forgotten ships sailed the seas, driving through the black night under towering pyramids of canvas? Or were they modern cynics, tolerating the sea only as a means of livelihood, thinking us mad to drive along hundreds of miles offshore in a vessel not much larger than their lifeboats? Again, we'll never know—but they'll never forget us, I'm sure.

8:30 p.m.: All hands are full of beans—only in a figurative sense, though, because tonight *Henri du Caribbee* gave us one of his usual superb dinners. But now we are all rid of what the Elizabethans called "the gross humors of the shore." We are well fed, well slept, and well exercised, and are certainly getting enough fresh air to satisfy any health addict. It is a wonderful feeling to be shaken down into sea routine, and except in a racing sense, time doesn't seem to matter.

But one of the reasons we are all so pepped up is our progress. We have covered one-quarter of the distance to England in less than 4 days and still move along at nine and better. Course is up to 082 degrees, bending more and more to the eastward, especially on the compass as the variation is increasing rapidly. The wind is southwest, around 20 knots; it dropped this afternoon but came back again, and now shows signs of freshening as the glass falls. The sea followed the same cycle: it got up a bit this morning, white breaking crests everywhere, went down with the breeze, now builds again. For the first time there is a chill in the air.

While this personal log does not reflect all activity, ship's work goes on constantly. This afternoon the port watch recorded in the log between 1400 and 1800: "Dried and bagged forestaysail and No. 1 jibtopsail, dropped and reset spinnaker to fix halyard, rove new line in preventer tackle, put flemish eyes in mizzen staysail halyard, sewed chafing gear on mizzen staysail, set it, sewed chafing gear on spare mizzen staysail, repaired No. 2 halyard winch." Although Dick did not mention it, I know there were countless changes in trim and readjustments of chafing gear—the whole boat is a cat's-cradle of lines and chafing gear. More damned strings! Preventer tackles on main and mizzen booms, plus a "go-fast" tackle on the main holding down the boom; balloon forestaysail sheet led to a main boom bale, chafing gear keeping it off the main sheet; double spinnaker halyards and a second foreguy in the clew as a jerking line—the list could go on and on. But somehow it all makes sense and works, although as you look around you are certainly reminded of the best way to stay alive at sea—don't fall overboard.

5th Day

43° 33′ N.
51° 32′ W.
Run: noon to noon: 205 miles
Average speed: 8.54 knots
Total run to date: 922 miles

Monday, July 7. 7:45 a.m.: At 2:45 this morning lights snapped on in the after stateroom; Dick in glistening oilskins stood by my bunk. "Oilies and two wool shirts," he said, and went out.

For a moment I lay trying to get oriented, listening: wind drummed through the rigging, water raced past the hull at my ear, spray—and rain—pattered on deck overhead. *Caribbee* was heeled well down and lurching as she climbed over and dropped beyond crests that had built during our time below.

The bunk was so warm—so warm and comfortable! And the cabin so peaceful! Never again will I criticize the ostrich; I only wanted to bury my head, too, and let her howl outside for somebody else. But somehow my feet hit the deck and I crawled into damp clothes and damper oilskins—has man ever devised anything nastier than wet nylon oilskins?—and high boots. And somehow made it up the ladder and into the cockpit before six bells struck.

It was cold. Black squalls lurked to windward, black and threatening even against a solid overcast. Not a star, not a ray from an almost full moon. The white of breaking crests driving out of the murk shone with an eerie radiance, and rain and spray stung.

The wind had backed into the south and freshened, so before the port watch went below a genoa was set and the spinnaker handed. Throughout our watch rainsqualls followed each other in a dreary procession, but none carried any real weight, although the wind gradually freshened. When we came below at 7:00 the seas had built some, but we were making good weather of it, steering easily, and logging between 9 and 10 knots.

Now, I write this while Henry clears the breakfast dishes. It is blowing a good solid thirty. The port watch is tying in a single reef. I am standing by, but Dick says they will need no help. Henry just commented: "Imagine three men reefing a boat of this size in this wind." Damned good men, I say—and also give credit to Rod Stephens, who suggested our reefing gear and procedure. With genoa working—and even the upper part of the main doing a share—*Caribbee* has hardly lost speed.

This weather change began at sunset last night. When we took over at 7:00 P.M. a ragged dirty cloud was to windward. It looked like a local squall but apparently was the forerunner of something more; ever since the track of the barograph has shown a very sharp drop, and it is continuing down steeply. Just before dark two Mother Carey's chickens appeared in our wake, darting and hovering, hopping and skipping over the surface of the sea. Naturalists call them Storm-Petrels, and according to old sailor superstitions they earned the name by appearing as the heralds of a gale. I feel about them like a small boy feels about graveyard ghosts at midnight: maybe they won't do me no harm, but I'd just as soon they go some place else. When I went forward for my final inspection at dusk they fluttered overhead like bats and I kept thinking I heard—but wasn't certain against the background uproar—faint bird cries. At dawn they were still with us, still fluttering and circling, apparently tireless. But not so we: the first light revealed a group like a Doré etching, miserable and cold, huddling in the cockpit under the lash of rain and biting wind.

Gone is yesterday's fair weather and "Bahama feel," with both watches anxiously awaiting a turn at bathing in the lee scuppers. At six o'clock the water temperature was down to 58 degrees—a 16-degree drop overnight!—and its color was a dark greenish black. There is a totally different aspect to this world from the tropical one we left a few miles back in the warm waters of the Gulf Stream; this is part of the world of drifting ice, of long winter nights, of fog and rock and raging gales.

Now we'll see how the other half lives, and maybe learn the meaning of "north" in North Atlantic.

FAR above the routes used by seamen to connect the populous continents of Europe and North America lie the lonely Arctic wastes, barren and forbidding, shrouded by ice and snow, a part of our world as remote from the thoughts of most travelers as a world in another solar system. Over the polar seas extend fields of ice that never melt, while the lands lie capped by glaciers hundreds of feet thick, creeping blankets which with the slowness of geological time reach the sea to break off and go drifting away at the mercy of wind and current. These, as icebergs, sometimes appear on man's highways as a reminder of the primordial forces still at work, mightier than man's defenses against nature, which we call civilization.

For nothing is more majestic or dangerous than a mighty berg of ice, glittering and unreal in sunlight, utterly deadly when hidden by night or fog. In describing their beauty, Nathaniel Bowditch in the prosaic *American Practical Navigator* rises to unaccustomed eloquence: "Icebergs assume the greatest variety of shapes, from those approximating some regular geometric figure to others crowned with spires, domes, minarets, and peaks, while

others still are pierced by deep indentations or caves. Small cata-
racts fall from the large bergs, while from many icicles hang in
clusters from every projecting ledge." But the bible of the U. S.
Navy Hydrographic Office does not forget the other aspect:
"They frequently have outlying spurs under water, which are as
dangerous as any other sunken reef. For this reason it is advisable
for vessels to give them a wide berth. . . ."

Like so many other things relating to the sea, the formation and
progress of icebergs follows a general pattern which can be described, yet never can be reduced to a precise formula. Most of
the bergs likely to be found on the North Atlantic shipping lanes,
originate from the glaciers of Greenland, where they are dropped
into the sea by a process called calving, an odd but somehow apt
term. According to Bowditch: "The size of the pieces set adrift
varies greatly, but a berg from 60 to 100 feet to the top of its walls,
whose spires or pinnacles may reach from 200 to 250 feet in height
and whose length may be from 300 to 500 yards, is considered of
ordinary size in the Arctic. These measurements apply to the part
above water, which is about one-eighth to one-ninth of the whole
mass. . . . The largest bergs come from the glaciers at Umanak
Fjord and Disko Bay, and their height will rise to 500 feet; but as
they lose in mass from that time forward, we cannot expect to find
them of such gigantic height when they finally appear near the
Newfoundland Bank."

After the bergs begin their drift, they follow a fairly regular
route past Cape Farewell on the southern tip of Greenland into
Baffin Bay, where they enter the southbound Labrador Current to
drift down the Labrador and Newfoundland coasts in a procession
as ponderous and stately as a parade of enormous white dinosaurs,
to finally arrive on the Grand Banks. Here, as Maury wrote in
The Physical Geography of the Sea, "the cold waters . . . press
upon the warm waters of the Gulf Stream, and curve their channel
into a horse-shoe . . . the great receptacle of the icebergs which
drift down from the north; covering frequently an area of hun-

dreds of miles in extent." And added: "clearly . . . the very seat
of that agent which produces the Newfoundland fogs."

The southward passage of ice is complicated and varied; the
number and extent of drifting bergs depend greatly upon weather
and upon strength and direction of intermingling currents during
the critical period. Many ground and disintegrate in the Arctic
Basin or along the rocky shores of Labrador and Newfoundland.
Others are obstructed by field ice, floating ice formed by the
freezing of the surface of the sea; still others are pounded into
fragments by gales.

But each year, according to a Hydrographic Office publication
entitled *Arctic Ice and Its Drift into the North Atlantic Ocean,*
approximately 7500 bergs calve from the glaciers of Greenland.
In an average spring 427 cross latitude 48°, the northern limit of
the Grand Banks, and 35 continue on past 43°, the southern limit.
. . . Consider a mass of thousands of tons floating deep in the
chill black water, lying quietly, only a slight curling of the sea
at its base, a segment of the past waiting to ambush modern man;
a bleak and lonely survivor of snows that fell on the polar ice caps
thousands and thousands of years ago, before Tutankhamen was
laid in his tomb, before Christ ascended the mountain, before
Columbus set sail . . . "The only sure sign of an iceberg is to see
it," states the bulletin. But "in a dense fog a berg cannot be seen
at any appreciable distance ahead of the ship, where it takes form
as a luminous white mass if the sun is shining; otherwise it first
appears close aboard as a dark shape." On a dark night thick with
fog, when the lookout forward literally cannot see a hand held
within inches of his face and the bow wave obliterates the sound
of breakers—driving, driving ahead, the first warning the crash
itself . . . for generations of seafarers it has meant one more ship
unreported, one more mystery of the sea. . . .

April, May, and June are the most dangerous months, according
to Bowditch, when bergs "have been seen as far south as latitude
37° 50′ N. and as far east as 38° W." By July of most years the

danger line has receded north of Newfoundland, yet as recently as 1950 on August 21 bergs were sighted in latitude 43° 30′ N., longitude 49° 00′ W. "Between Newfoundland and the 40° parallel floating ice may be met in any month," states Bowditch as a precautionary reminder.

Many are the stories of encounters with icebergs, and the deceitful conditions in which they are found. One account appears in the journal of Lieut. John Steele Park, R.N., written on board the brig *Carshalton Park* during a passage from Jamaica to England in 1826: "*June 29th.* A light breeze from the southward, with foggy '*Bank weather,*' as the sailors call it. At eight o'clock this morning it cleared away, and I took altitudes for my chronometer, which made the longitude 49° 42′; and, at the same time, we discovered an island on the starboard beam, 3 or 4 miles off. Shortened sail, hove the ship to, and sent the mate to see what it really was; for, although I had no doubt of its being an iceberg, yet it certainly looked something like land; and I did not wish to leave it in any kind of uncertainty. The fog, which had cleared away at eight o'clock, and left a beautiful blue sky, returned suddenly when the boat was about halfway from the ship. The mate, an active, skilful seaman, had a compass with him, and he apprehended no danger; but pushed on for the island, instead of returning, when he saw the fog spreading. Hour after hour passed away, and no appearance of the boat. Night came on, dark as the grave, with a cold, benumbing drizzle, and a fog so dense that we could scarcely see across the deck. My grand object was to keep the ship as near the same spot as possible. All day and all night we kept the bell tolling, and fired a great gun occasionally: a tar barrel was also blazing at the main-yard arm, but all was unavailing. I shall never forget the terrors of that night. I reproached myself as the cause of their destruction; and I prayed most earnestly for daylight and clear weather. I thought daylight would never come, but it came at last, and the fog was thicker, if possible, than the day before. The most sanguine now began to despair. About five o'clock something was heard, like the blowing of a conch shell, but so faint and indistinct that we thought it was only the echo of the great noise we were making on board. However, it was discovered the sound was coming nearer and nearer . . . In a few minutes the splash of oars was heard, and in five minutes more the boat was alongside, with all hands safe and sound, thank God! but cold and hungry enough. The mate tells me he rowed round the iceberg, which he thinks was about 300 feet in length, 150 feet in breadth, and 40 or 50 feet above the surface . . . streams of water were gushing down its sides, and they had only got a few yards from it, on their return, when (to use his own words) 'it took a sally and fell over on its beam ends.' Our last sight of the ice, when bearing S. W. 3 or 4 miles, was in lat. 42° 13′, lon. 49° 44′."

Few disasters in maritime history excited public imagination like the loss of the White Star liner *Titanic* in 1912. Widely advertised as the Queen of the Seas, she was the most advanced ship the world had seen: the largest passenger vessel afloat, the fastest, the most luxurious—and the safest. Her builders boasted of her invincibility, calling her unsinkable. There were floodproof compartments, double bottoms, watertight doors, and every other device naval engineering had developed. On her maiden voyage she sailed for New York with 2224 aboard, the passenger list studded with famous names. Yet at 2:20 A.M. of April 15th the black water of the North Atlantic closed over the proud funnels as she carried 1513 people down with her. . . . The unsinkable ship—the very title a challenge by man to his ancient enemy, the sea—had passed over an "outlying spur" of a drifting berg; passed over so gently that many passengers were not aware of the collision, but the steel plating had been ripped from bow to stern as though by a giant can opener, and the elaborate compartmentation was of no avail. . . . Again the sea had defeated man.

Yet the tragedy had one beneficial result—the establishment of the International Ice Patrol, financed by several nations but op-

For moderate breeze and calmer water: genoa, main and mizzen.

For heavy weather and rough seas: The double head rig of jibtopsail, forestaysail, main and mizzen.

With the wind abeam or slightly ahead: ballon jib, main, mizzen staysail and mizzen.

With the wind abeam or abaft: spinnaker, main, mizzen staysail and mizzen.

CARIBBEE'S LEEWARD SAILS

erated by the United States Coast Guard. Now cutters patrol the Davis Strait area each spring and early summer, counting and identifying bergs before they come far enough south to endanger navigation and forecasting the rate and direction of drift. This data is incorporated in chartlets issued weekly by the Hydrographic Office which show the extent and nature of dangerous ice.

Aboard *Caribbee* was the chart for June 3, diagraming in neat red symbols and red lettering ice reported to that date: solid fields extending along the coast of Labrador and sealing the Straits of Belle Isle; drifting growlers and bergs scattered from Cape Farewell to mid-Newfoundland. Later reports received just before we left Bermuda stated: "Nothing dangerous south of 48 degrees." We should be safe enough.

Yet it was impossible for me entirely to forget the sight and sound of glaciers at Spitzbergen calving into the frigid waters of Temple and Magdalena Bays, seen before the war: the thundering roar of fission, the slow-motion rise of the geysers of spray, the sluggish and fantastic forms of the drifting masses. Nor could I forget a later brief glimpse through swirling fog of the desolate waste of pack ice that stretched to the pole. For to most men ice is somehow terrifying, elemental and alien, an almost subconscious fear inherited from our remotest ancestors. Nor could I forget that all attempts to precisely catalog the sea and its mysteries are fallible and that, despite all vigilance, somewhere ahead could hide the maverick berg, the stray that in the vastness of the ocean had slipped away from the carefully branded and tabulated herd.

☆ ☆
☆

3:50 p.m.: No noon sight; overcast solid: fog, water dripping from everything aloft, even the tail of Sylvester Junior, the black kitten with the shoebutton eyes who has ridden the mizzen jumper stay ever since the Cat Cay Race. Our run by dead reckoning—fairly accurate, we believe—was 208 miles. So we have had three consecutive "200" days, a grand experience. Now things are not so promising. The barometer has leveled off and the wind lacks weight.

It has been a fairly busy day. About eleven this morning the wind strengthened to around 35 knots and the port watch shifted from genoa to double head rig, setting the small jibtopsail as there was every indication it would freshen more. The main had already been reefed, as noted in the last entry. Speed held at well over nine. Then shortly before noon we ran into fog and the wind dropped into the upper twenties, so they went to the big jibtop.

When our watch took over after lunch the wind moderated further; we first set the mizzen staysail but handed it on being headed, and proceeded to reverse the sail-handling routine of the other watch, shaking out the reef and going back from double head rig to genoa. The sails were wet and heavy. Oilskins make any job twice as hard: air temperature is now 58 degrees and water 55, so waterproof clothes are necessary, yet as soon as you wear gear that keeps out the damp the slightest exertion causes damp within—a miserable steaming sweat.

At this moment we are close hauled and forced slightly below course, but despite a rather long swell from the southwest underlying a smaller chop we are making almost eight. Fog blows across from the weather side like curling smoke; it has a penetrating chill that goes to the skin. Visibility is sometimes a hundred yards, sometimes a boat length. There is tension in driving blindly ahead, the man forward staring into a gray void. Even the spray of the bow wave vanishes into nothingness before it falls back into the sea. Our senses begin to play tricks on us: we imagine we see looming shapes, or hear horns, or even feel currents of colder air, as from an ice box suddenly opened.

A catsup bottle encrusted with barnacles and a piece of timber shaped like a natural crook frame from a Caribbean sloop suddenly appeared and vanished again, reminding us we are not alone on the ocean. Our dead-reckoning position puts us slightly north of the steamer lanes and I hope we are—being run down is certainly the greatest danger of the passage. And we are in waters where it happened frequently enough when the fishing fleet was thickly clustered on the Tail of the Banks. Radar is supposed to be a consolation to small-boat sailors, yet since its introduction I am almost more afraid of steamers. Now they plow ahead faster than ever while lookouts are less alert. And although radar will probably detect another steamer—but not always, as several recent accidents seem to indicate—it is likely to overlook a wooden sailing craft, a fact I know to be true from watching radar screens and from talking to men of a great deal more experience. In fact, on the very pilot chart we are using there is an insert in red titled "Search and Rescue Operations" which says that "operators of disabled wooden craft . . . should hoist on a halyard . . . any metallic object which would assist their detection by radar" as patrol vessels and planes "thus can continue searches in darkness and during other periods of low visibility." It is a chilling thought to remember converging with the steamer night before last until we flashed the sails; if we had not seen each other and altered course we inevitably would have come together. It is strange to think of two vessels setting forth from ports thousands of miles apart, sailing courses that might vary a thousand times, and meeting at a precise point in the vast expanse of the Atlantic. It seems almost impossible but has happened with terrifying frequency.

Yet somehow I enjoy fog. It has a quality of association with the sea—of people and places close to the sea. I think of it rolling across the flats at Nantucket, slowly swallowing the boats, the shore, and then the houses, feeling and smelling like the sea itself. I remember it in Nova Scotia, and on the Skagerrak, and along the coast of Maine—always in connection with boats and the men who sail them. And out on the ocean the narrowed horizon intensifies the feeling of aloneness, of being in a world of your own, and brings you even closer to your shipmates.

But I hope to hell it doesn't last long!

5:15 p.m.: It has moderated still more. We are sailing full and by and have dropped below 7 knots on the Kenyon. As the breeze lightens, the swell from the southwest bothers *Caribbee* more. If there is wind behind the swell I wish it would hurry and arrive. Yet we can't complain: we are out of the area where we might expect light variable winds and slow going, and now are in a position to catch the westerlies and really boil the rest of the way. We are well into the "Roaring Forties," although that term for the band of west winds—"The Counter Trades"—which encircle the earth between 40 degrees and 60 degrees, properly applies only to the Southern Hemisphere where the westerlies howl virtually unchecked by land. But for this month in the North Atlantic the pilot chart shows the wind averaging only 20 per cent from the easterly quadrants, and the U. S. Weather Bureau's booklet on *The Preparation and Use of Weather Maps at Sea* declares under "Prevailing westerly winds" that "the tabulated results for that portion of the North Atlantic included between the parallels 40° and 50° N. and the meridians 10° and 50° W. show that winds from the western semicircle (south to north-northwest) comprise about 74 per cent of the whole number of observations."

As so far we have had almost nothing but winds from the south and east, percentagewise our chances for westerlies grow better each hour. With the run to date, it could mean a very fast passage —during the past 2 days there has been plenty of happy talk of a new record: "Carrying the mails" is the slogan. By desire and by circumstance we have gotten farther north than the great-circle route from Bermuda to the Scilly Isles but our position should now pay off. To date we have sailed to keep *Caribbee* moving at maximum speed for the given wind condition, and win or lose I believe in the policy. We could have held higher without the spinnaker a good deal of the time, but at a sacrifice in speed.

It is odd how you begin to speculate on the other boats the moment you slow. While we were traveling well all was optimism: we gave little thought to the competition except to feel we were "murdering 'em." Now, within a few hours, the cockpit discussions consist of endless speculation on what the others did, what conditions they might have had, and where they are. It is agreed we must have opened up quite a lead, and that is the important thing at this stage of the race.

We are on the edge of the Grand Banks, that wonderful but now nearly despoiled treasure house of the Atlantic, whose riches supported whole nations through the centuries. The Cabots named Newfoundland "Baccallao," the Basque name for cod, so thick were the fish. And during those same centuries the Banks developed the finest sailors the world has known, hardy fishermen sailing from the ports of Europe and North America. There is no counting the keels that have woven the tapestry of history over this remote plateau of soundings in an inhospitable part of the ocean, or the men and ships whose bones lie on its bottom. It is one of those places where I feel a sense of the past, of those who have gone before.

I write this from my spot at the top of the companionway, huddled under the spray hood. Jack just said I look like the prompter at the opera. He sits on the after cabin trunk with the foghorn at his feet.

Fog swirls by. The stern rises and falls against the murk, swells suddenly appear to lift us and disappear within a few feet, the centerboard trunk sighs in my ear, and big drops trickle from the main boom down the back of my neck. Despite the visibility and damp we are relaxed. It is the first watch in several where we haven't hung on tooth and claw and hoped *Caribbee* wouldn't throw us.

Frank just relieved Bobby at the wheel. Bobby stood up and stared out at the fog and muttered: "Put a little sherry in this and Henry could serve it for chowder."

My turn to call the jib.

7:30 p.m.: This is the end. All sails are down as we roll and slot mercilessly. Nothing else has changed: the fog lies like a heavy blanket, the swell glides in from the southwest, the barograph pen continues its even way—but there is not a breath of wind. We wallow helplessly, lighting cigarettes and watching the smoke for a premonitory curl, and peer out into the murk as though expecting to see wind beyond. Meanwhile the needle of the Kenyon placidly rests on "0."

It happened so suddenly *Caribbee* almost suffered damage before we could get things under control. A few minutes before seven I felt the breeze lighten. We had been averaging about 6.5 during the previous hour. I happened to be sitting in the cockpit and leaned down and looked at the Kenyon and said jokingly to the helmsman: "Get going, boy; you're under six." Before he could answer there was no wind at all. Not a breath. It was quicker than turning off an electric fan. All hell broke loose, taking us completely by surprise: the main boom went slam-crash across the deck and back again, threatening to jerk the traveler out by the roots; the nylon genoa folded back against the spreaders and filled like thunder and folded back again; and the mizzen boom did its puny best to yank off the stern. Having been close-hauled for several hours and headed below course, we had taken off all preventer tackles in case we wanted to tack, so it was a mad scramble to get in the genoa, subdue the main boom enough to lower the sail, and drop the mizzen.

And I must admit I never had so odd a feeling in my life as those first moments of looking at poor *Caribbee* stripped naked, masts tracing wild arcs in the fog as we wallowed without steerageway. I guess I felt as Lincoln did when he said he was too old to cry, but it hurt too much to laugh.

The port watch glumly took over at 7:00. Henry had been caught short in the galley but suffered no serious losses: we ate, but not cheerfully, and Henry summed up our feelings when he said in a tone of great disgust: "I never saw anything get so monotonous so fast."

But we were able to laugh when Frank gave a demonstration of *Samuel Pepys* "banking her turn around the Azores," flinging up great clouds of spray as she planed past on a southerly route at a fabulous rate of knots.

The one thing you can't lick on a sailboat is lack of wind. And that's what we've got. So our booming run ended not with just a bang, but with a bang and a slat.

6th Day

44° 33′ N.
50° 00′ W.
Run: noon to noon: 92 miles
Average speed: 3.83 knots
Total run to date: 1014 miles

Tuesday, July 8. 1:45 a.m.: Our watch has been on deck since 11:00, and the rain has not stopped for a second. It is an icy misting rain, but at least it has knocked down the fog and let in some breeze. The calm spell lasted until almost 9:00; then the rain began and a bit of air stirred from east by north. The port watch got under way on the port tack, that being the closest to the desired course of 089°. Now we slip along, steering about 120 degrees magnetic, sometimes above, sometimes below, but certainly well bore-sighted. Our only consolation is that being forced to the south will get us off the Banks quicker—we have all formed a great dislike for this particular piece of water. As someone said a few minutes ago, "The Banks are only fitten for cod, a notoriously unintelligent fish."

None of us can ever remember being colder. My hands were so numb I had to warm them under oilies and sweaters for several minutes before beginning to write. Probably the sudden transition from Gulf Stream warmth has something to do with our suffering. We're mostly hot-country boys anyway. But our chills are not wholly imaginary: the 2300 log entry shows an air temperature of 45 degrees, cold enough for an Eskimo out on the water and exposed to a steady rain. I cannot help feeling ice is near, yet

Bowditch says bergs have no discernible effects on air or water temperature.

Frank and I just went over the barograph chart of the past week. Before we left Bermuda there was a dip, but on the second of July, at the time of the start, the recorded barometric pressure was 30.20. While we had clear skies and fresh winds it continued to rise, reaching a high of 30.35 Saturday noon. That was when we were boiling along under spinnaker and taking baths in the waterway, with the wind between south and south-southwest at around twenty. From that high it began to drop, slowly at first, but quite sharply from midnight to noon of Monday, when it went down at 29.93. Again the weather behaved in accordance with barometric indications: it was during that period skies became overcast and the increasing weight of the wind forced us down to reefed main and double head rig. About noon the track leveled off, remaining steady as the breeze tapered and we shook out the reef and reset the genoa, but began to climb again during the afternoon. Then about the time the wind let go entirely there was a vertical jump of five-hundredths, a slight dip an hour or so later when the light breeze came in from the east, then another smaller jump. Since, there has been a slow steady rise. At midnight the pressure was 30.12. We are almost exactly on the 30.00 normal pressure curve shown on the pilot chart. All of which adds up to nothing we can interpret at this moment. Has anything in the history of man caused more speculation or conversation, or had more prayers said to it, than the weather and its high oracle, the barometer?

On deck there is some discussion as to whether a Nordic type would be superior to a Latin on a night like this: the consensus seems to be that a bare blonde fräulein, well plumped by pastry and dumplings and ensconced under a feather comforter, would have it all over a señorita no matter where.

But the only female anywhere around might be one of the Mother Carey's chickens circling our wake. I am now sure the

faint cries I heard the other night came from them. It is an odd
sound, suited to an odd little bird. They are barely visible and
seem unreal. Although the moon is almost full only a wan glimmer shows through the overcast. Somewhere people must be
enjoying bright moonlight; perhaps even someone might be
thinking enviously of us, muttering: "Those lucky guys are having
a lovely moonlight sail." And so we are. But without the moon.

8:40 a.m.: Conditions are the same. The cold misting rain has
not let up. At 6:00 the other watch went about; now we are close-
hauled on the starboard tack, steering anywhere between 045 and
055 degrees magnetic, speed varying between 4 and 5.5 knots.
The barograph has continued its upward trend, now passing
30.20. It is a raw morning. Visibility is less than ¼ mile. A swell
has set in from the north; it is colliding with the remains of the
southwesterly swell of yesterday and causing something of a
bobble. Hurts us in this light windward going.

It is hard to keep up racing tension. Came on deck earlier to
find a cockpit bull session, all hands laughing and talking, the
helmsman casually joining in. So for once I turned heavy skipper
and "broke it up" Navy style. Now feel embarrassed although I
know everyone in their hearts agreed with me. Despite the im-
pression I might have given in these notes by relating bits of
conversation and levity, *Caribbee* has been sailed as conscientiously as any boat I have ever been aboard even for a short race.
We have not only driven day and night as hard as we might
during an afternoon race on Long Island Sound, but it has been
more than merely carrying sail: all hands have stayed alert to
shifts of wind and the other factors involved in keeping a boat
going her best. Whenever we carry a spinnaker or are close on the
wind with a genoa a man is forward, calling, and a second man
stands by amidships. Usually only the helmsman and the man
relieved are in the cockpit, and the helmsman talks very little.

But this transition has made our spirits sag, and consequently
lowered our racing efficiency. It is a terrible temptation to huddle

down out of the rain. A light head wind and a jump of a sea with 2000 miles to go is enough to cause a let-down. Yesterday we were talking of a new record and today are getting nowhere. Our competitors to the south may still be carrying the old breeze, streaking past. The recent Bermuda Race was a good example of the vagaries of wind on the ocean, even when boats were in sight of each other; then we watched smaller competitors come from out of sight astern and go out of sight over the horizon ahead while we lay becalmed, lacking even steerageway. So *Janabel* or *Marabu* or *Samuel Pepys*—or perhaps all of them—might at this moment be moving along at close to hull speed, while we stay right here. Still, that is something different, something over which we have no control. We can't feel too bad if we lose that way, but we would never forgive ourselves if we lost by minutes and could think back and remember where we ourselves had thrown away hours.

Now we go as well again as these conditions permit.

9:50 a.m.: Just finished my wheel trick. The wind was never more fluky on the Chesapeake—it is jumping all over the place. It sounds ridiculous but we spent the first fifteen minutes of our watch debating the proper tack. On being forced down to 020 degrees on the starboard tack, we prepared to come about, as the port would be nearer the charted course; but when we got ready to come around we were lifted right up to 060 degrees.

We are back in that old racing groove, everyone on his toes. At the moment Bobby is forward calling the genoa and acting as bow lookout. The fog has again shut down, but the strength of the wind remains about the same: we are logging it at 6 to 8 knots.

It is amazing how different boat and crew feel when keyed up. *Caribbee* moves through the water nearly a knot faster in identical conditions, and we are all much happier. Even personal discomfort is forgotten in the challenge of not missing a shift that might mean many seconds in our total elapsed time. We still have the mental hazard of worrying about the others, but it is inevitable that they will have some soft going too. Maybe they're in this same area of calm—after all, no swell rolls in to show wind anywhere to the south—and are suffering identical conditions. And maybe *Caribbee* can be made to keep going better than they, so actually we continue to open a lead. Maybe. At any rate, that is the way we should sail it and that's the way we are sailing it. And we all feel better.

It wasn't what I said a while ago that made the difference. Every man aboard knows as much about racing as I do. My remarks only made them remember what these miserable conditions made us all temporarily forget. That's the wonderful thing about a crew of real sailors: you don't have to explain anything, from sail-handling to tactics to staying on the ball. I would be willing to bet right now there won't be another let-down, no matter how long it takes to get to Plymouth.

The barometer is climbing nearly as rapidly as it fell last week. Which makes me hope the westerlies are close behind; I always associate west winds with a rising glass. Meanwhile the northerly swell has pulled around into the northeast and gotten considerably bigger. So maybe our next prize package will come from that direction. A nice nor'east gale would be about the only thing that could make this slop a pleasant memory.

I wonder why the manufacturers of oilskin pants don't take into consideration a very frequent and necessary human function, especially in weather cold enough to enforce the wearing of oilskins? Shedding layers of garments to find suspender straps is a terrible chore, making even more difficult the task described by Frank as "getting at one inch of plumbing through two inches of insulation."

Frank recently made another valid observation, which I trust was recorded by Mother Carey's little feathered friends. They no doubt conjured up this weather after hearing me wonder how they would taste *en brochette*. Watching them scamper over the swells like sandpipers on a beach, Frank said: "I like them because they're the only other things crazy enough to be out here with us." But, on second thought, maybe a Mother Carey's chicken wouldn't consider that very flattering. In fact, they might get damned annoyed by the comparison.

Ain't nobody out here but us chickens, and they're mad at us.

1:35 p.m.: Leaning back expanding after another of Henry's meals. We may have complaints about fate but none about our cook. Hot biscuits, pies, baked hams, soufflés—the works. Always hot, always good, always on time, and all turned out on a non-gimbaling alcohol stove.

Another watch is behind, but not many miles. At 11:15 we tacked on being forced down to 020 degrees, a course which not only took us away from where we wanted to go but headed us almost directly into the swell, so *Caribbee* plunged bows under and stopped dead. Now doing better although the course is highly variable and speed averages between 3.5 and 6 knots.

Had something of a start shortly before lunch. We heard a foghorn but were unable to determine the bearing until a trawler suddenly appeared under our starboard bow. She was close enough for us to read her name, *Igaratza,* and was on what seemed at first to be a collision course. I was at the wheel and automatically executed the well-known maneuver of getting the hell out of the way—I know all about a sailing vessel holding course and also know where several sank doing it. But her net was towing astern and she had bare steerageway, so we cut close across her bow. A big crew was on her foredeck; all hands stopped work to wave and shout and we yelled back, although neither group could understand the other. I believe they were Portuguese. After the first fright it gave us a nice companionable feeling to find fellow humans packed away in the same box of gray cotton. Within a few moments the *Igaratza* had disappeared astern, but as a tangible souvenir we acquired a gull. He detached himself from the flock waiting for the trawl and now hovers in our wake staring down reproachfully at a trail of tin cans, well polished. He had better take the hint and leave while he has the strength. Even a seagull couldn't exist on what goes overboard from this ship.

During the final few minutes of our watch I sat on the bow pulpit as forward lookout. Not much in sight except a narrow circle of water, but water to me is perpetually fascinating. On these Banks the sea is gray-black and actually looks cold. Today it is very confused, fairly large swells coming in from a dozen directions to pile up into steep pyramids which collapse as patches of white foam. By suddenly appearing from under the blanket of fog even a normal swell seems mysterious and fearsome, the embodiment of impersonality and power. Nothing could be more different than the aspect and feel of the Grand Banks of Newfoundland and the Grand Banks of the Bahamas, one so dark and cold, the other so bright and warm. Here the water is murky and opaque, and looking down I remembered crossing the Bahama Banks from Norman Cay to Nassau on a calm day: the old *Temptress* seemed to be magically suspended in air, or somehow to be gliding over a sheet of the clearest glass, so our shadow on the sand two fathoms below was as sharply defined as any silhouette thrown on a sheet, and it looked as though you could reach down from the bowsprit and pick up starfish without wetting your arm.

Which reminds me: last night our Andros parlimentarian dressing for deck was a sight worth coming here to see. Basil won't swim even in the Bahamas until "summer," which by his definition is mid-August. So when he got out of his bunk and found the cabin like a deep-freeze locker he began to pile on the layers —first heavy long underwear, then two thicknesses of socks, two of woolen pants, two of sweaters, and a nylon oilskin suit and rubber knee boots. Then two more sweaters and—so help me!—a heavy rubber oilskin suit! And two knitted watch caps, with a sou'wester lashed on top! He could just barely waddle up the companionway steps. Frank asked innocently as he appeared on deck: "Do you put on socks between the layers of boots?"

11:35 p.m.: So ends a frustrating watch and day. About half an hour ago were finally forced to drop the genoa to prevent damage. Now we slat back and forth without steerageway; there is no discernible motion to the air except that being fanned by the mainsail on each roll. Slat and bang, roll and slat, each reef point pattering against the canvas, boom straining against preventer tackles—and I spent weeks girding my mental loins for driving before gales! Now the only decision involving the safety of the ship is whether to lower sails to keep them from slatting to ribbons.

The saddest sight is the character at the wheel, completely useless yet unceasingly hopeful. No creature ashore or afloat is a more woeful spectacle than a racing helmsman without wind, all ready to go some place but nothing to go with, while the sails droop in folds.

During the last hour I kept remembering an observation by John Hall, a Bahama cook, who looked out of the galley during a spell of hard head winds to say: "You eats what the cook serves." And in yacht racing you certainly do: I can't think of a comparable situation in any other sport. If you run out of wind, you stop. Period. There is no question of relative swiftness, or lack of preparation or skill, or any human virtue or failure. It is like a racing car opening up a big lead and then running out of gas—no, because that would involve human or mechanical error. It is more like a cross-country runner getting well ahead of the pack, moving smoothly and strongly, morale and confidence high, feeling fine . . . and suddenly grinding to a halt, powerless in the grip of a magic spell that froze him like Lot's wife while the others caught up.

And we certainly have ground to a stop. All during the afternoon and early evening the wind was very spotty while the confused sea persisted. A few faint breaths appeared to move us along at speeds of 5 knots or better; we would become hopeful if they lasted more than a few minutes, thinking perhaps the change had come, but the puff would die and the needle of the Kenyon drop down to 2 or even less. So for perhaps another twenty minutes we would wallow along to the accompaniment of drumming reef points; then another cat's-paw of breeze would steal out of the fog and the whole cycle of movement, hope, and disappointment would begin again.

Now we are flat, deader than Imperial Caesar or a doornail or anything else you might care to name. Our little world is very little indeed, a gray cone surmounted by the masthead light. The fog closes in all around. We can hear Mother Carey's chickens but cannot see them. Their cry is at once harsh and plaintive, something like a whippoorwill's call. I'll swear a few minutes ago one close astern jeered: "Yak-yak-*yak:* ha-ha-ha-ha-*HA!*" on a rising note of derision. Maybe he was right about giving us the ha-ha but that crack of yak-yak was unfair. Deck conversation has ceased. Long silences are broken only by the explosive ejaculation of a single four-letter word. Even there we don't seem to show much originality, although Bobby did display inventiveness toward the end of the watch by coming through with a five-letter word. But as it was only in a plural form—a masculine-gender noun that is invariably plural—perhaps he doesn't deserve too much credit.

When I get to hearing things in bird talk I'd better make like the ostrich. Hope to hell I can sleep.

THE sea is never wholly still. Always there is movement on its surface or within its depths: the long slow pulse of the tide, the

"Boss, don't know what the stern is doing . . ."

". . . but the bow is going like hell!"

seeping of cold water toward lower levels, the lazy swell of a distant gale, the irresistible flow of mighty currents, the serrated ranks of waves driven along before the wind. Long before human eyes saw or began to comprehend any of its mysteries the sea rolled unchecked over what became the land, by its power and alchemy forming the world as we know it now.

There is on this planet no other force to compare with the sea for creation or destruction. It was the cradle of the first life, and may well be the repository of the last. There is nothing so beautiful in repose or awesome in anger; nothing so beneficial to man or so ruinous to his projects; nothing to inspire greater confidence or more abject terror; nothing so simple or so complex.

Of all the wonders of wide waters, the phenomenon of current is the most fascinating. "There is a river in the ocean," wrote Matthew Fontaine Maury, the founder of modern oceanography. "In the severest droughts it never fails, and in the mightiest floods it never overflows; its banks and its bottom are of cold water, while its current is of warm; the Gulf of Mexico is its fountain, and its mouth is in the Arctic Seas. It is the Gulf Stream. There is in the world no other such majestic flow of waters. Its current is more rapid than the Mississippi or the Amazon, and its volume more than a thousand times greater. Its waters . . . are of an indigo blue. They are so distinctly marked that their line of junction with the common sea-water may be traced by the eye . . . so sharp is the line, and such the want of affinity between those waters, and such, too, the reluctance, so to speak, on the part of the Gulf Stream to mingle with the littoral waters of the sea."

From the earliest days of navigation in the Caribbean the existence of a mighty current was known and utilized. Columbus discovered himself in the grip of it, and Peter Martyr a few years later tried to analyze the source and effect. Every Spanish galleon bringing home treasure had on board the *Derrotero de las Antillas,* a highly secret book of sailing directions. The recommended route took advantage of the current well to the north of the Straits of Florida, but no chart of the northern reaches existed until the

the indefatigable Ben Franklin, in 1770 when he was postal director, published one to speed mail between New England and European ports.

Curiosity about the origin of the Gulf Stream increased with knowledge of its extent. In 1804 Captain James Manderson of the Royal Navy issued *An Examination into the True Cause of the Stream of Florida* and named the Mississippi River as the "prime mover of the Florida Stream." This caused a new wave of speculation. One Captain Livingston, a shipmaster whose name frequently appears in the pilot books of the nineteenth century, replied by pointing out that the Mississippi emptied into the Gulf of Mexico no more than "a three-thousandth part of the water which is discharged in the Strait between the Florida Reefs and the Bemini Kays," and went on to refute the theory further by noting on the basis of Manderson's theory the velocity of the Stream might be calculated by the rise and fall of the floods of the Mississippi, while in "August, 1818, the River Mississippi was uncommonly low, and I never saw the Gulf Stream run with greater velocity."

In *The Physical Geography of the Sea* Maury supported Livingston in his argument, but disagreed with the Captain's own theory that the flow of water depended on "the motion of the sun in the ecliptic, and the influence he has on the waters of the Atlantic." Maury also disagreed with the learned Dr. Franklin, who was of "the opinion that came to be most generally received and deep-rooted in the minds of seafaring people . . . which held that the Gulf Stream is the escaping of the waters that have been *forced* into the Caribbean Sea by the trade-winds, and that it is the pressure of those winds upon the water which drives up into that sea a head, as it were, for this stream."

In turn Maury believed the Gulf Stream depended only partially upon the pressure of the trade winds and the "head of water" in the Gulf. He pointed out "when we inject water into a pool, be the force never so great, the jet is soon overcome, broken up, and made to disappear." He saw the Stream as a vast "conducting pipe" with the "furnace" in the "torrid zone," bringing water from "the cauldrons of the Mexican Gulf and Caribbean Sea" to make Erin the "Emerald Isle" while "in the same latitude on this side the coasts of Labrador are fast bound in fetters of ice." Thus he believed temperature was the prime motivating force, together with a difference in density due to greater salinity.

Present research tends to support Franklin and those "seafaring people." Measurements by oceanographers with fantastic modern instruments—such as the geomagnetic electrokinetograph, which measures water flow through determining the amount of electricity generated by its passage across the earth's magnetic field—point to wind as the major force behind the Gulf Stream.

Visualize the North Atlantic as a giant circular basin, its lower and upper limits the equator and the polar circle, its sides the American continents and the coasts of Europe and Africa. From right to left—east to west—across the bottom the trade winds blow with steady relentless pressure, as you might blow on water in a hand basin. This sets up a surface movement which is known as the Equatorial Current, a drift that flows across the ocean near the equator, continues along the Northern shore of South America, and finally funnels through the openings between the West Indian islands to bank up in the Caribbean. Because of this piling of water against the western shore the whole surface of the sea has been sloping up on a gradient of about 3 inches for each 1000 miles, but along the shores of Central America it is forced to an elevation of several feet. Something has to happen, and it does, the result being a terrific surge through the gap between Cuba and the Yucutan Peninsula, and thence on through the gully separating Florida and the shallow Bahama Banks. No water goes into the Gulf of Mexico, as it is a pocket offering no egress. Nor does the Gulf contribute to the Stream—which makes "Gulf Stream" a complete misnomer.

This gigantic jet of tropical water—40 miles wide and more

than 1000 feet deep—is like nothing else in the world, flowing at rates that recently have been determined to be as high as 9 knots in narrow bands within the main stream. It sweeps up along the coast of North America, roughly following the 100-fathom curve on a northerly course; at Cape Hatteras it swerves off to the northeast; and off the Grand Banks of Newfoundland changes course again, this time to almost due east. Here also it alters character on colliding with the intensely cold waters of the Labrador Current flowing south from polar regions. There is some mixing and a widening and slowing of the main body of the Stream, so beyond the Banks the remaining current is known as the North Atlantic Drift. But there is plenty of punch left: the Drift divides north of the Azores, one branch flowing along past the British Isles and Scandinavian Peninsula, the other swinging south to pass the Canary Islands and the shoulder of Africa, where the northeast trades take hold and start the whole cycle again.

Thus the outer perimeter of the Atlantic basin is constantly circulating as a huge lazy whirlpool, impelled by easterly trades to the south and prevailing westerlies to the north. In the center there is a vast calm eye called the Sargasso Sea, so stagnant its beds of drifting weed frightened early sailors and gave rise to legends of missing ships being held fast forever.

This is a greatly oversimplified sketch of the Atlantic and its mightiest current. Innumerable other factors enter in, such as the Coriolis force, the tendency of wind and water to be pulled by gravity and the spin of the earth clockwise in the northern hemisphere and counterclockwise in the southern; and the constant flow of waters of different temperature seeking their proper depths; and the mixing of waters of varying salinity. The whole complicated relationship is a study that has occupied the lifetimes of many able men, yet we are far from solving the mysteries of the sea.

My own interest in ocean currents went back to a winter day in 1933, when I picked up a glass fishing float on the beach of

Great Exuma, one of the Bahamas. I held it in my hand and looked out over the Atlantic, visualizing the thousands of miles it had come since drifting away from a net in the Bay of Biscay, and thought of the forces that had acted upon its iridescent surface, and once again was overwhelmed by the wonder of it all.

Since then I had spent many days and nights in or near the Gulf Stream, that "river in the sea." I had sailed past Cape Corrientes on the southern coast of Cuba, which the U.S. *Coast Pilot* names as its point of origin; had ridden it north from Havana to Charleston; had bucked it out around Cape Hatteras; and had crossed it more times than it would be possible to remember.

Now on *Caribbee* we approached its end, at least insofar as name is concerned, the point in its career where it locks in struggle with that icy giant from the north, the Labrador Current. It is a battleground that has treated men harshly through the centuries: almost constant fog in summer and blinding blizzards in winter; calms, gales, drifting ice, confused seas, violent changes in temperature and crazy shifts of wind. Long-dead John Purdy wrote in his *Memoir of the Northern Atlantic Ocean:* "The navigation about and to the southward of the Newfoundland Bank seems to require all the seaman's spirit, skill, and vigilance; for here, in particular, he may have to combat with the contending elements."

And we were to continue to be victims of the battle.

7th Day

44° 40′ N.
47° 38′ W.
Run: noon to noon: 86 miles
Average speed: 2.79 knots
Total run to date: 1100 miles

Wednesday, July 9. 5:00 a.m.: In the pale dawn light four figures sit in a row along the starboard side of the deckhouse, oil-skin-clad, sea-booted, multi-sweatered. They stare out into the fog, watching oily swells appear in endless procession. There is not a ripple of breeze on the backs of the swells. All sails lie along the decks like broken wings—and about as useful. Everything is clammy cold and drips.

When we came on at 3:00 the port watch had just set sails after 3 hours with them down. We moved along for perhaps 30 minutes, while the moon tried to break through—and did to the extent of taking on an outline. It even warmed slightly, and as we crept along at perhaps 2 knots we hoped the turn had come. But then nothing: tried to maintain steerageway under genoa and mizzen staysail, main furled, but not even that would work.

From below Basil's snores reverberate. When he first started we jumped to man the foghorn in answer. Now we listen only with envy; we think how nice it is to be asleep.

We stay cheerful but somehow the strain is greater than during bad weather. This calm frays the nerves as nothing else I have ever experienced.

7:25 a.m.: For the four hours we were on deck Frank logged in the "estimated made good" distance column: 0400—"0"; 0500—

"0"; 0600—"¼ mile"; 0700—"½ mile." Under "steered by compass" is the terse notation: "All over." And under "comments" he wrote: "Had debate as to whether we moved more than ¼ of a mile in 4 hours and the skipper pointed out these things mount up faster than you think and we might have done one mile."

About half an hour before we came off watch a faint breeze struck in from the quarter; rushed to make sail and even got out the spinnaker gear. Everything on deck again in 15 minutes. Seemed like sails were up and down every hour on the hour—or maybe half-hour.

The sun is trying to shine; it lacks color and outline but a pale silver path across the water is better than an even murk. Also it is a reminder that a sun shines elsewhere in the world, and maybe we'll eventually get out to it.

3:00 p.m.: For the first time in a very long time—literally, and to us it seems even longer—we actually move. About 10:00 this morning a gentle breeze came in from the east, dead ahead, but at least enabling the port watch to get on some sail and stop the interminable rolling and banging. Although it was a trifle unfavorable Dick and Basil chose the port tack to get the hell off these Banks, if possible.

Soon the fog lifted to a high mist, and around noon the sun was bright enough for Frank to get sights. There was a great shedding of oilskins and spreading of wet sails. Then the wind veered to about southeast, forcing us to come about. Now we steer 070 degrees instead of the 090 degrees desired, so we continue farther north whether we like it or not. We have been averaging 5 knots, but as I write this we are going back into another band of fog and the wind lightens.

It is curious to reflect on the breaks of racing. By playing it boldly we may have lost all: we came north to find wind and instead have gone flat. Those to the south may be moving comfortably along in bright sunshine, never suffering from the cold, and not getting into fog heavy enough to kill wind. It may turn out our very speed was our greatest enemy, especially by encouraging us to carry a spinnaker and go north of the great-circle route in anticipation of breezes fresh enough to more than compensate for the extra distance. Now we are trapped. With the wind hanging to the south of east the port tack would be completely disastrous, taking us back over our course and inevitably putting us astern of the fleet. Yet we cannot lay course on the starboard tack either, and thus are forced up and up into higher latitudes. Which is getting your bad luck with compound interest.

7:45 p.m.: At six o'clock we had been one week at sea.

A celebration was in order, so both watches and the cook assembled in the cockpit for a *Trans-Atlantic Special*—half Barbados rum, half canned orange-and-grapefruit juice, well shaken but no ice. A potent and warming beverage.

All hands were in high spirits, depressed only by our "40 and 8" progress—8 miles in 40 hours. It is not quite that bad, of course, and it is good we can joke about it instead of snapping at each other. I have never seen a group with better dispositions or morale—again the mark of real sailors. Living on a small boat is one of those arts that develop along with the more obvious skills.

This is the first time I have ever served cocktails during a race. On board *Caribbee* the liquor is not put away; it is always there for anyone who may want a drink (a privilege never abused), but I do not offer it. Drinking at sea is one of those fetishes that vary from boat to boat: I have crewed on vessels whose skipper loudly proclaimed there would be no drinking and actually locked up the liquor (and immediately all hands—even virtual teetotalers—developed horrible thirsts and began to grouse); and aboard other vessels where Martinis appeared before lunch and the skipper just as loudly proclaimed he wasn't going to miss his usual snort just because he happened to be racing (no grumbling on the part of the crew but considerably less efficiency).

As in all things the happy medium seems best: on *Caribbee* we drink moderately at sea when cruising in good weather; we rarely drink when racing. But a Trans-Atlantic Race is a special case. Dick and I discussed the matter at length before leaving Bermuda and agreed three weeks or thereabouts would be a long time to be wholly dry. He believed a regular afternoon get-together of all hands a very valuable thing to prevent any tensions from developing between individuals or watches. Having this in mind was one of the reasons for adopting the system of two 6-hour day watches; losing a half-hour below every other day won't hurt anyone, and certainly we see little enough of the opposite watch during the remaining 23½ hours. This afternoon it worked fine: we are in such good shape a couple of cocktails produced a wonderful effect. There was much laughter and kidding and swapping of stories, just like old friends meeting again—which surprisingly enough is a rather apt way of putting it. For a week the watches have done little more than pass each other on the way to either food or a bunk—and if there is anything we're mutually faster at than getting to the table it is getting to the sack. So I feel the cocktail half-hour a great success.

Previously the wind had diminished and we shifted from genoa to drifter, a very light-weight, full-cut nylon jib made principally for reaching, but flat enough for windward work in very faint breezes. Because it is of lighter material and less affected by rolling, it works when the genoa will not. With it we cannot point quite so high, but it kept us moving when otherwise we would have been dead in the water.

Suddenly feel very sleepy. The rum and dinner are working.

8th Day

46° 26′ N.
46° 04′ W.
Run: noon to noon: 125 miles
Average speed: 5.21 knots
Total run to date: 1225 miles

Thursday, July 10. 12:35 a.m.: The sea is as smooth as an inland lake—in central Siberia. It is cold, very cold, and the faint breeze is strictly from the tundras. Overhead the moon struggles to show through a high overcast but only succeeds in looking bleak and forlorn.

Can't get over the North Atlantic—at least for the moment. There is no swell from any direction; no tumble, no surge. As Frank observed a few minutes ago, "It's flatter than a platter. . . ." What breeze there is hangs around southeast, up or down a point as it freshens or eases, but is never strong enough to put the slightest ripple on the surface. Only the upper parts of the sails are working. It is almost eerie to glide along noiselessly at between 4 and 5 knots. Earlier the wind had more weight, for the port watch logged an average speed of 6.8 for the hour ending at 2100; 7.2 for 2200; and 6.8 for 2300. On taking over, we jinxed it, falling by midnight to 5.2.

Somehow am sleepier than at any time on the passage. It is sheer agony to stay awake; I am writing this by flashlight for something to do. While waiting for my wheel trick it was hard to avoid toppling overboard; I huddled forward on the pulpit, trying to keep my eyes from watering too much to be able to see the jib, holding on the headstay for dear life—maybe literally. Undoubt-

edly the rum has something to do with it as I was completely relaxed and slept heavily during my watch below, but the silence
and the piercing cold have a hypnotic effect.

We approach Flemish Cap, an area of shoal water similar to
but much smaller than the Grand Banks. Geologists consider both
part of a submerged mountain range broken off from the American continent, of which Newfoundland is a visible part. The
average depth of the Cap is around 80 fathoms, of the Grand
Banks much less. Once in an old pilot book I read a theory that
the Banks were formed by rubble dropped from icebergs brought
down by the Labrador Current and melted by the Gulf Stream.
Undoubtedly that meeting has contributed sediment, but more
important has been the effect on marine life, and thus indirectly
on the affairs of man and the destiny of nations. Even recently
diplomats have squabbled over fishing rights, for here through the
centuries have swarmed countless millions of fish: the currents
bring plankton, tiny marine organisms that form the basis of the
whole chain of life in the sea; plankton attract larger animals
which feed upon them; these in turn fatten cod—just like car-
toons of a string of bigger and bigger fish pursuing each other
with gaping mouths. Early navigators wrote of ships being
stopped by fish, so thickly packed were the schools—no doubt an
exaggeration but not a very great one, for at one time they could
be scooped up with baskets or anything else handy, and large
merchant vessels had to follow the smacks like Chesapeake Bay
"buy boats" to take off the catch before the fishermen sank from
sheer weight. Now the Banks are almost depleted. If we did a
"bit of fishing" as has been facetiously suggested as we lie becalmed our chances of catching anything would be very slim indeed.

Also we are close to sailing the "deep blue sea" in a very literal
sense. Everyone is so accustomed to the distortions in the charts
of our old friend Mercator they forget the slant of the North
American continent toward Europe. So actually, although *Carib-*

bee has been several hundred miles offshore and has come over a thousand miles since leaving Bermuda, our course has paralleled the easterly trend of the land. When crossing the Banks we were back on the continental shelf. But at Flemish Cap begins the open abyss of the Atlantic, a true "point of no return."

There is a pale band around the horizon to the south and east where the moon apparently shines. Here we have a solid canopy of dark cloud.

2:00 a.m.: We are finally out into the clear. The "pale band" became sky. Astern lies a curtain of cloud and fog. The moon shows, still somewhat diluted, and a few stars with frosty, misty halos. But to lessen our joy the wind has backed toward the east, so we are forced off to 050 degrees. Desired course remains 090 degrees—we have no choice except to go farther north and hope for wind, even though a high and almost stationary barometer makes us fear we are in the grip of a stagnant high-pressure area.

We debate the drifter versus the genoa. Whenever the speed drops below four we get ready to shift, then a puff comes along to make us feel the genoa is more efficient. And so it goes by the hour—with five spinnakers below waiting for those westerlies encountered by almost every other sailor in these parts since John Cabot in 1497!

7:25 a.m.: A brilliant sunny morning, crisp and clear; one of those "highs" in high latitudes such as we had 3 years ago when crossing Sweden by the Göta Canal, and later among the skerries of the Gulf of Finland.

8:20 a.m.: The sea is very smooth, the smallest of undulations from the southeast running in under others from the northeast. In places it is slick, in others slightly ruffled, yet the apparent wind remains fairly constant in both force and direction. We steer 060 degrees and average between 4 and 5 knots.

At 0800 heard a weather forecast from Newfoundland. It predicted "Light variables over the Grand Banks; off the south coast of Labrador wind southwest at 15 knots." That's for us, and hope 'tis an indication of more wind to the north than to the south. Maybe this vacuum extends right back to Bermuda.

Since we have gotten clear of the fog *Caribbee* has never stopped, making my previous hope rather futile. Still, in areas where great volumes of warm air and cold water meet there is bound to be fog. Here winds warmed by the Gulf Stream to the south and the continental land mass of North America to the west blow over water directly from the Arctic. And such fog does not necessarily kill the wind; in fact, Maury states "As a rule, fogs and gales increase both in numbers and in frequency as you recede from the equator." I'll gladly trade some of one for some of the other, any time. Guess which.

11:45 a.m.: A real working morning: both jibtopsails, forestaysail, spinnaker, balloon forestaysail, and mizzen staysail spread on deck for drying. The brand-new baby jibtop is mildewed and smells—shows how things must be watched and even then can get ahead in circumstances beyond your control. This is the first drying day since we came on the Banks, yet sails stowed unbagged and spread as loosely as possible have already begun to go. No real harm done yet—just the new look lost.

Frank spent two hours aloft checking the track, pins, tangs, splices, blocks, and fittings, and looking for chafe. There is no more vital a member of a crew than the man who can go aloft in weather fair or foul, and whose knowledge of rigging keeps all in order against the hour of test. Everything was in fine shape. The only masthead job was reseizing the spinnaker blocks. We use double halyards, one on either side of the mast, so in case of failure one is always backing up the other. They also give us better control of the sail when hoisting or lowering.

So far I would say the main problems of shipkeeping on a passage of this sort are mildew and chafe. Plus of course fatigue in wood or metal. The first two can be kept under control by constant vigilance; we make hourly inspections for chafe, and after every change in trim make a circuit of the deck to see that all points of constant or intermittent contact are protected. Mildew even during prolonged periods of damp weather can be minimized by spreading sails below, and making sure there is some circulation of air between the folds of canvas. And of course we sun damp sails on deck whenever conditions permit. Fatigue is something else again. Inspection will detect surface failures, such as cracks, but no amount of care and watchfulness can warn of internal flaws or approaching disintegration. Metal tires. It can stand only so much. Without warning a trusted fitting in apparently perfect condition can let go: the mast might go over the side, a bad leak might develop, steering gear or rudder might fail. In preparation for a test such as this, any questionable items should be replaced, and later inspection should be constant. Then it is permissible to be fatalistic—at first leave nothing to chance, afterwards don't worry.

While Frank was aloft I sent up my Contax camera with an ultra-wide-angle lens fitted and gave a photography lesson from the deck until the watch below objected to the shouting. Short-focal-length lenses allow much more detail aboard ship. There is a story of a famous lady photographer backing right overboard, and I sympathize with her—about half the time when using a normal camera you can't get what you want without being able to hang about 30 feet out in space. The wide-angle lens helps.

At this writing it is lovely on deck. The breeze is cool but the sun warm enough to encourage stripping to the waist—although at the moment I feel perhaps I am rushing the season a bit. But it is good to take off the red flannel undershirt worn day and night ever since we hit the Banks. I almost expected to find it had developed a capillary system.

1:45 p.m.: Every day as soon after noon as possible Frank posts the day's run on a small chart attached to the cabin bulkhead by scotch tape. It has been fascinating to watch the pencilled line grow—at first by very noticeable leaps, lately by creeping bounds. "What did we make?" becomes the chant before

Frank puts away the sextant, but he is reticent until all the figures are in hand, and even then will say nothing: like the high priest in some ancient ritual he crosses from the navigator's nook to the chart, shielding it with his body as he adds a dot and draws a line from the previous dot. Then we crowd around, and he gives us the magic number—the mileage our blood, sweat (or chills), and tears have wrung from Father Neptune in the preceding 24 hours. It is the most dramatic incident of the day, a moment of great glee: "We must be murderin' 'em!" or great pessimism: "Christ, I'll bet we're behind the whole bloody fleet!" or prayerful optimism: "Maybe they're back in the fog, slatting, while we work out into this new wind!"

Today our run by accurate observation—beginning with a star fix at dawn, sun lines during the morning, and a noon sight—was 125 miles. Thus for the "day" (a sailor's day of 24 hours) we averaged 5.21 knots—not bad considering the conditions, but not good if the others had more wind. If they had identical, probably damned good.

As we tow no recording log our day's run and hourly average are not exact accounts of the distance we actually sail. In these baffling conditions—especially when beating to windward if a whorl of the Labrador Current should be against us—we might sail 60 miles to make good 30. Daily distances are reckoned in a straight line from the preceding day's noon position. Thus at the end of this passage east we probably will have sailed at least 10 per cent farther than the distance the record will show.

Our Kenyon speedometer in the cockpit is reasonably accurate at around 6 knots, having an error of 7 per cent on the high side which is corrected before logging. The helmsman's estimate of distance made good is entered at the end of each half-hour wheel trick, and has worked out with enough accuracy against daily fixes to give us confidence in our dead reckoning. We will tow a regular spinner log the last couple of days approaching the English coast.

The Royal Ocean Racing Club rules which govern conditions under which we sail permit radio transmission. In theory we should be able to maintain contact with the shore, or at least other vessels. In practice we can do nothing of the sort. Frequencies allowed yachts are not monitored by ships, nor are they capable of enough range to reach coastal stations. I have tried several times to contact the United States Coast Guard cutter acting as a weather-reporting post at station "Dog," which should be within range of our transmitter, but can get no reply. Our failure to establish radio communications is no surprise: it is what we expected before the start. Too many government regulations surround the use of radio for it to be of much value to a small ship without elaborate preparations and equipment.

Each day at noon we run the engine for about an hour to charge batteries. Although we did not remove our propeller, the shaft was pinned to prevent accidental turning in case the clutch slipped. So although we have electricity, our dependence on the elements for progress and ourselves in emergencies is the same as it would have been centuries ago. There is no difference between the ocean of 1492 and 1952. Even the refinements of modern navigation—sextant and chronometer and books of tables—are useless if clouds obscure the sun and stars. Wind and weather are still the factors that govern our destiny.

Today after the usual position-posting ritual Frank and I studied the track charts of the Bermuda-Cuxhaven Race of 1936. On the eighth day the leaders were south of this position but about the same distance from England. Not much consolation in that, except after calm going near Bermuda they found plenty of wind —too much for most at times—in the higher latitudes. So maybe our turn will come.

Here below there is no motion whatever. A glass filled to the brim would not spill a drop. On deck it is still drying weather; the sun is bright and the same light breeze holds from east-southeast to east, so we continue north willy-nilly while the barograph

"The spinnaker work has started.... For the first time there are complaints below. Bulkheads creak and groan.... Parachute spinnakers are efficient brutes, but the strains they set up are incredible. Often I wonder how wood and metal can be engineered to withstand the strains imposed."

"We remain time minded in all things. Even here on an empty ocean, far from the sight of anyone, we clock our sail changes and try to make them as fast as if we were in close quarters."

climbs higher. It now reads 30.50. We must be trapped in the
center of a high. "You take the high road and they'll take . . ."
Nuts.

8:00 p.m.: Always the compensations: this morning the port
watch—poetic group!—noted in the log: "Beautiful dawn; sun
red, sky clear." Now the starboard watch appreciates the sunset.

The sky is almost completely cloudless; there are a few wisps
of cirrus high in the south, a few more in the west—right over
the horizon where the sun is disappearing—and a couple of fat
cumulus puffs directly opposite. Overhead the sky is a most amazing shade of blue, very bright, very deep. Around the horizon except to the west there is a corona of pale lavender, deepening to
purple where the sky joins the sea. Over the sun the clouds are
rose. All these colors reflect and combine in the water, and take
on a peculiar golden sheen, especially toward the sun.

There is a wonderful quality—a "feel"—to the air. It has a
pleasantly dry chill bite, the same as a frosty fall morning in the
north woods. Those red flannels are back on; also corduroy pants,
a heavy flannel shirt, and an eiderdown jacket. But no gloves and
my hands are not uncomfortable.

I write this sitting on the forward end of the deckhouse. The
drifter is the sail pulling us along at the moment, but the genoa is
hanked on the stay ready to be hoisted if a little more breeze
strikes in. Everything is snugged down for the night should a wind
pounce upon us from this innocent sky.

Suddenly I look up as *Caribbee* rolls and everything slats. The
main boom bangs and the reef points beat their tattoo. Frank, at
the wheel, asks: "Were those just three isolated swells?" I look to
the east and see no more. The sea remains flat. But three long
swells did roll in from some place over the rim of the world, impelled by some unknown force far away: the first shouldered us
up and rolled us to port and the next two arrived in perfect syn-
chronization to slap us back and forth as they slid under. I look
at the sails and call: "All full again." A movement ahead catches

my eye. The night shift of Mother Carey's chickens is arriving on schedule. During the day we have seen many gulls, some of them the same fat Arctic gulls I once saw swimming along the edge of the polar ice pack, 'way up at 82 degrees north. This is a relative world: I suppose they will report seeing a sail boat "down south" when they rejoin their pals. Also we have sighted a shark, a school of blackfish, the masts of a steamer hull down over the horizon, and a small southbound whale cutting across our bow. This part of the ocean is positively crowded.

Now the color of the sky has changed. By my watch it is almost 8:30, and ahead it is nearly dark. The sky is a very deep blue, almost purple, while astern it is rose and lavender. And the sea ahead and astern matches the heavens above. Thus we sail into the night.

Yes, the compensations: I wouldn't miss being here for anything in the world. True, there are times when I gnaw my nails and swear at our luck and lie sleepless in my bunk—but I wouldn't trade a minute of it for anything.

10:35 p.m.: At 10:00 the moon arose redder than I have ever seen it before. Made me remember the calypso song: "The moon came up in blood." Now it is brilliant, casting an equally brilliant path across the water. But no air stirs. Before the moon appeared every star reflected as in a pool.

The sails hang limp. Not even the drifter is lifting. If there was any swell we would have to drop everything. It is clear, calm and cold, lovely for everything except racing.

Unaccountably I have suddenly remembered the eggs shipped ahead, those precious eggs coated with plastic and now speeding across the Atlantic by steamer. It is vital we get to England before they go the way of all eggs—and unfortunately they are crated with our shore-going clothes: our dinner jackets, our "town and country" suits, our spare shirts. I can picture the headwaiter at Claridge's as I ask for a table: the averted eyes, the nose raised to an elevation even higher than usual. Horrors! And here we sit.

My concern stems from Henry's telling me today the eggs shipped ahead to Bermuda have gone bad. Three years ago on the Baltic cruise we carried similar eggs unrefrigerated for four months and lost nary one, but this time they were poorly packed and many were broken in transit. Washing removed the protective plastic coating and then they were like any other eggs.

This scientific age is fine until something goes wrong. Such as the coating on eggs. Or airplane engines. Or pilot charts.

☆ ☆
☆

THE sea is never wholly still. This is true not only of currents and invisible flowings and reflowings of liquid masses adjusting themselves in hidden depths, but of the surface as well. For even on the calmest days, even on one of those rare occasions when the eye cannot detect a ripple along an exposed beach, the visible face of the sea is actually stirring in some variation of the undulating pattern of movement men call "waves."

Waves are so much a part of the concept of the sea that the very words "wave" and "sea" have developed a curious relationship of virtual interchangeability, confusing to landsmen. The *sea* is as Falconer described it in his *Universal Dictionary of the Marine*, published in 1771: "a great congregation of waters." But, as he also points out, *sea* is "variously applied by sailors, to a single wave; to the agitation produced by a multitude of waves in a tempest; or to their particular progress or direction." Thus in 1641 Evelyn wrote in his *Diary:* "We sailed again with a contrary and impetuous wind, and a terrible sea." Or *sea* can mean large heavy waves, as Stanyhurst noted in 1582: "Theire ships too larboord doo nod, seas monsterus haunt theym." In sailor-talk waves opposing a course form a "head sea," waves with tumbling crests form a "breaking sea," and so on: the unabridged *Oxford English Dictionary* sums it up by saying that *sea* is used to describe surface conditions "with an epithet indicating the roughness or smoothness of the waves, or the presence or absence of swell."

Waves have been rolling over the oceans of the world since the dawn of time, restless and relentless, tirelessly reflecting the mood of the heavens above. Since Neolithic man first ventured forth into open water nothing has concerned the seafarer so directly, yet scientific analysis of the origin and nature of waves and related phenomena is a very recent thing, based on the experience of amphibious warfare and small-boat operations during World War II. For no matter how carefully an operation against enemy territory might be planned, or how thorough the preliminary bombing and naval bombardment, a beachhead could not be established unless the condition of the sea permitted. Thus the success and safety of an army might turn on the slope of a beach, and how a swell behaved upon it; or the speed of waves advancing from a storm centered a thousand miles away.

As a result of intensive study and the compilation of data from countless sources, in 1947 the U. S. Navy Hydrographic Office with the assistance of the Woods Hole Oceanographic Institution published a slim volume called *Wind Waves at Sea, Breakers and Surf*. In it is assembled all the knowledge of the ages, yet so complex is anything concerning the sea—even something so familiar and apparently simple as a wave—the first paragraph begins by admitting "It is difficult to frame a definition, in everyday terms, that will cover all the types of phenomena that are commonly called 'waves.' " Yet as definitions are necessary to any study, the authors continue to describe them as "successive ridges with intervening troughs or valleys which, in the case of wind waves, advance in undulatory motion." But there are waves of origin other than wind: the so-called "tidal waves" of hurricanes, which have nothing to do with the tides but are formed by the banking up and sudden release of water; or huge "tsunami" rollers generated by submarine landslides, which radiate with tremendous speed and power, on one occasion traveling from Java to the English Channel in 32 hours and drowning 36,000 people on the way; or the tides themselves, lifted by the gravitational effect of moon and sun, waves thousands of miles between crests but on the open sea only a foot or so high, ceaselessly running around the world in the Southern Ocean to spill over into the other oceans and flow north at perfectly predictable rates, varying in height and speed only when they encounter the shelves of continents.

But "wind waves" are the ones of most concern to the sailor, for "the old rule still holds and always will, that it is the waves of a storm, not its winds, that the mariner has to fear." In World War II wind waves tore the steel bow off the heavy cruiser *Pittsburgh* and sank destroyers, as they have overwhelmed vessels since man first sailed the seas. Wind waves become breakers which have dashed in the glass of the light tower on the Island of Uist in the Shetlands, 195 feet above the sea, or have thrown 7000-pound boulders over a 20-foot wall at Cherbourg; wind waves on the open sea have been clocked at speeds of 70 knots, and as swells surging in on the shore of Africa have attained lengths of 2719 feet, over half a land mile.

The growth of wind waves is one of the most fascinating—and in the latter stages awesome—manifestations of the sea. The cycle from calm to raging gale has recurred since the first formation of this planet, yet the exact relationship of wind and wave has never been repeated.

But the pattern is similar. Visualize the sea utterly flat and smooth, as far as the eye can detect: clouds reflecting by day, stars by night. The first faint "cat's-paw" of breeze raises tiny ripples, capillary in nature, being due to surface tension, not to the force of gravity. With every passing puff these ripples appear and disappear instantly, a delicate tracery watched for by every racing sailor during a calm. It has been estimated it requires a wind of from ½ to 2 knots to generate them. When the breeze in-

creases and they reach a length of about 0.68 inches from crest
to crest, and a velocity of about 0.76 feet per second, a transfor-
mation takes place: by some process not quite understood capillary ripples become gravitational waves, capable of growing into
moving mountains such as those described by Thomas Gates in
1609, who near Bermuda encountered a sea that "swelled above
the clouds, and gave battle unto heaven."

After the alteration has taken place waves continue to receive
energy from the wind and to increase in size due to the direct
push against their upwind slopes, but the whole process of building from ripples to a storm sea is not a simple matter of wind pressure. For while the wind is exerting force ahead against the crest,
it is blowing against the particles in the trough as they move
against it; and, so long as the waves are traveling more slowly
than the wind, there is a suction effect on the leeward slopes
similar to the effect on the leeward side of a sail.

In the open ocean the masses of water constituting waves do
not move bodily ahead, as optical illusion makes the casual observer believe. If storm waves at sea did behave as breakers on a
beach, where the whole mass does advance, "the ocean would not
be navigable," as the Navy publication flatly states. Nothing could
be fashioned which would be capable of withstanding a gale, and
civilization would never have expanded beyond the area where
man was first cradled. Instead, each individual water particle
making up a wave moves ahead only a short distance as it is lifted
by the crest, to recede as it descends into the succeeding trough,
ending at almost its original position. Thus water particles exhibit
an orbital movement except where crests are blown forward by
the sheer power of the wind.

As the wind continues and the waves grow, in deep water there
are only three factors theoretically capable of limiting the size of
development: the strength of the wind, its duration, and the
"fetch" or distance it can work on the sea. But unfortunately for
the precise tables in *Wind Waves at Sea* formularizing the

"heights of waves, in feet, theoretically produced by winds of various strengths blowing for different lengths of time," or "blowing over different fetches," and other tables on "the correlation between the age and steepness of growing waves," ideal conditions for the production of the theoretical never exist at sea—as the authors hasten to emphasize on the first page.

But theory or no, a gale blowing over the sea soon produces a mighty train of waves, steep in the early stages, lengthening out and becoming higher as time and distance extend. Minor variations of wind direction and force—the savage squalls which scream through every storm—transform the surface into something far from the regular procession of stately crests imagined by the landsman. All during the process of development newer and smaller waves are constantly developing on the older and longer ones, so each towering peak is really a combination of an indeterminate number of smaller waves of successive generations —the result being a confused turbulent heaving of jagged peaks and tortured valleys and bursting crests, without true regularity or flat surface anywhere, the whole overlaid by spindrift, droplets of water torn off the surface and blown along like horizontal rain. There are secondary ridges, peaks, and valleys running on top of the primary series and either series may be traveling in any direction in relation to the wind at the moment. Adding to the confusion "the lateral breadth of the individual wave may not be more than three to five times as far as it is from one crest to another, and sometimes no farther than it is from crest to crest, with their ends merging into valleys in a wholly irregular pattern." Thus twenty or more sets of waves may be running with different periods, speeds, and directions.

Yet despite the factors in actual practice which prevent the theoretical maximum of development, the *U. S. Naval Institute Proceedings* in 1934 published an article on "Great Sea Waves" stating that "during a prolonged period of stormy weather" in the North Pacific the U.S.S. *Ramapo* encountered "an enormous wave, the highest that has ever been reliably reported, with an estimated height of about 112 feet . . ." part of a sea "advancing at 55 knots. . . ." It is awesome to conceive a wall of water whose crest would surge into windows on the ninth floor of a modern apartment building traveling across the ocean as fast as an express train—a gray sullen mountain topped by frothing white, roaring ahead of the gale. Awesome and frightening, somehow primordial, a reminder of the rudimentary forces during the dark and lifeless period of the formation of the earth.

Strangely, the largest waves do not occur during hurricanes or typhoons, although the confused sea in the calm eye may be the most dangerous and destructive a sailor can encounter. One of the requirements for the development of giant waves is wind steady in direction, and the circular and progressive nature of these most ferocious of storms prevents the wind from remaining long at any one point. For the record, on the seas of the world "the vast majority of waves are considerably lower than 12 to 15 feet, and waves much higher than 20 to 25 feet are not usual anywhere." But it is "well established that waves may grow to 40 or 50 feet—or even higher when a really severe gale extends over an area great enough to have an effective fetch of 600 to 800 miles."

Research has shown the "largest storm waves" have been about the same height in the North and South Atlantic as in the "Southern Ocean," the unbroken sweep extending from South Africa to Australia, as the "stormier latitudes of all oceans experience equally severe gales" and a "fetch of 900 miles probably is sufficient for the generation of the largest of storm waves reliably reported anywhere, no matter how strong the wind." But on the Southern Ocean seas do become longer, waves 600 to 800 feet between crests being fairly common, with occasional giants of 1200 to 1300 feet observed; while on the North Atlantic even the most severe storms do not ordinarily produce waves more than 450 to

550 feet long. Curiously, however, the longest swells have been recorded along the shores of the Atlantic.

Wind waves frequently outrun the body of the storm that generates them, preceding as messengers of impending disaster. Irish peasants long called such outriders "death waves." But when wind waves continue beyond range of the gale, or after the wind has died down, they are called *swells*, and as such have continued 2500 miles before finally dissolving upon the shore. Even in this process they have a definable character, becoming *breakers* if they collapse "as a result of advancing into shoaling waters or of dashing against ledges or breakwaters," and *surf* if they break in a "more or less continuous belt along the shore, or over some submerged bank or reef." Surf sometimes develops far from the land, as over Borkum Ridge in the southern part of the North Sea, "where the seas break heavily in depths of 10 to 15 fathoms (60 to 90 feet) during onshore gales," or, due to currents, "along the Newfoundland Banks, off Ireland, and at the mouth of the English Channel where the depth is something like 100 fathoms."

Wind Waves at Sea points out that a seaman "may never, in a lifetime, encounter waves of the great heights . . . even if his voyages regularly cross and recross the stormier parts of the oceans in stormy seasons." Yet always behind the calm there is the threat, the latent power, the implacable and impersonal force. On *Caribbee*, sailing out into the stormier latitudes of one of the stormiest of oceans, we had to be prepared for whatever the gods might have in store—as have all sailors since the first ship ventured forth on wide waters.

9th Day

46° 53′ N.
44° 24′ W.
Run: noon to noon: 80 miles
Average speed: 3.33 knots
Total run to date: 1305 miles

Friday, July 11. 4:40 a.m.: For the 4 hours between 11:00 and 3:00 the port watch entered in the log a quartet of uncompromising zeros. Not a foot did they move. In Dick's hand there appears the notation in the column headed *weather:* "Barometer: 30.52. Wind: none. Conditions: cloudless sky, sea calm, bright moonlight." Under *comments:* "Dropped all sails." So they sat on deck inhaling the clean pure air and admiring the view, consoling themselves by forming a bucket brigade to the galley, no doubt dwelling on the beauties of the night as they munched.

We took over at 3:00 and maintained the status quo, doing some munching ourselves, and were even forced into reluctant admiration of the beauty of the night. For nothing is more delightful than contemplating the path of the moon across a calm sea, feet up, a cushion at your back, a ham-on-rye firmly clutched in one hand and a steaming cup of cocoa in the other. Such a combination inspires the noblest thoughts of which man is capable, and soothes the stomach as well.

But a little before 4:00 we sat up abruptly and looked at each other in questioning wonder. Could that be breeze? Could that faint stirring we imagined wafted against cheek and neck actually be breeze, that rare and precious commodity known to move boats? We said nothing but stealthily crept to our stations: the main went up first, a white triangle slowly expanding in the moonlight; then the drifter; then the mizzen. And wonder of wonders! we moved. Not a ripple showed on the water, yet the Kenyon needle lifted to 1.8, inspiring Frank to note at 0415: "Fastest we have ever gone in a flat calm."

The moon is still high and still there is no discernible wind, yet we have not stopped. Aloft a vagrant current must be working on main and drifter; they are full while the mizzen hangs in folds. Never before has that ancient sailor's term of "ghosting" seemed so apt: it is almost supernatural to glide along without visible means.

Ahead a long low band of dark cloud extends all the way across the sky, black and somehow ominous, although it may be only a trick of the sun still below the horizon. Our bow points at the center of it, and each minute it looks blacker and solider as the sky beyond takes on the rose and lavender tints of coming dawn. Perhaps it is only a bank of fog. The top is flat, and now I can see an end to the south. We crawl toward it, watchful.

Suddenly England seems one hell of a long way off.

6:45 a.m.: We sailed under the cloud. It lifted with the sun, and the threat went out: no line squall, no fog—nothing but a poor forlorn little bank of stratus masquerading as something tough. For 2 hours not even a kitten's paw had printed the surface, but as we went beneath, the wind dropped down from its perch on the upper spreaders—not with the leap of a tiger, but at least the pounce of a good husky Siamese tom, and the sea lost its maddening mercurial sheen.

Now we reach along on course at 4.5 knots. The wind has steadied at north and shows signs of freshening; we carry the drifter—I should say balloon jib when it performs its designed function—sheeted to the end of the main boom, and the mizzen staysail also draws. Frank figured a new great circle from the point where we found ourselves after flopping clear of the Banks.

Present leg is 095 degrees magnetic. Hope we will be able to follow this track better than the last.

It is amazing how spirits lift with any sign of progress. Anyone watching a movie of this might think we were nearing the finish of a tight New York Yacht Club squadron run. In fact, earlier this morning it occurred to me there was something pathetic—or perhaps slightly ridiculous—about the intensity with which we work every puff for every yard. The competitive spirit is an amazing thing, hard to define or analyze, yet it has been a prime motivating force during all recorded history. The will to win—or excel, or however it may be put—has always furnished a drive stronger than almost any other. Applied to yachting, I believe part of it stems from a man's attitude toward a boat: in a very real sense, a crew dedicates themselves to the service of an inanimate object. Night and day, in fair weather or foul, they tend its needs. There grows a relationship of possessiveness, of fierce pride, of love, a process of virtual deification ending in a conviction of invincibility. And the better the sailor and the better the boat the more intense becomes the feeling. There is not a man aboard who at this moment is not convinced *Caribbee,* given identical conditions, can beat any boat afloat anywhere. So it is hard to see her going anything but her best.

Or maybe the reason we work so hard is no more complicated than we know we have to get to England to continue eating, a habit we would be most reluctant to abandon.

8:35 a.m.: My watch below but too excited by moving again to be able to sleep. The wind has backed into the north and freshened somewhat, being logged at 0800 by Dick as north 8 knots. He estimated *Caribbee's* speed for the preceding hour at 5.9 knots, so we convert most of what the gods send us into mileage towards England.

I am back in my bunk after assisting in a spell of energetic sailshifting, seeking to settle the relative efficiency of spinnaker versus ballooner in this light going on this point of sailing. As Dick entered in the log under *Comments:* "At 0805 set spinnaker, true wind abeam, apparent wind 2 points forward of beam. Struck spinnaker, set drifter, reset spinnaker. Experiment indicated spinnaker best in these conditions." So it was, by two-tenths of a knot —enough better to favor the spinnaker when laying course, but not enough to warrant sagging off below.

When the sea is smooth a fast boat seems to make her own wind by leaning into the true breeze, bringing it farther and farther ahead as she gains speed, in turn creating more wind. It is one of the grand sensory pleasures of sailing.

10:50 a.m.: Napped but awake again feeling quite rested. Stuck my head up through the after hatch to find we still move well, having averaged 6.9 knots for the hour ending at 10:00. The wind has gone ahead, and now is northeast by east at 10 knots. It is clear and sunny with an air temperature of 58 degrees. Dick and the boys have shifted back from spinnaker to balloon jib and a small sea is beginning to build.

It is very pleasant to lie here and listen to water sing past the hull planking at my ear—that gurgle is the loveliest sound in the world—and for the moment I am content. I contemplate with satisfaction a passage of well over a thousand miles without a mishap to crew or ship. So far not so much as a Band-Aid or a laxative pill has been issued from the medicine chest; with sterile needles threaded, morphine syringes loaded, and anything else you can name in the way of modern drugs ready for any emergency or illness Cruising Club doctor Paul Sheldon could anticipate, we remain healthy. Like our five spinnakers and no wind! But no complaints this time.

The advance planning and preparation has worked out. I believe we have aboard every carpenter's, plumber's, mechanic's, and rigger's tool that could possibly be needed for any repair below or aloft, and Cap'n Nick has done an equally good job of providing spares. Last winter I went through my library and copied down lists of gear carried by other people who have made

similar passages, which were amended by the Cap in light of
Caribbee's requirements.

More or less the same system was used in the galley and navi-
gating departments. In the former Henry prepared sample menus
and a list of stores; the Bermuda Government by special arrangement lifted customs charges, permitting us to store in a bonded
warehouse the crates of food shipped ahead from New York, and
then load directly aboard in Hamilton harbor. These crates were
numbered against a master list. Therefore before opening we
knew the exact contents, and as each item was stowed away its
location was noted on the same master list. Henry checks off stores
as we consume them. Thus we know exactly where to go for a can
of cherries or tuna fish or any other item of food, and exactly how
many of each are left aboard.

Frank did the same with the charts and other navigational
equipment required, sending to Bermuda what was needed for the
race to England. And in both departments additional crates have
been shipped ahead to Cowes by steamer to be held for our
arrival.

As I write this I see with the clarity of perspective the details
that were worked out before we ever sailed from New York for
Newport, and now realize why I was so glad to hear the starting
gun in Bermuda. Those on the committee boat that day would
probably have conceded *Caribbee* looked ready for the passage
ahead, but neither they nor any other casual observer would have
realized the planning that brought us to the line, or what we had
stowed away on board: food, equipment, sails, spares—an endless
list.

Before the start only one item bothered me: water, the most
vital of all. Because she is a centerboarder and has the shallow
bilges characteristic of her type, *Caribbee's* tanks hold only 140
gallons. The Cruising Club of America required 10 gallons per
man for the Newport-to-Bermuda course, about one-quarter the
distance, and I was afraid there might be a comparable require-

ment for the Trans-Atlantic Race. It was a great relief to find the Royal Ocean Racing Club circular specified only 15 gallons—Imperial gallons, of course, slightly larger than American—but we made up the difference by taking on 2 additional gallons per man in 9-ounce Coast Guard approved sealed cans, which form a perfect emergency ration and stow well.

Because of prior experience with water consumption on both *Carib* and *Caribbee* for fairly extended periods, I felt secure, but well before sailing warned every prospective crew member we would have to get along on less than a gallon per man per day, usually regarded as the safe minimum. We drink all we want but are careful to avoid waste; Henry uses salt water for washing dishes and for cooking whenever possible, and even mixes salt and fresh for dishes where straight salt water would be too strong. No one has felt any inconvenience, I am sure. I even allow myself a fresh-water bath each day, filling an 8-ounce tumbler three-fourths full and using 2 ounces for brushing my teeth, 2 ounces for washing my face, and 2 ounces for my body.

By a coincidence, as the starboard watch finished breakfast this morning the second small tank of 20 gallons went dry. Frank immediately whipped out his slide rule: nine men have consumed 40 gallons in 9 days, an average of .495 gallons per man per day—or, as Frank said looking up from the rule: "Hell, call it a half gallon." Thus our 140 gallons at present consumption would last 31 days even without rationing. But as the remaining water is divided between two 50-gallon tanks, and one conceivably could spring a leak—or a pipe elbow break or a valve go bad—we will continue to observe present restrictions.

One restriction is on fresh water for shaving, and the ship is divided into shavers and nonshavers. In the former group we have the skipper, the port watch officer, the navigator, our new ensign, Cap'n Nick, and Henry. The remaining three sport whiskers of varying quality, from the somewhat nebulous mustache and sideburns of Bobby to the plow steel, high-tensile beard of Basil—a real menace to my favorite scarlet Hudson's Bay blanket which covers his bunk. After each watch below he appears with red fuzz hanging on his chin, a sort of auxiliary beard creating a red-and-black plaid effect. Dick suggested I make him comb out the wool each day and keep it in a box, so the blanket can be rewoven when we finish.

Now we are all well in the groove I honestly think we could stay at sea indefinitely and stay content—always with that proviso about racing. Our stock of conversation is inexhaustible, if not always ennobling: last night at dinner there was a heated discussion on the nature, uses, application, and results of that ancient aphrodisiac, Spanish Fly. Thinking back, maybe the remark about staying at sea indefinitely isn't accurate without another proviso.

I begin to feel sleepy although haven't much time left in my bunk. So far have been pretty good about sleeping—once or twice have taken half a Seconal to help because at sea sleep is next to food in importance. We all make good use of our watches below. Which reminds me of those beautiful phrases from World War II, and wonder what unsung genius created them: "sack artist" and "chow hound." Could anything be more descriptive, more truly visual? Shakespeare never did better. The language is still alive.

Time to sleep.

2:30 p.m.: Still moving and still laying course, but now close-hauled. Again there is quite a change in the weather, and in the color of the sea. This morning over the shoals of Flemish Cap it was much lighter in shade, almost a jade green. Now it is cold and black, the elemental and forbidding sea of the lonely northern wastes. The wind has pulled around into the northeast and kicked up whitecaps which have a gray and sullen look. Occasionally one catches the bow just right and comes aft as icy spray. But the barometer hangs steady and there is nothing to indicate anything heavy behind.

Our watch came on deck at 1:00 to find the last of the reaching breeze, and immediately shifted from balloon jib to genoa, struck

"Every modern convenience aboard Caribbee, even running water—in fact, if you weren't careful it would run you right over the side. A glorious sensation.to lie on deck abaft the main shrouds, the spinnaker overhead bellied out against the blue sky, the water singing past below."

"The spinnaker pole is well forward because our course and speed puts the wind on the beam. It is surprisingly warm: this air is coming to us from those sunny blue reaches towards the equator."

the mizzen staysail and flattened down. At the time a solid bank of fog was ahead. We put on oilskins and prepared to be wet. It was only a narrow band; we sailed through it and a couple of smaller patches, and are again in the clear, although a high haze makes the sun indistinct. Astern the fog bank looks like smoke from burning autumn leaves spreading flat and thick across a valley. As I write, Jack announces from the wheel: "Fog bank ahead." So there is, but it appears less dense than that astern—so probably will turn out exactly the opposite.

Although glad to be moving, I must confess being disappointed that we are not going with started sheets. I always mistrust a wind from northeast, anyway. It wouldn't have to freshen much to make us uncomfortable, or much beyond that to stop us cold—cold in more ways than one, as it is blowing off ice fields not very far away. Still, it is ungrateful to complain. Lately our supplications to the weather gods have altered from prayers for those lovely sou'westers to anything at all—please, Mr. Aeolus, please send us wind: just any old stray breezes left in your bag, anything that will fill our sails and send us on our way. . . . And now we must not mind if it is dead on the snoot. I always remember a passage in Claud Worth's *Yacht Cruising*, that grand old classic, to the effect if a man doesn't like going to windward he isn't a man, or a sailor, or something. Yet despite my admiration for the good doctor I say show me a man who likes going to windward and I'll show you a man who spends most of his nights afloat anchored in a snug harbor. For beating to windward on the open ocean in a hard wind is just that, a beating, hard on men and gear, and unrewarding on the track chart. Short distances are an exception for a little windward work is exhilarating, and a race without an upwind leg is no contest at all, either on the ocean or on an inland lake. And we of *Caribbee* welcome it, as we did during the opening stages of this race—there is no surer way of separating the men from the boys. But now is no time to start again.

Frank appeared as I wrote the last sentence and announced our day's run as 80 miles. Eighty miles! *Kon-Tiki* did about as well drifting! And here we shift from drifter to spinnaker to genoa and back again, adding mizzen staysails and balloon forestaysails for good measure, and end up with a day's run like a bloody raft's! I find it hard to believe after my enthusiasm of this morning, but Frank reminds me the sails were on deck most of the night, and produces dismal figures showing we advanced only 2 miles between evening and morning star fixes. Damned discouraging. As of noon we had covered 1305 miles. Even on the basis of the handicap distance we have 1565 left to go. That's a lot of ocean.

The wind is suddenly damp and raw. Patches of fog are all around. Overhead haze thickens. The sun has gone blurred and silver. A sea builds.

4:40 p.m.: Just finished a wheel trick. Moving well but not laying course. Steering about 105 degrees magnetic, which is 10 degrees low.

There is some fog but it hangs close to the water. The masthead fly is clear, and beyond the sky shows blue.

For awhile the fog was thicker and a lookout stood ready with the horn. According to the pilot chart the main steamer lanes between New York and the English Channel are a hundred miles to the south, but the routes to Scotland and Scandinavia cut right through our present position. I am sure we are now clear of danger from stray icebergs but steamers will remain a hazard during bad visibility all the way to the finish.

10th Day

47° 50′ N.
43° 01′ W.
Run: noon to noon: 83 miles
Average speed: 3.46 knots
Total run to date: 1388 miles

Saturday, July 12. 2:05 a.m.: This watch the miserable quint-essence of futility. Came on deck at 11:00 to find sails slatting. Lowered genoa. Later tried drifter, but no luck. Dropped every-thing. Then a faint breeze struck in. Frank settled the cockpit argument about whether sails would fill by saying: "We might make a couple of hundred yards on the puff." So set everything again—to make 200 yards on nearly 2000 miles! I doubt if we covered even 100 yards before all sails were on deck again. We now roll under bare poles.

Two birds came abroad during the last sail drill, apparently blinded by the spreader lights. One flew into the drifter and fluttered down into the water. The other slid down the main and landed on deck. I believe it went under the dinghy but don't give a damn.

To stay awake is torture.

9:10 a.m.: Oily flat calm. A misting rain fell earlier, but the sky is clearing. Have not had steerageway for more than a few minutes in 12 hours. Sails have been down most of the time. They are down now. A swell large enough to roll us considerably slides in from the north.

Breakfast garbage thrown over the side is finally disappearing astern. The starboard watch is sitting in the cockpit debating whether we save our time on it. One theory is that as it is of very light displacement it rates high; the other is that as it has a very short waterline it rates low. But it is nice to find we go faster than something, even paper cartons and tin cans.

The four of us sit looking out over the heaving ocean watching for any stray cat's-paws that might ruffle the surface, occasionally glancing up to see if the masthead fly indicates a faint stirring of breeze aloft. With this swell it would take more than a mere breath to waft us along; we would have to find something fairly solid to hold *Caribbee* steady enough for the sails to work. Consequently we are about as relaxed as it is possible to be when utterly frustrated. But even frustration is not enough to spoil the appetite or sense of humor of this crew: we talk of everything from weather to sex to food in Sweden versus food in Denmark to spear fishing in Martinique to whereabouts of other boats to sex to weather. Frank is working on the invention of a rubber trysail with rubber sheets which would connect with a large unbalanced rudder and scull us ahead as we slat in a flat calm. He estimates it will drive us at ¼ of a knot. I have ordered one for the next Trans-Atlantic Race. We also discuss means of providing a conveyor belt for the port watch so food can be more conveniently transported from galley to cockpit, to save the tread on the companionway steps now wearing thin as a result of the traffic. In fact, the capacity for reducing stores shown by the port watch is a never-ending source of awe and topic of conversation. Each of us daily has a new tale to enhance the legend of these supermen: I tell of seeing Bill Sherar carrying a stack of sandwiches, holding them by pressure at the ends; the stack looked like a fully extended concertina, and he had to turn sideways to get up the steps. Frank avers they use a system like volunteer firemen at a good barn-burning, passing up chow with the will of a neighborly bucket brigade. Bobby claims they have worked out a special rotation system for their watches: one half hour at the wheel, one half hour watching the jib, one half hour in the galley, and one half hour in the head. When it is flat calm, like this, they leave a man topside as lookout and the other three go to the galley, indifferent to the pitiful moans of the character left on deck but bribing him into remaining on duty by tossing up peanut butter and strawberry jam sandwiches at 6-minute intervals. Jack Littlefield—now known as "The Cobra" because of his ability to strike pancakes off a platter faster than the eye can follow—contributes his bit in reverent tones. As we consider him the only man on our team capable of offering competition in a free-for-all eating contest with the giants of the port watch, we are discouraged, and console ourselves with a can of pineapple rings.

So it goes. Seconds tick into minutes, and minutes extend into hours. Meanwhile for 5 days we have gotten virtually nowhere. Down deep I have always wanted to know what it is like to cross an ocean completely dependent on the vagaries of wind and current. Basically, our problems are identical to those of Cabot, or Hudson, or James, or any of the ghostly procession of men and ships who long ago sailed these seas at the mercy of the elements. Last winter while trying to decide to make this passage I was writing a book on the old voyagers; a desire to share their experiences and life—and in a measure their hopes and fears and hardships—must have unconsciously influenced my decision. And now, despite momentary discouragements, and periods of discomfort, I am happy to be following in their wakes. Even though we have comforts and facilities and equipment and food beyond their wildest dreams, the requirements of the eternal sea remain unchanged, and we who inherit their traditions and some of their skills know a feeling of kinship. And long after this race has been finished and the winner declared, these will be the memories that matter.

11:05 a.m.: Nothing has changed except the sun peeped through the overcast for a few minutes, enabling Frank to get an unexpected sight. Also the swell is diminishing so we roll less, a boon no doubt appreciated by those below trying to sleep, and by Henry, who works in the galley.

Have been looking over the *Pilot Chart of the North Atlantic Ocean* for July. We are in a 5-degree block where the percentage of "calms, light airs, and variable winds" should exactly balance the percentage of winds "of at least Force 8"—2 per cent calm, 2 per cent gale. And where easterlies are normally so scant that the chance of not being able to lay course is only 1 in 10. And where winds of Force 4, Beaufort Scale—11 to 16 knots—should blow 58 per cent of the time from between southwest and northwest, inclusive. And still another chart, one prepared by the British Admiralty for lifeboat use, notes for our region: "Winds usually from a westerly quarter and often stormy." Yet here we continue to flop helplessly, the five spinnakers gathering marine moths or flying teredos, or something, while the pen of the barograph traces across the paper in a perfectly level line.

I believe we are in the center of a vast stagnant high-pressure area. I visualize an expanse of thousands upon thousands of square miles of ocean lying nearly mirror-smooth; fog over some, sun over some, overcast over more. Riffling this vast area are occasional local breezes, just enough to tantalize poor sailors anxious to be on their way. Sometimes the vein of wind may peter out after 15 minutes, as did the faint slants we set drifter to last night; and at other times the local adjustment of conditions might last for several hours, as did our northeast breeze of yesterday, protracted and fresh enough to kick up whitecaps, yet not changing the over-all picture. So this whole expanse of ocean centering around 45 degrees north latitude and 45 degrees west longitude must be like a checkerboard, with squares of wind and squares of calm, and wind alleys leading from one square to another, but even these dying into a dead end when the purely local inequalities of pressure are neutralized. But this is just a layman's hunch; the whole theory of weather baffles me despite attempts at understanding. And, from the frequency with which forecasts are wrong even in coastal waters where meteorologists have unlimited facilities and reports at their disposal, weather baffles men nearly as much as when the ancient Greeks were making offerings to Poseidon, Shaker of the Earth, and Zeus, King of the Immortals.

But if my hunch is accurate, the other boats must be experiencing similar conditions, now pulling up, now dropping back a few yards or miles. Yet from an objective point of view it is hard to conceive anyone could have had worse conditions for so protracted a period, so consequently the others must have closed the gap we opened during the first 4 days—and I believe it must have been quite considerable—or perhaps have even gone ahead. And there isn't a thing we or any other boat or crew could do about it. We are enacting a new version of the old story of the hare and the tortoise, where the hare loses not because of indolence and sloth, but because he is paralyzed by the fickle finger of fate; perhaps on the outer perimeter of this high-pressure area wind is blowing toward a low, and chance has put our competitors there.

The *Pilot Chart* also reminds me by a series of dated red lines that hurricanes do sweep across this part of the Atlantic at this time of year, although here too the percentages are against the possibility. But my faith in percentages is being shaken. And the longer we sit here like sitting ducks the more chance has an opportunity to operate. Grim thought.

Frank, hardy soul, has just taken a sponge bath on deck and is now wearing shorts.

1:50 p.m.: At 12:15 the sky darkened to the southwest and a few ripples appeared. Some low scud came over. Never was such joy shown at what seemed a change: on drifter, main, and mizzen, helmsman hopefully alert, the rest of us fussing over trim. Lasted all of 5 minutes, during which actual and definite steerageway was achieved. Then the darker clouds were past and we were left with the same general overcast we had earlier, which promises nothing. The sea is flatter than it has been yet—the barest of underlying swells, so sails stay up, hanging in limp folds.

Our noon position gives us an advance of 83 miles for the 24 hours, an average of 3.46 knots. As Frank noted in the log: "Find more easterly current than most data would indicate." We certainly must be in the grip of a favoring drift. For once that "silent, imperceptible and therefore dangerous" sliding of the surface of the sea, as Blunt called it, is not dangerous but friendly, our one ally. For without a fair current we could not possibly have come so far. The pilot chart shows our position at the approximate point where the southern side of the Labrador Current joins the northern extremity of the Gulf Stream, not in collision, as over the Grand Banks, but in seeming harmony as part of the North Atlantic Drift. So at least in this we are lucky. A foul current could have put us back on the Banks—or even landed us stern-end-to on Cape Race!

After lunch Henry was asked if he had ever seen eight men eat so much. He said he hadn't, but that if we didn't decrease our present rate of consumption of stores or increase our progress over the bottom, he would soon never see eight men eat so little.

7:35 p.m.: It goes on. Still not a breath. The water lies like oil, like molten metal, only small undulations moving the surface. To the west the sunset is pale, although there is a reddish band under the cloud layer tinting the sea in that direction.

We cannot move. Despite the fact life goes on normally and even cheerfully there is something of a nightmare unreality about being utterly helpless. Modern man has so freed himself from a feeling of dependence on the elements that it hard to adjust himself to being at their mercy. It just doesn't seem it could happen to us, much less go right on happening, with nothing to be done about it. Those poor eggs sitting among our finery on the dock in Southampton!

This afternoon two small brown whales came close, one diving under the boat. The water is very clear. Leaning over the side we could not only see the whale lazily sliding under the keel, but our rudder, and the propeller feathered and obediently standing up-

and-down in the deadwood. It is like being suspended over a blue void—too literally true to be stated as a simile. Hanging in this blue world are not only *Caribbee* and her whale friends but thousands of small brown jellyfish, tiny little thimbles which squeeze themselves ahead, easily outdistancing us. I watch them with a certain wry dislike, not being able to forget my casual remark long ago that after man had finished atomizing himself into oblivion jellyfish would undoubtedly inherit the earth.

Before dinner Dick and Bill swam. Water temperature is about 60 degrees. For some obscure reason, perhaps because it is better to think of certain things when they are behind, I remember that foggy night on the Banks when the air temperature fell to 45 degrees. Makes me shiver to think of it—in more ways than one.

8:05 p.m.: Interrupted the last entry to try to scoop in an imagined breeze. It took 15 minutes to wear ship by backing the drifter. Now we have steerageway, I think. Wrong. Helmsman was just asked by man forward to come up 5 degrees. Answer, by Bobby from the wheel: "Friend, I don't have the slightest control over her." Jack, sitting on the pulpit watching the jib, protests, declaring bubbles are going by. Bobby finally notes response to rudder by swing of compass, concedes steerageway. Sluggishly *Caribbee* creeps up to 105 degrees magnetic. Frank sticks his head through the companionway and exclaims: "Boy, we're moving! At least a knot!" Pause. Then wistfully: "She sure loves to go when there's anything to go with." We trim the main slightly, change the lead on the drifter sheet. Bobby exultantly: "She's showing 2 knots on the Kenyon." Jack stares up at the drifter. Frank and I fuss over trim, over leads, watching masthead fly and ribbon on the stays. "No higher," calls man forward. "No higher," repeats helmsman. Pause. A trail of bubbles shows astern. "Let her go off a little," calls the man forward. "Coming off," replies helmsman. Silence. We run out of the pattern of ripples which have been showing on the surface. No more bubbles appear under the stern. Around *Caribbee's* sides the water again lies smooth, a small underlying swell shimmering the last light reflected from the highest clouds into patterns like watered silk. The wind sock and the ribbons droop listlessly. As we roll slightly the reef points begin their tattoo against the idle canvas. We lie absolutely dead in the water . . .

I write this in the cockpit, using a very dim flashlight. The night is overcast, but warm. To the west there is a faint band of blue, laced by the palest rose. Ahead there is no division between sea and sky: all is a uniform gray, the weld of the two oceans imperceptible.

10:55 p.m.: The end of another weary watch. Have not progressed a mile in the whole 4 hours. But in the last 20 minutes a faint southwest breeze has struck in, so now have on ballooner and mizzen staysail. We turn the ship over to the port watch with steerageway, a rare achievement.

ONE of the most fascinating documents produced by man is the "Pilot Chart of the North Atlantic Ocean," which reduces to colorful and precise symbols those concepts which further divide the sailor's world from the landsman's. For a pilot chart is literally a road map of the sea, its highway markers blue arrows showing the strength and direction of the wind, and the flow of currents; its danger signs red lines indicating the track of past hurricanes, and the limits of floating ice; its traveled highways black lines routing steamers; and its way stations heavy red circles pointing out the lonely outposts of weather ships.

There are other symbols, and other colors, too, for compressed into an area 26 by 38 inches is almost everything that affects navigation on the North Atlantic, from 5 degrees south of the equator to 60 degrees north; from Cape São Roque on the shoulder of South America to Cape Chidley, far up along the icebound coast of Labrador; from the fjords of Norway to the steaming beaches of equatorial Africa. At a glance the navigator can determine normal barometric pressure off Tampico, the likelihood of fog approaching Cape Sable, the probable temperature of air or water close to the Cape Verde Islands, the possibility of a hurricane in Martinique, the distance ice extends south of Cape Farewell, the magnetic variation at Gibraltar, the northern limit of the Gulf Stream or the rate of flow of the Labrador Current, the percentage of calms near the Azores, or the approved track for low-powered steamers between Europe and ports on the Gulf of Mexico. He can find the strongest part of the northeast trades or the extent of the 100 fathom curve off Ireland, the frequency of gales at latitude 50° north longitude 30° west or the best route for a sailing ship from the Lizard to Cape Horn.

Only with the help of a pilot chart can anyone visualize the vastness and complexity of that most varied of oceans, the North Atlantic. Among other wonders can be traced the doldrums, the vast section near the equator characterized by squalls and light baffling winds; and the steady flow of the trade winds from Africa to the West Indies, the artery which carried life from the old world to the new; and the warm sweep of the Gulf Stream eastward, with its division off the coast of Europe, one branch flowing north to make habitable lands which would otherwise be barren, the other branch turning south to complete the gigantic circuit to the Caribbean.

Nothing else so conclusively demonstrates the gradual accumulation of knowledge, and the debt of each generation to those who went before. For a pilot chart is the result of countless thousands of observations made by the forgotten men who through the years have probed the eternal mysteries of the sea. "On the 23d of April, 1776, the heat of the sea was 74°, our latitude at noon, 28° 7' N. Next day the heat was only 71°; we were then in latitude

29° 12′.″ "In March I experienced a strong current setting about ESE between the Caymans and the Isle of Pines. Both my mate and myself separately calculated it to set about 60 miles per day, or 2½ per hour." "On the 4th of September, 1820, John Lamont, a fisherman of Bute, found, near the Cumrays, a bottle, containing the following label: 'Off the coast of Iceland, July 27, 1820, lat. 62° 10′ 0″ N., long. 19° 20′ 0″ W. of Greenwich: this bottle was thrown from the *Merioneth*, whale-fisher, in order to ascertain the direction of a current setting strongly off shore. Whoever finds it, will do a service to navigation by publishing the place where, and time when, it was found. R. MORRIS, Captain.' In the month of August, therefore, this bottle was carried by the current in a S.E. direction, to the North Channel of the North Sea: and thence, by the tide of flood, to the Firth of Clyde."

The man who began compilation of the vast data lying untabulated and unused in ships' logs was Matthew Fontaine Maury, then an obscure lieutenant. Because of an accident that left him unfit for sea duty he was put in charge of a house rented by the Navy in 1831 which had been dignified by the title of Depot of Charts and Instruments. The "Depot" was simply a storehouse for navigational equipment to be issued naval vessels. But Maury was more than a storekeeper; he immediately conceived the idea of expanding the services of his office and suggested shipmasters submit reports of experiences and observations so the data could be digested, compiled, and published for the benefit of all. The suggestion was enthusiastically received by mariners of every nation. Maury distributed many special log books, and within 5 years had received twenty-six million reports. To a great extent the publication of his first "Wind and Current Chart" ended aimless passages with fate and chance wholly in charge; as Maury wrote in the introduction to the first edition of his masterful work, *The Physical Geography of the Sea:* ". . . the young mariner, instead of groping his way along until the lights of experience should come to him by the slow teachings of the dearest of all schools, would here find he had already the experience of a thousand navigators to guide him on his voyage. He might therefore set out with as much confidence as to the wind and currents . . . as though he had already been that way a thousand times." Before Maury, the usual sailing time between England and Australia was 124 days each way; after his charts were published, outward passages averaged 97 days, and the return 63. One of his diagrams, showing winds girdling the globe in various belts at different latitudes, "combines in its construction the results of 1,159,353 separate observations of the force and direction of the wind, and a little upwards of 100,000 observations of the height of the barometer."

Therefore Maury deserves his title of "The Pathfinder of the Seas," and the credit line the U. S. Navy Hydrographic Office still prints upon every pilot chart: "Founded on the researches made in the early part of the nineteenth century by Matthew Fontaine Maury . . ." Other maritime nations might well do the same, for all modern pilot charts only continue the work he began, as all hydrographic offices are outgrowths of the humble Depot of Charts and Instruments.

So as we on *Caribbee* studied the wind roses in each 5-degree square of ocean ahead and astern, and tried to evaluate the effects of current, storm, or calm, we were again only following in the wakes of vanished men and ships, acknowledging our debt to the past. And, because of them, we had expected and were prepared for our sudden transition from hot to cold, from the sunny skies of the Gulf Stream to the fog of the Newfoundland Banks and the icy waters of the Labrador Current, from the long swelling seas of the open ocean to the confused chop of soundings.

Yet in our admiration we had never wholly forgotten that all efforts of man to reduce nature to a formula are fallible. We had not overlooked the fact that the strength and direction of wind as recorded in the "roses" was tabulated on a percentage basis, and that percentages can work over short periods in odd ways and

still be correct. Within certain limits we had been ready for anything—almost anything, I should say: anything except what was
actually happening to us.

11th Day

48° 32′ N.
41° 48′ W.
Run: noon to noon: 63 miles
Average speed: 2.62 knots
Total run to date: 1451 miles

Sunday, July 13. 4:50 a.m.: Came on deck at 3:00 to find the port watch apologetic about lack of wind and a tangle of gear from the last spinnaker jibe, a few minutes earlier—it was easier to forgive the latter than the former. The 'chute hung in limp folds, needing more than a mother's loving care. Fortunately, another zephyr soon came in, this one from something south of west, so we jibed back and now show 3 knots on the Kenyon. To keep moving we have to sail high of course—anywhere from 110 to 125 degrees while the great-circle track calls for 095 degrees. But if we try to come down the spinnaker collapses, the swell sets us rolling, and we go dead.

This is my wedding anniversary: may the day bring comparable luck.

5:30 a.m.: A pale dawn. The sun is probably up somewhere but *Caribbee* crawls along under a cover of cloud. Neither sea nor sky shows wind, or any prospect thereof. The barometer is steady at 30.45.

We maintain steerageway thanks to Frank's tireless energy forward calling the spinnaker: "Up 5 degrees, up 3 more, down 5 . . ." A few minutes ago he directed: "Bring her down a gnat's eyebrow." Jack from the wheel asked: "What's that in degrees?" and promptly got the answer: "One and a half." So we creep along

127

past Portuguese men-of-war, assorted jellyfish, and other marine curiosa. Off the port bow a group of seagulls ride lazily and allow us to overtake them.

We have reached the nadir in racing. A man coming up from below exclaimed: "Say, look at the bubbles go past!" And was answered by the helmsman in bored tones: "Yeah? Which way?"

6:30 a.m.: A light but seemingly true breeze from about south-southwest is sending us along on course at 4 knots. We have just changed from the rope to the wire spinnaker pole afterguy. When it is very light and especially if there is a chance of having to jibe we use linen, but as soon as it freshens shift to flexible stainless steel with a rope tail. Some skippers are against wire because it is impossible to cut with a knife if a man goes overboard; while I acknowledge that drawback, its nonstretching and non-parting qualities overbalance the fault, at least in my mind. Having had experience with both under a variety of conditions, I believe in a wind of any weight no ocean racer should use anything else.

The whole surface of the sea shows ripples. It is a relief. That oily sheen of utter calm can become maddening. For the first time in my sailing life I have learned what it must have meant to the old-timers to run into prolonged calms and light variables. We become upset because we may be losing a race, but now I find it possible to visualize a similar situation when moving literally was life or death. In yellowed logs and journals are countless stories of crews perishing from scurvy, from thirst, from starvation, just because a ship could not cover a few miles. The clumsy vessels sometimes lay in the doldrums for weeks while men went slowly mad and leapt cursing to break the shimmering mirror below. Before the days of antifouling bottom paint, ships unable to reach port sank beneath their crews after teredos had riddled the hulls. Water turned bad, cargos rotted . . . and neither prayer nor blasphemy availed. If every circumstance has its compensation, mine lies in a feeling of kinship with men of the past which could

"Henry Davis, recently renamed 'Henri du Caribbee' by his grateful flock. 'Never has so much been consumed by so few' was his epitaph on the Bermuda Race, and we daily rise to new heights of gastronomic endeavor."

"A couple of days ago to the great sorrow of all hands I had to decree rationing: stove on at night only at three o'clock change in watches, a cold lunch, and no more baking.... From now on Caribbee will be sailed with the desperation of men willing to risk all in a desperate gamble—no Plymouth, no pie...."

be achieved no other way. Yet the situation is not wholly comparable despite Henry's remark when the whales were underneath: "Instead of watching them we'd better catch one." We still have plenty of food and plenty of sweet water, and *Caribbee* can glide miles on faint airs that would not have moved a cargo vessel of the seventeenth or eighteenth century one foot.

Bobby just commented this 3:00 to 7:00 watch now ending is one for the log as the first in days where we have gone 4 whole hours without losing steerageway. We really have become grateful for small favors.

Much warmer. As we go below the breeze drops again. Speed is under three.

1:35 p.m.: Back on deck after a really good sleep, principally inspired by the song of water moving along our topsides—the finest sailor's lullaby in the world.

As our watch finished breakfast a new breeze sprang up from south by east, so before turning in went up to indulge the joy of motion. A cockpit discussion with Dick resulted in another spinnaker-versus-balloon jib experiment. Two days ago in even lighter going with the apparent wind approximately two points forward of the beam we found the new parallel-cloth spinnaker two-tenths of a knot faster, but by coming up 10 degrees—a little less than a point—the jib picked up the difference. Then we were able to lay course with the spinnaker, so there was no question about which was best. But this morning with the spinnaker we were forced 25 degrees below course even with the pole against the headstay, and the argument reopened. I held out for the jib, Dick for the spinnaker, so we shifted back and forth, steering carefully and watching the Kenyon. Carrying the 'chute we were making 6.2 knots at 070 degrees; with the jib we came up to course, 095 degrees, and made 6.5 knots. Since by sailing 20 degrees off course the distance to be covered between two points increases by 6.4 per cent, and at 25 degrees off becomes 10.3 per cent greater, there was an enormous difference in relative efficiency. But most interesting was in this particular going we actually sailed faster under ballooner than spinnaker, again showing how a fast boat can make her own wind by pulling it farther and farther ahead, consequently increasing its apparent velocity, and thus in turning raising her own speed.

So with *Caribbee* moving along on course better than she had for days I could lie in my bunk fully relaxed, and soon slept. But before dropping off I thought again of something that has been in my mind ever since the start: when either watch is below the other can be content in the knowledge that the boat is being kept going at her maximum ability. Dick commented this morning he never had the feeling so strongly, and it is certainly reciprocated. I believe the only serious criticism some sailor ghost riding aloft and watching might have is on the score of overeagerness, especially in undertaking the expected blood-and-thunder northern route. It was never our plan to come so far above the original great circle, of course; we no more intended to cross Flemish Cap than to go around Greenland. Looking back, falling off below course to carry a spinnaker when the wind first freed, before getting on the Banks, was about the only place where we had any choice. Before and after, conditions dictated. In my notes is a quote from an Uffa Fox book analyzing conditions on the North Atlantic for July. After pointing out that 80 to 90 per cent of winds "are westerly or north or south, which means a fair or beam wind, and as these vary from force to 4 to 6 (16 to 27 miles an hour)" so "they are ideal for fast passages . . . being enough to drive a small sailing vessel along at her maximum speed and yet not enough for reefing as they are abaft the beam," he continues, to say that "*Dorade* and *Landfall* in the 1931 Trans-Atlantic Race could just lay course close hauled at the start as the wind was south-east, but after this it remained astern and never forward of the beam all the way across." Ah me! We sure as hell picked the wrong year to race across the Atlantic.

A long smooth swell is rolling in from the southwest, quite a sizable one. The sky is overcast. There was a slight dip in the barograph track during the early hours but now it has leveled out. At the moment we are laying course and making better than 5 knots, but a few minutes ago Frank chilled us with the announcement that the day's run ending at noon was the worst yet, a miserable 63 miles. No comment.

7:45 p.m.: Henry is clearing away the dinner dishes and I relax in the main cabin for a few minutes before turning in. Feel well packed and very gay. At noon Dick entered in the log: "As the master did not hold Divine Services crew were employed in various tasks beneficial to the ship: sewing canvas, marking genoa track, etc." In a different hand at the end—Frank's precise print —is a small bracketed note: "Don't be overmodest; also reducing weight in stores."

To continue from the ship's log: at 1900 there is another entry, this one in Bobby's sloping script: "Skipper's 13th wedding anniversary. Starboard watch prepared hors d'oeuvres. Port watch presented cockpit dodger of own manufacture. Speech by Mc-Kinney. All hands consumed delicious brew by skipper."

It was quite an occasion. I suspected something afoot when I was barred from the galley about five o'clock, and was certain of it when Basil came on deck about six with not only his hair slicked down but the red blanket fuzz combed out of his beard. I lost no time shaking up a *Trans-Atlantic Special,* and all hands magically appeared in the cockpit. First Bobby brought up the offering of the starboard watch: a ring of canned lobster arranged around a cup of very peppery Bahamian sauce, and an Edam cheese quilled all over with olives, pickles, and cheese cubes stuck on toothpicks. Most welcome. Basil was introduced as toastmaster, and after a very touching oration presented a hand-sewn canvas dodger for the cockpit. Also most welcome. Afterwards all hands toasted Zib in Gosling's Best Barbados, and wished me another happy thirteen years, and I said I thought they would be if we had finished the race by then, and we got very happy and noisy and threw olives and bits of cheese to the seagull on duty, so he could join the party, too. Then each watch went below in turn to find Henry's contribution a huge casserole of stewed chicken and mushrooms, with rice and *petits pois* on the side, topped off by apple pie and wedges from the Edam.

So now understandably and justifiably I relax on the cabin cushions, filled with peace and fondness for my shipmates, and allow myself sentimental thoughts as well as luxurious contemplation of my waiting bunk. Nice? It *is* the only life.

By coincidence, we are halfway across.

12th Day

49° 19′ N.
39° 11′ W.
Run: noon to noon: 112 miles
Average speed: 4.66 knots
Total run to date: 1563 miles

Monday, July 14. 7:50 a.m.: We crawl along under a pall of dirty gray cloud over an oily sea the same color. It feels almost as if the two could close and trap us forever. There is barely a line of separation at the horizon: all is drear and chill. The only sense of motion comes from a succession of swells rolling us from side to side in monotonous repetition. To the old southwest swell has been added a smaller sequence from the north. For minutes at a time the breeze will have strength enough to keep sails full and *Caribbee* steady. Then the conflicting swells synchronize: one glides up and shoulders us sharply to port; another is waiting on the starboard beam to heave us back, and wham! off we go in a series of wild gyrations. Everything aloft slats and slaps, the boom jumps against its preventers, the helmsman swears, and the Kenyon needle drops toward zero. Finally the offending rollers go scampering gleefully off toward the horizon and *Caribbee* picks up speed and proceeds toward England with the air of a dignified old gentleman who refuses to acknowledge he has been tripped.

During the past 8 hours the wind has progressively gone ahead, forcing us farther and farther from course. Before midnight we could actually lay course carrying a mizzen staysail. Through the early hours the sheets were gradually trimmed, literally an inch at a time. Again we go north, willy-nilly.

11:15 a.m.: England lies thataway, somewhere beyond the starboard rigging. We're off for Iceland. Not only does the wind remain light, but constantly shifts against us, adding injury to insult.

12:05 p.m.: Sun! Suddenly the whole aspect of the day has changed, and with it our viewpoint. All is now blue and sparkling. Tiny points of light dance on ripples that run up and down and across the backs of the swells. Shorts are *de rigueur* if in the sun and out of the breeze. But in the opposite situation long under-wear and sweaters are still necessary. The watch on deck are stripped down but make sure their jobs keep them in sunshine.

As the sky cleared we had a start: Bobby sighted smoke on the horizon, a thick blob pluming high. It did not look like a steamer behaving normally so our first terrible thought was that one of our competitors might be afire just over the horizon. Frank never made it to the lower spreaders so fast, but then could plainly see it was a steamer blowing her tubes. We have settled down again, but our reaction proved fire at sea is still the sailor's greatest dread.

I write this sitting amidships with my back against the cabin. Somehow I feel like a fat old possum blinking at the light after a long winter sleep—punctuated by a few random nightmares. It is good to be alive: to have the sun warm against back and shoul-ders, to see a gentle breeze filling the sails, to hear the song of bow wave and bubbles along the hull. Often I think, as I feel my own spirits lift or lower with the mood of the skies, how closely man is attuned to nature, despite centuries of civilization. And how in this man resembles the sea, which also takes its moods from the heavens above: both reflect the will of a dominating yet largely unseen force. Perhaps this is the key to the relationship between man and the sea, the never-ending fascination that lies in mutu-ally unfathomable complexity.

We move, we move. The breeze is veering toward the south—"going 'round with the sun," as the old-timers would have said—while the barograph track shows a continuing dip. Perhaps it means this stagnant wind system is about to break up, and we will have a change in conditions.

The swell no longer bothers us. It has been over an hour since the mainsail had the wind spilled out; again the canvas bellies in a smooth curve and drives us on our way. From the lower reef points my trusty red flannels flap in the breeze, adding what a fashion editor might call a note of color. Or perhaps might even describe as "an accent." But in fact you could go further and say those red flannels not only have accent but character—although perhaps the precise nature of that "character" should not be defined. Still, somehow it makes me think of another of the wonders of small-boat sailing and the change it effects on human personality.

All of us are adults with definite standards of privacy and cleanliness. Ashore it would be unthinkable to wear the same underclothes day after day—and night after night—while cheerfully crawling into a bunk still warm from another bathless character in his underclothes. Yet at sea you never give it a thought.

The theory is sometimes advanced that boats and bodies stay cleaner because there isn't any dirt away from the land. Probably true. But the total scrapping of the fetishes of our prophylactic civilization goes beyond that: it is a point of view, part of the alchemy of a small vessel. For we who love the sea in any of its parts, right down to the most sheltered gunk hole in a landlocked bay, also share a love for boats, and others who feel about them as we do. Much of our veneer disappears and we revert to a more basic life. Humans lived together in close contact without benefit of chrome-and-porcelain fixtures for more centuries than it has been years since they were considered necessary. So after a day or two at sea you become only a healthy satisfied animal, blissfully forgetful of germs lurking in nonsterile surroundings, and thoroughly enjoy yourself. Come to think of it, maybe humans have to be a little dirty to be happy—scrubbed children never seem to be enjoying themselves as much as grubby ones.

Somehow the same subtle change takes place in relation to

personal comfort. Imagine driving an automobile sitting oilskin-
clad in a cold rain, or uncomplainingly climbing the roof on a
stormy night to fix the radio antenna, or crowding into a room
smaller than a closet at home—a cubicle shared by eight others,
festooned with damp sweaters, tired socks and limp boots; alternately livingroom, diningroom, library, community center,
bed- and bathroom; sometimes right-side-up, sometimes left-
side-up, sometimes trying to toss you like corn in a popper—and
loving it.

It is not only we as a crew of dedicated fanatics. Over the years
I have seen it happen innumerable times: I have seen the most
carefully enameled females come aboard boats far smaller than
Caribbee and be completely at home. They slop around happily
in a tiny galley and wrestle with a smoking kerosene stove when
they haven't voluntarily entered their all-electric kitchen in years;
they huddle through misting rain and driving spray while their
coiffures trickle down the back of the neck; and struggle in and
out of girdles crouched in the forepeak, falling over coils of rope,
sail bags, and the spare anchor. And immediately forget that by
their shore-going standards a day must begin and end with a hot
tub. All part of the alchemy of sailing.

Yet any relaxation of what skippers of yore called "the articles
of cleanliness" must not be confused with a lack of neatness. For
neatness on deck and below is essential to a happy ship: uncoiled
halyards, trailing sheets, and loose gear in the waterways are no
worse than a clutter of personal effects below. In fact, neatness—
in its comprehensive sense—is practically a matter of self-
preservation. Consider: on *Caribbee* we are nine. We have been
at sea nearly 2 weeks. We could conceivably take that much more
—or even longer—to finish. Thus for a period of a month we must
exist wholly off what we have carried; off our own fat, so to speak.
In a sense it is like marooning nine men in a small cottage for that
period, with a penalty of death for stepping off the front porch.
All necessities must be thought of in advance, and put away to

leave living space. Yet beyond the point of cubic content—and that in comparison to the smallest of cottages—the simile is hardly apt. For a boat is more complex than any house: we are driven across the sea by our sails, which in turn depend upon an intricate web of steel, wood, and linen. To keep all in order, we must not only have the skills to use the tools, but must be steeplejacks and tightrope walkers. At any moment, despite inspection and care, there may be a failure through fatigue or chafe; we must have aboard all the tools and replacements for any possible emergency. We must carry cooking fuel and other fuel to generate our electricity; we must have the charts and instruments to determine our position on the trackless ocean; we must carry clothes to insulate us from every type of weather, medicines to heal or cure. Spare toilet-washers are as important as extra turnbuckles in the larger scheme of things: and sail twine and flashlight batteries and hacksaw blades and snatchblocks and vitamin pills.

This vast assortment must be tucked and chocked away to ride securely in any weather, due consideration being given to damage from sloshing bilge water, accessibility, and relative likelihood of need. And above, around, and with it the nine of us must eat, sleep, and work. Thus I say neatness is mandatory.

Beyond neatness in general maintenance is what might be called neatness in personal housekeeping. It is always interesting to watch a new shipmate's method of putting away gear on coming aboard: his shaving kit, his toothbrush, foul-weather clothes, camera, shore-going shirts, and the rest. A lot can be deduced about his abilities as a seaman for, with few exceptions, the tidiest below are the most capable on deck. When a man stows his own gear with due regard for the convenience of others, you can be sure he will be considerate in every other way, even at the helm when you are forward smothering a jib in bad weather.

2:40 p.m.: This may be it!

We are really going. The last entry was interrupted by the wind chopping around into the south and freshening. The watch on deck fell over themselves scrambling to trim sheets. Now we cook along at 6.8 knots on course—on course!—while the breeze shows every sign of hardening further. 'Way up high, small clouds scurry over from southwest and the barograph records a steady decline.

As usual, the excitement of being under way kills tiredness. Our watch sit around the cabin table although Henry has long since cleared away the remains of lunch. A few minutes ago Dick came down to make a log entry and I had a look. It ended: "Starboard watch busy supervising navigator changing barograph paper instead of doing sack duty." This is too good to miss, even for sleep. After all, you can't spend your whole life in a bunk, especially when *Caribbee* tears along for the 50th parallel of north latitude. It doesn't happen every day—especially the tearing along.

But even if we sit out a part of this one we still claim a record for our watch, thanks to the superb devotion to sack duty shown by our worthy navigator and watchmate, Frank MacLear. After being relieved on one of those cold foggy Grand Banks nights he made it from wheel to bunk in seven seconds, a magnificent achievement which involved traversing half the length of the main deck, descending the companionway, making a sharp left turn past the chart table, ducking into the after stateroom, removing his oilskins, and getting between the blankets. Of course this record is not uncontested: carping critics of the port watch point out that while they concede from the speed of his take-off he could have done all I have listed, the time claimed would not have permitted the removal of hip-length boots as well, and Basil insists he was not wearing boots when called for the next watch on deck. We put this down to sheer jealousy, unworthy in men to whom we concede superiority in all matters involving a knife and fork.

While on the subject of bunks, I should add Dick and I have set new standards for the maintenance of a hot bunk. I don't know exactly how it started, or even when, but gradually we have come to fuss over our mutual sack like a couple of old maids. Before going on deck I smooth the sheets just so, tuck in the blankets, fluff the pillows—including a small pillow of unknown origin, whose lingering perfume probably inspired all this—and fold back blankets and sheets with geometric precision. Dick has a slightly different technique, especially on the placement of the pillows. Whatta sack! During the bad watches I see it dancing over the sea as a thirsty Arab sees the oasis over the desert, a mirage of infinite beauty and desirability. Turned sheets and fluffed pillows! Shades of Cape Horn!

5:15 p.m.: Dick's five o'clock log entry exults: "Really under way again at last. Over 8 knots with slightly cracked sheets." We carry genoa, main, and mizzen, and steer the new great-circle course of 106 degrees, while the sea stays calm and the sun lowers to a lovely dusk.

After a couple of hours of sleep I find myself rested and relaxed, but somewhat confused as to time and place. It doesn't seem possible we near 50 degrees north, for this is another of those days that remind our Bahamians of home. At noon Bobby said it was like going through Crooked Island Passage, and Basil, ever loyal to Andros, was reminded of crossing the Tongue of the Ocean. In any case, as we approach the threshold of the true northern wastes we enjoy the first really good weather and sailing since we were swallowed by the fog off Newfoundland. Somehow those miserable days of slatting and groping through the murk have already assumed a dreamlike quality, yet the closely spaced daily-position dots on the track chart prove they were real enough.

There is a stir on deck, and we heel a little more. From the wheel Dick calls forward to report the Kenyon needle nears nine: I cannot understand Bill Sherar's reply, but there is no mistaking the incredulous glee in his voice.

Except for the one brief lapse soon after we went flat, I do not believe any crew ever worked harder or more conscientiously. For hour after frustrating hour and day after day we have shifted and trimmed sails to each minute shift of wind, eking out every possible foot and mile. As so often happens, the harder we work the less we have to show for it. While we were tearing off the miles for what looked like a record passage things were comparatively easy; with a fresh wind steady on the quarter we could have covered the distance we have made during the past week in 2 days without moving from the wheel, and forever after pointed with pride to our achievement. Yet at the will of the gods our labor produces only an infinitesimal extension of the line across the chart on the cabin bulkhead.

Still, we remain time-minded in all things. Even here on an empty ocean, far from the sight of anyone, we clock our sail changes and try to make them as fast as if we were in close quarters. Yesterday Dick reported with justifiable pride the port watch had shifted from balloon jib to spinnaker in 50 seconds—from sail on deck to set and drawing. This morning the starboard watch hung its collective head in shame for taking 1 minute 45 seconds in shifting from balloon jib to genoa. The halyard snarled with the ballooner halfway down—and afterwards we agreed it should have been hoisted again while the foul was being cleared so we would not have been without a headsail for the 30 seconds necessary to untangle.

9:15 p.m.: Alas! Gone is the joy from Mudville: the breeze is dying. From our glorious eight we are down to six, with every indication of less. During my past trick at the wheel we went through several holes in the wind as real and well defined as holes in a road. They show on the water like oil slicks. On entering one, the genoa goes hard aback against the spreaders, pressed there by the head wind our speed creates; we glide across, gradually slowing, until we re-enter the dark water on the far side, where wind ripples show. There the old breeze takes hold as though nothing had happened, the genoa fills with a bang, and we go merrily away until we fall into the next hole. But it seems only a matter of time until the doughnut will be all hole, and we will again be hungry.

Shortly before dark we passed a rusty tramp steamer at close range, and discovered this sea which we have constantly recorded as "smooth," or "flat," or "calm," is not really any of those things. For the little steamer was making something of a fuss about it, alternately plunging anchors under forward and raising stern high with a great feathering of foam from her propeller; and then squatting aft to expose a bewhiskered expanse of dirty red forefoot. She came at us from the horizon with the incongruous air of a child's wind-up toy running across a floor, up and down, up and down, until she passed close enough for us to read her name, *Bauta,* and wave at the men on her bridge, and then continued to see-saw her way across the swells toward the setting sun. Somehow she seemed slightly ridiculous and wholly unreal, and we were filled with pity for the characters aboard held in thrall by chipping hammers, coal dust, and canned Brussels sprouts.

As I produced the cocktail ration Frank remembered this is Bastille Day, so to *Janabel* and the spirit of La Belle France we drank a standing toast, optimistically raising our glasses in a direction vaguely over the starboard quarter. Is she there, out of sight over the rim of the world, or is she somewhere ahead, nearer the finish line than we? As I write the questions I can feel my tension mount; other sports measure competitive uncertainty in seconds, minutes, or at the most hours—we will have no answer for days or even weeks.

10:05 p.m.: The wind has become light and variable.

11:00 p.m.: The wind is almost gone.

11:35 p.m.: Wind gone. Sails down.

☆ ☆
☆

ABOVE the ocean of water lies the ocean of the air. For, as Maury opens *The Physical Geography of the Sea:* "Our planet is invested with two great oceans; one visible, the other invisible; one underfoot, the other overhead." Neither can be considered alone: each is so dependent on the other they are literally one, equally mysterious, equally unpredictable, equally complex.

Yet for centuries man missed the relationship. It was the sea, the liquid tangible familiar sea that was friend or enemy, dependent upon mood. Even philosophers ignored the fact water is the slave of wind, faithfully mirroring the will of the heavens, obedient to their every whim. The sea which raged through dikes and overwhelmed ships was the culprit, the cruel sea, while the sly wind went blameless; it was the sea to which prayers were directed: "Lord, have mercy, for thy sea is so great and our ship is so small."

Air is possessed of as many tangible and measurable qualities as water. It is a mixture of transparent gases—largely nitrogen and oxygen, but including argon, carbon dioxide, hydrogen, neon, helium, krypton, and xenon. It has definite weight: a cubic foot at ordinary pressure and temperature scales 1.22 ounces, or one 770th part of an equal amount of water. It exerts measurable pressure on the surface of the earth: some 15 pounds per square inch. When it is heated, it increases in volume, and thus becomes lighter. When it is cooled, its volume is diminished, and it becomes heavier. It is capable of carrying in suspension varying amounts of water vapor, at times visible as cloud or fog.

The first requirement for a basic understanding of the phenomenon of weather is to visualize air. Think of it as a clear liquid, a fluid having as definite a character as syrup, capable of flowing from one level or place to another in response to certain immutable laws. This flowing, entirely a matter of readjustment of pressure, of filling depressions in the atmosphere, we call wind. And the key to all is the simple fact that heated air rises.

As wind is the master of the sea, so is the sun master of the wind. For the creation of wind is wholly a matter of atmospheric pressures, and these pressures in turn are created by the action of the sun on the envelope of air which surrounds the earth—that other ocean, a gaseous sea some 200 miles deep, at the bottom of which we humans live. In these characteristics of air lies the whole secret of the heavens. For ceaselessly the rays of the sun act upon the land and sea areas of the earth, a complicated process of heating and cooling, of rising and falling pressures, made further complex by the spinning of this planet through space, and the seasonal inclination of the poles.

Picture the earth as a vast ball spinning along with the vertical axis roughly at right angles to the face of the sun. As it turns, the whole procession of continents and islands and oceans and lakes is presented to the solar rays; even more important, some parts are always closer to the sun than others—the middle of the ball, the equator, receives direct sunshine, while the poles know only oblique rays. Thus around the earth at the equator a band of earth and water is constantly heated, while the poles are capped by eternal ice. This is the most important single element in the weather of our planet.

As air is warmed over the equator, it increases in volume and expands, flowing outward at the higher altitudes toward places where the surface air is cooler. Since this overflow of air at high altitude removes weight from the layers of atmosphere below, the pressure on the surface is reduced. Thus along the equator there is a band called the *equatorial low*.

To make a necessary digression, surface pressure is measured by a simple instrument called the barometer, discovered in 1643 by Torricelli while serving the blind Galileo as hands and eyes. They found that a tube closed at the top and open at the bottom, filled with mercury and stood vertically in a dish of mercury, would maintain a column of mercury about 30 inches high. Correctly they explained the phenomenon as being due to the weight of the column of air resting on the liquid in the dish, a shaft of air rising mile upon mile into the sky. Consequently when warm upper air flows away from an area, and there is less weight aloft.

the barometer shows a low reading; when cool air presses down with increased density, the barometer is high. And, as one of those inflexible laws, winds flow from highs to lows; nature abhors a vacuum, and the lower the pressure, the nearer a vacuum.

Thus over the equator a column of heated air is constantly rising and spilling into cooler zones to the north and south. At the poles, cold air is sinking toward the surface. As the upper air flows in over the poles the barometric pressure becomes greater; so surface air moves away from the high-pressure area at the poles toward the low-pressure band at the equator.

If the earth were not turning, in the northern hemisphere warm air would drift northward at high levels and southward in the lower atmosphere. All surface winds would blow directly toward the equator. But here the concept becomes complicated by rotation and gravity. Air heated near the equator does rise and drift northward, but is deflected and appears as a westerly wind at high levels. As it moves northward it loses heat fairly rapidly and sinks. At about 30° north much of it descends to surface level, where it fans out, some flowing south, some north. The part that goes south is acted upon by the same Coriolis force which influences the currents of the sea—the deflecting influence of rotation that pulls objects to the right in the northern hemisphere, to the left in the southern, best comprehended by trying to draw a straight line across a piece of paper revolving slowly on a phonograph turntable. In the same way, the descending air that has fanned out toward the north becomes a west wind.

Meanwhile, the southward flow of surface air from the pole appears as an east wind. By the time it gets to 60 degrees north it meets the warmer northward-drifting west wind coming up from the 30-degree band. The latter is driven upwards over the cold air, and another vertical adjustment takes place. Essentially the same process takes place in the southern hemisphere, except the direction of deflection is reversed.

Thus the earth is divided into several well-defined areas of wind and weather, all stemming basically from the influence of

"The whole boat is a cat's-cradle of lines and chafing gear. More damned strings! ... But somehow it all makes sense and works, although as you look around you are certainly reminded of the best way to stay alive at sea—don't fall overboard."

"Gone is yesterday's fair weather and 'Bahama feel' . . . There is a totally different aspect to this world from the tropical one we left a few miles back in the warm waters of the Gulf Stream; this is part of the world of drifting ice, of long winter nights, of fog and rock and raging gales."

solar radiation on the atmosphere. Along the equator extends the area of low pressure which sailors call the *doldrums* and which Bowditch describes as occupying a position between the high-pressure belts to the north and south, a barometric trough where "the pressure, save for the slight diurnal oscillation, is practically uniform, and decided barometric gradients do not exist." This area, lying between the two systems of trade winds, was the terror of the sailing ship navigators. "Here the winds sink to stagnation, or rise at most only in fitful breezes, coming first from one point of the compass, then from another. The air is hot and sultry. The sky is often overcast and showers and thunderstorms are frequent." Many were the men who perished in the grip of the doldrums, death a welcome relief from the tortures of thirst, scurvy, and starvation.

North and south of the doldrums lie those broad highways of trade and adventure, the *trade winds,* "the most constant of winds for they sometimes blow for days or even weeks with slight variation in direction or even strength." These were the winds that carried Columbus across to the New World, and which until the development of steam power wafted the commerce of nations. In the northern hemisphere sailors found the northeast trade, in the southern the southeast trade, each blowing from the 30-degree subtropical high toward the low of the equator, deflected in accordance with those natural laws already explained. It is safe to say the trade winds have had as much influence on the development of civilization and the destiny of man as any single force on this earth.

On the outer margin of the trades, along that same parallel of 30° latitude, where the equatorial air cools and sinks, a belt of high pressure encircles the earth. Here also "the barometric gradients are faint and undecided and the winds correspondingly light and variable." This area was known to sailors of the past as the *horse latitudes,* for in it ships were so frequently becalmed and in want of water that cargoes of horses had to be thrown overboard. Unlike that of the doldrums, however, the weather is usually clear and fresh, lacking the oppressive humidity of the equatorial belt, and the periods of stagnation are likely to be intermittent instead of continuous.

Beyond these Calms of Cancer or Capricorn, a more dignified name for the horse latitudes, the barometric pressure diminishes. Thus currents of air flow poleward, only to be diverted by the rotation of the earth into the *prevailing westerlies.* In the southern hemisphere, where there is little land to complicate the basic global circulation of the atmosphere, the westerlies "exhibit a persistency approaching that of the trade winds," and blow throughout the year so strongly the latitudes in which they are encountered are called the "Roaring Forties." In the northern hemisphere they are often disrupted by other factors, yet still through the years have been consistent enough to earn the name "passage winds," or "counter trades."

So for centuries navigators have planned their voyages to take advantage of the winds, a concept further dividing the sailor's world from the landsman's: a view of the earth as segmented into broad highways of wind, moving in different directions in different latitudes, each with entirely unique characteristics. Thus during the age of sail, ships plying between Europe and the United States directed their course south until they encountered the northeast trades off the African coast, and sailed westward with strong fair winds, then curved up along the coast of North America to benefit from the Gulf Stream and prevailing southwesterlies. And, when returning, kept in those same westerlies to ride home with equally fair winds.

Thus plotting a passage in a ship at the mercy of the heavens is like planning a battle, a weighing of strategic variables and probables: of wind and calm and current. Yet in the final analysis the master of the sea is the wind and the master of the wind is the sun—while the sailor is slave to all. He can only curse or pray, according to his nature and his faith, while hoping for the best.

And on *Caribbee* we could do no more.

13th Day

49° 47′ N.
37° 07′ W.
Run: noon to noon: 86 miles
Average speed: 3.64 knots
Total run to date: 1649 miles

Tuesday, July 15. 4:40 a.m.: With the first light the sea is so calm that every detail of the clouds is reflected. The water is exactly the same color as the sky, a mirror extending toward the horizon in every direction, stirred only by the slightest underlying swell. Overhead the sails hang in limp folds. Despite all efforts at the helm we drift around in circles, sometimes pointing toward England, sometimes Iceland, sometimes Bermuda.

But as I look out over the sea, I am at peace. There is not even a sense of impatience, or frustration. The first moments of dawn are always so utterly beautiful, so full of promise, it is impossible to be other than grateful for the privilege of being alive and able to enjoy. I wonder what man has achieved by his civilization, his towering cities and his sense of urgency, that compensates for the loss of moments close to nature? Is the dictator more to be envied than the shepherd who stands on the mountain, canopied by stars? Is the man of wealth better off than the fisherman who glides out of a West Indian harbor at sunrise? Such questions have troubled men since they could think, yet remain unanswered, as they always will, for in them lies the essential riddle of humanity.

As I write, a large school of porpoises is passing in stately procession. I first saw a family of four close under the stern: a mama and papa, no doubt, and two fat babies. They seemed in no hurry whatever, but looked us over carefully before strolling on to the north. Now I realize this is no quiet family junket but a parade; as far as I can see backs are breaking the oily surface sheen. Suddenly I understand why mariners of the Middle Ages could mistake a line of porpoises for a sea serpent: a moment ago the resemblance to a long snaky body was startling. Maybe I did see it! Sure! It had the head of a lion, the wings of a bat, the talons of a hawk, and—yes, carried a purple umbrella with pink polka dots!

I must tell the others! But wait: yesterday the boys decided this continued calm was adding an odd gleam to my eye, and they would have to put me in irons à la Captain Quigg when I cut "southwest" out of the compass card, or began making paper dolls from the pilot charts. So maybe I'd better not tell them what I saw. They might not believe about the umbrella.

6:15 a.m.: We were just treated to a spectacular show by the heavens. In the pale glow of dawn we could make out a streak of cloud to the southwest. At first it looked like a narrow band along the horizon, but as the light strengthened it lifted. Finally we could see the band was actually the bottom of the cloud canopy under which we lie. As we watched, it lifted higher and higher, dividing the sky into two parts, one gray and overcast, the other blue and bright. Then suddenly the cloud seemed to pull apart like the sliding roof in a nightclub patio, and *Caribbee* was flooded by dazzling sunshine. Now overhead the sky is very blue, laced only by a few wispy cirrus clouds.

But we gained no speed: beauty doesn't make a boat go.

7:30 a.m.: The sunshine was brief. The cloud cover has closed again.

2:45 p.m.: It is impossible to convey the complete frustration of these crazy shifts of wind. We log them as "light variables" and have ceased recording each change of sail or course.

As an example: at one o'clock when our watch came on deck

we found *Caribbee* on the starboard tack with the genoa set, averaging 2 knots on a course between 045 and 050 degrees. The desired great-circle course is still 106°. Thus the wind came from almost exactly the point where we wanted to go—a dead muzzler, with practically no choice of tacks. We shifted to the drifter, hoping for a couple tenths of a knot, and got it at about the same heading. Then the wind backed until we were forced up to 020 degrees, at the same time freshening enough to raise our speed to 4.3. So we tacked and went back to the genoa, and for awhile lay course making 5 knots. But not for long. Within minutes the wind began to veer, pushing us down through 115, 125, and 140 to the present heading of 172 degrees, while our speed dropped under three. Now again there arises the question of tack, and whether to shift back to drifter.

In the last Trans-Atlantic Race, 2 years ago, Erroll Bruce kept a "Crew Endurance Diagram" on *Samuel Pepys*, recording in graph form morale and ability in terms of exhaustion brought on by successive gales and hard driving. He started at the top with "Very confident," and "Cheerful," and went down through "Easily irritated; mistakes frequent" and "Very tired" to "Too tired to sleep; bad mistakes." During each spell of "Rough seas" the curve of the graph descended; during each period labeled "Calmer" it went up sharply. Now I wonder how they fare? If they are having identical conditions I'll bet that graph is reversed: morale up for "Rough seas" (if any) and down for "Calmer."

8:15 p.m.: For the first time in days I have the feeling we are actually gaining on England. Each noon we gather around the chart on the cabin bulkhead with an "it can't happen to us" sensation in the pit of the stomach, but tonight Frank ordained the setting ahead of our clocks by one hour. Now we are in "Zone Plus 2" time, meaning we have crossed the meridian 37° 30′ west of Greenwich, and consequently are roughly only 2 hours away by the speed at which the sun travels.

Zone time is a Navy concept, and a useful one, corresponding at sea to the time bands on land: Eastern Standard Time, Central Standard Time, and the rest. In the old days, a ship's clock was set at 12:00 when the captain, squinting at the sun through his sextant to make sure it had reached the highest point, suddenly shouted "Noon!" When zone time is used, minor local differences are ignored through a band of 15 degrees of longitude, the distance the sun moves—or appears to move—across the surface of the earth in one hour. Thus there are 24 bands, or zones. For convenience, they are labeled "plus" up to the International Date Line, 180 degrees of longitude, halfway around the world from Greenwich, and "minus" the rest of the way, through the areas of east longitude. So gaining an hour of time is the equivalent of gaining 15 degrees of longitude, definite proof we are getting somewhere.

The barometer stopped falling last night when the wind died, and has been steady all day. Now it begins a slow rise. All afternoon we were tantalized by magnificent clouds, great towering masses of cumulus that seemed certain harbingers of wind. For hours we crept from one to another, peering at each as hopefully as a drunk looking into empty bottles. And with no more luck.

14th Day

50° 29′ N.
35° 40′ W.
Run: noon to noon: 66 miles
Average speed: 2.79 knots
Total run to date: 1715 miles

Wednesday, July 16. 1:30 a.m.: I have just had the odd and somewhat eerie experience of holding in my hand a Mother Carey's chicken. They somehow symbolize to me the freedom of the open spaces, and the wildness of the sea itself. Through the years I have watched them scamper up and down and across the waves, seeming to revel in the danger of breaking crests. Always before I have noted their arrival with a feeling of misgiving, sharing the old superstition that they portend a gale. Now, as they have appeared each evening since we left the Gulf Stream with the regularity of the sunset, my credulity has worn thin. But I do not cease to marvel.

They are small birds, no bigger than a starling or a swallow, and have an erratic flight, rather like that of a bat. It does not seem they could travel any great distance, yet now we are over 600 miles from land. The one I held had flown into the drifter, blinded by the spreader lights; it skidded down to the deck, fluttering desperately against the sail, and then crouched in the waterway. I was standing at the lee shrouds so it landed at my feet. It is hard to say which of us was more startled.

We looked at each other, and I remembered reading their legs are not strong enough to support them on the ground. There wasn't any alternative to extending the helping hand. So I can pass along to an eager world the information a Mother Carey's chicken coming on board in mid-Atlantic squats on deck with wings half-extended, and when picked up doesn't shake any more than you do. It is a strange little bird, sooty-gray all over, except for even darker wings and tail, and a white spot on the rump. The beak is black and sharply hooked; the feet are webbed, useful for support when feeding on the surface, giving them the appearance of running over the sea. Actually, the feet are brought down together with a patting motion while the wings are kept spread, but the appearance of walking is supposed to be the origin of the name Storm-Petrel, a corruption of Saint Peter. And while on the subject of corruption of names, Mother Carey's chicken undoubtedly stems from "Mater Cara," the Blessed Virgin Mary of medieval sailors.

Like many superstitions, the legend of bad weather in connection with the appearance of Storm-Petrels around a ship has at least some basis of fact. As they feed principally on plankton floating on the surface of the sea, and the passage of a vessel creates an area of smoother water, during gales they tend to hunt in this area, while during fair weather they range far and wide.

Of course, I'm not superstitious. But before tossing my friend out into the night I reminded him he owed us something of a debt of gratitude, and respectfully requested he let us have a bit of wind out of any old gales that happened to be lying around. Or at least put in a good word for us with his boss, generally reputed to be Davy Jones.

2:50 a.m.: Our watch on deck will end in another 10 minutes. The port watch has been called, and below is struggling to get awake and into its clothes. They will probably have to spend the next 4 hours contending with the same miserable conditions, worse than anything short of a hurricane. Never before have I understood so well the meaning implicit in the words of Master Fletcher, preacher, written during Drake's voyage around the world: "We often met with adverse winds, unwelcome storms, and even less welcome calms."

Conditions are unchanged. Calm, a light variable slant, calm again. Sea smooth except for a small underlying swell. Periods when we make 3 or 4 knots, periods when we slat; periods when we lay course of 106 degrees, periods when we are up to 020 or down to 130. When a faint air stirs we hoist the sails, when it dies they must come down again before tearing themselves to ribbons. Up main, up drifter, down drifter, up genoa, down genoa, up drifter, down everything. Port tack, starboard tack, wearing around because not enough headway to tack. Hour after hour, getting nowhere.

7:30 a.m.: Awakened by Henry at 6:20 just as port watch dropped the genoa, giving up the ghosting (oops!). Now, after huge breakfast of pancakes and Canadian bacon, on deck to the usual oily calm. In order to avoid future repetitiousness, have completed a contest for a new word to replace "oily." Among the suggestions: "diesel calm," "lubricating oil calm," "600-W calm," "liquid Vaseline Hair Tonic calm." None seems quite suitable.

But more important, have discovered the reason for the oily look of the sea: millions upon millions upon millions of tiny jellyfish. What from deck level looks like the floating scum around a fueling dock turns out to be little blobs of jelly, each touched by a dot of brilliant blue. We have scooped up a bucket of water, and in that one bucket there must be thousands of the creatures.

The 0500 log entry concludes: " 'Eyes' observed in water." We have been looking for those "eyes" for days, ever since Frank and Dick remembered it was the "eyes" that brought them wind last year, after *Malabar XIII* had been becalmed. They are convinced the "eyes" did it, and now we are practically trapped by a solid mass of them. They are larger versions of these same jellyfish, and do look something like staring blue eyes in certain light.

Well, we've had a Mother Carey's chicken aboard, and now we have "eyes." But the barograph doesn't show wind, the sky and clouds don't show wind, and damned if any of us have any right to be as cheerful as we suddenly are.

10:00 a.m.: This morning has reminded me of a winter day on the Chesapeake, where Bunny Rigg and I have sat in a duck blind for many similar days. We would get out with the first faint light, cold and sleepy, and set out the decoys and ready our guns and wait for the dawn. Under us the water would be smooth, but frequently with a slight swell from the southward like this. As the sun lifted above the horizon there would be a pale shaft of silver across the water, but then it would disappear behind the canopy of clouds. Above the horizon there would be a dark band of gray.

Nothing would stir. We would stand at opposite ends of the blind, huddled in sheepskin coats, and stare at the sky and the water. A few black ducks might move down the center of the bay, flying low and fast, and a lone whistler might circle just out of range, but the guns would remain in their stands. The day would grow brighter, and we would first loosen and then take off the heavy coats, and then perhaps a layer of sweaters. Later we would have a swig of brandy chased by a cup of coffee, and watch the morning breeze trace faint patterns of ripples on the water, and the decoys begin to bob. The sun would show through gaps in the clouds, but was never bright because it was being filtered by even higher clouds . . . And through the whole day we might not get a shot, but still would go home that night with a wonderful feeling of satisfaction and accomplishment.

I remember once trying to explain to a lady who thought hunting cruel and wicked that hunting meant more than killing, more even than the test of skill involved in laying a pattern of shot around a flying bird, or dropping a buck with one clean shot— more than any of the implications included in any definition of "sport." There are the other satisfactions—the compensations.

And that parallel certainly holds in sailing, too.

1:45 p.m.: Moving, for a change. For the last couple of hours we have enjoyed another of those wind streaks, the only things that have teased us ahead during the past week. To noon, the run for the past 24 hours was 66 miles, an average speed of 2.79 knots. Words fail me.

Before lunch we were treated to a very funny show: the port watch finally decided the time had come for a bath, regardless of temperature and consequences. About 10:00 Dick came on deck and rigged the nylon bathtub Ernest Ratsey had presented *Caribbee* before we left Newport. His theory was that as the air is warmer than the water, allowing the tub to stand a couple of hours would make it the next thing to a steaming shower at the Waldorf. So he lashed it to the windward rail and poured in buckets of water, and went below for another nap.

At 12:00 a procession appeared, the entire port watch, complete with towels and a look of determination. To encourage them, Frank got out the ship's thermometer and demonstrated that while the temperature of the sea alongside was a mere 62 degrees, the tub had risen to a comfortable 65 degrees. Dick had unfortunately underestimated the air temperature.

Basil was chosen as the first victim, and as he carefully inserted a toe Dick poured in an extra bucket of water. There was a scream that must have scared bonefish off the flats in Middle Bight, Andros, and Basil went back down the companionway faster than one of those same bonefish. A minute later he reappeared wearing the heaviest sheepskin on board, but I will say he finally shucked it and got in the tub.

Real devotion to the common cause!

4:20 p.m.: Oddly, the wind still holds, although it is still highly variable and probably will drop with the sun. But at the moment we are showing 6 knots on the Kenyon, and feeling properly grateful. I was just on deck between naps, and found the wind southeast by south at around 6 or 7 miles an hour—a good full Force 2, Beaufort scale, maybe even touching Force 3. The barograph track is absolutely level.

The watch on deck still works at chasing the wind around the compass—the eastern half of the compass, of course. At 4:00 Dick logged for the preceding hour: "Drifter, balloon forestaysail, main, mizzen staysail & mizzen; struck mizzen & set spinnaker; headed—struck spinnaker & mizzen staysail, set drifter; changed from drifter to genoa. Now hard on wind steering 111°."

When I was up the boys were being entertained by a new variety of porpoise, cute little fellows with grayish-blue backs and cream bellies, a sharply defined line of color running from snout to tail. Like all porpoises, they roll over to give us a good look, and slide under the bow and dart off only to come rushing back, meanwhile grinning like kids on a picnic. They really seem to have fun, and I hope if I'm reincarnated it is as a porpoise. What could be better for a sailor?

10:35 p.m.: The breeze holds. Two hours ago we decided it had freed us enough to carry a spinnaker. Now our largest sail towers overhead, a huge pale mushroom somehow faintly luminescent against the dark sky. We rush through the night.

Suddenly all the joys of sailing, all the wonderful sensory satisfactions of silent movement, come back stronger than ever. I sit here at the head of the companionway wanting the moment never to end, but to go sailing on across the sea forever. Such is the complexity of the nature of man: of not wanting the very thing he seems to want most. For days I have prayed to move toward our destination; but as soon as we do, all the pleasure returns, and I don't want it to be over.

It must have been that way in the ships of old. We read of 90-day passages, of 120-day passages, of men taking years to circumnavigate the earth, and feel full of pity. Yet time is such a relative thing that there must not have been a sense of hardship—and always there were the compensations. The best proof is that ships never lacked the men to sail them.

I put down this notebook for a minute and made a full circuit of the deck. Frank is forward, sitting on the pulpit, looking up at the bellying expanse aloft. He says nothing: there is no sea to make steering difficult, and the sail stays quietly asleep. Under the bow there is the sound of rushing water, a rhythmic plash. Twin fans of water radiate from each side of the hull, glowing weirdly with pale green phosphorescence. Single drops scatter out over the black sea like globules of cold fire.

There is no light on deck except the compass. Behind it Bobby sits at the wheel in tense concentration, while Jack crouches in the waterway within reach of the spinnaker sheet. They too are quiet, as though afraid to break the spell. A commodity as tenuous as a breeze might vanish at a word! And the Kenyon touches eight, and the backstays hum, and astern lies the wide silver path we trace for a few fleeting moments across the ocean.

This afternoon the drinks were poured and glasses raised precisely at 6:00, saluting 2 weeks at sea. As though by invitation—perhaps a messenger from Davy Jones, sent by our friend the wayfaring Chicken—the largest whale of the passage chose the moment to surface alongside. He was quite a guy, altering any philosophical comments that might have been made into an argument on his over-all length. IIe circled us lazily, leaving a wake like a battleship, snorted in derision at so puny an object as *Caribbee,* and took off due north.

11:55 p.m.: It lacks 5 minutes until midnight. The breeze remains about south, but has become light; in fact, it shows every sign of going the way of all the others. Our speed has dropped to five, and I suppose it is now only a matter of time until we begin to roll helplessly.

Until this passage, I didn't fully realize the horrors of slatting. Without doubt, it has been the worst feature of this past period of calm. You begin to listen for it even when below, a subconscious dread that kills sleep. From your bunk you visualize the exact pattern of what is happening on deck . . . You hear a murmur of voices as someone detects a faint breath of air and a patter of feet as the whole watch moves around trying to determine its direction. Then the creak of the main halyard, and the rattle of the coffee-grinder winch aft as the drifter is sheeted. The aimless rolling stops, and there might even be the sound of water moving past the topsides. You know that the helm has come alive, and that the needle of the Kenyon has crept up past "1," past "2," perhaps even to "3." From below you share the hope of the watch above, that perhaps "this is it," the first faint outrider of the wind which will drive us on to England. You might doze. But then there is a changed sound on deck, perhaps a call from the helmsman about the jib, or the sound of a winch, but you come awake knowing the wind is dropping, dropping, and soon it will begin . . . and it does. First there is a patter as the reef points slap against the canvas of the mainsail, an insistent sound like rain on a taut surface, or even the roll of distant drums. It is the sound you have been dreading, yet knowing would resume . . . Then the slashing jerk and crash of the main boom straining against tackles, and the thunder of the jib rolling full and aback . . . then the sound of sails being lowered and loosely furled. And again the aimless rolling . . .

Yet maybe I'm wrong. In the few minutes it has taken to record past anguish the breeze has definitely freshened. A moment ago a Mother Carey's chicken somewhere aloft called something. Maybe he was reading over my shoulder and saying: "This poor character has had enough: turn on the breeze!"

We heel to a new strength of wind. Again *Caribbee* rushes through the night.

WITHIN the broad zones of weather that girdle the earth are endless variations, for something as capricious and elusive as air refuses to be reduced to a formula. Even the trades, those most reliable of winds, may be fickle: as Bowditch says, "Their uniformity should not be exaggerated."

So although the seaman's world of winds may begin with the humid calms of the doldrums, and extend progressively northward through the easterly belt of trades, the light variables of the horse latitudes, the brave westerlies of the temperate zone, and the frigid easterlies of the polar wastes, there are vast seasonal and even daily variations within the zones. For altering the theoretical behavior of the atmosphere are as many factors as there are objects on the surface of the earth: the islands and continents, the oceans and rivers, the forests and the plains—even the newly plowed field or the paved highway, for each reflects the rays of the sun in its own way, and each affects the ocean of air above and around it.

In 1820 John Purdy summed up the winds of the earth in his *Memoir, Descriptive and Explanatory, of the Atlantic Ocean:* "The Winds are divided into *Perennial, Periodical,* and *Variable. Perennial,* or *Constant,* winds are those which always blow the same way; such is that easterly wind, within the tropics, commonly called the *Trade-Wind. Periodical* Winds are those which constantly return at certain times: such are land and sea-breezes, blowing alternately from land to sea and from sea to land. *Variable,* or Erratic, Winds are such as blow now this way, now that, and are now up, now hushed, without regularity either as to time or place: such are the winds prevalent in England." And, he might have added, throughout that band of latitude, roughly midway between equator and pole, men call the temperate zone.

The north temperate zone, as the name implies, extends from the tropics of the south to the polar areas of the north, the same general area as the prevailing westerlies. Lying between the two extremes of hot and cold, it is affected by more variation in temperature and pressure than any other area of the globe: it is a battleground of conflicting systems, subject to the moods and dictates of each—from the blizzard originating in the Aleutians to the hurricane sweeping up from the Caribbean, from the steaming heat of deserts to masses of air chilled by eternal ice. It is also the most heavily populated and traveled zone of our planet, where the behavior of weather most affects the destiny of men and nations.

Since the earliest days of history philosophers have attempted to reduce the phenomena of the heavens to a formula. "In the Spring may men sail," wrote Hesiod in the eighth century B.C. "When first on the topmost spray the fig-tree leaves appear as the footprint of a crow for size, then is the sea navigable." In the fourth century B.C. Theophrastus compiled a book on weather signs: "If the sun has a hollow appearance, it is a sure sign of wind or rain . . . When the west wind is accompanied by lightning from the north, it indicates either storm or rain." And in the Bible appears a 2000-year-old version of the current doggerel, "Red sky at night, sailor's delight; red sky in morning, sailors take warning." St. Matthew wrote (xvi: 2–3): "When it is evening, ye say, It will be fair weather: for the sky is red. And in the morning, It will be foul weather today: for the sky is red and lowering."

Down through the centuries the lore has accumulated—the scientific observations of the savants and practical knowledge of the sailor and the farmer—until man has finally achieved some comprehension of the laws behind the weather, of what makes the wind and the rain, the calm and the storm.

Man has learned, for example, that the constant cycles of weather in the temperate zone, the recurrent phases of warm and cold, of clear sky and rain, of hard wind and gentle breeze, are caused by a constant procession of "lows" and "highs" moving from west to east, periodic waves of varying pressure, each with definite and definable characteristics, and each with equally definite results. In the language of meteorologists, lows are called *cyclones,* from the suggestion of Henry Piddington, President of the Marine Courts in Calcutta, whose *Sailor's Horn-Book for the Law of Storms* was of inestimable value to the masters of

"Visibility is sometimes a hundred yards, sometimes a boat length. There is tension in driving blindly ahead, the man forward staring into a gray void. Even the spray of the bow wave vanishes in nothingness before it falls back into the sea. Our senses begin to play tricks on us: we imagine we see looming shapes, or hear horns, or even feel currents of colder air, as from an ice box suddenly opened."

"On these Banks the sea is gray black and actually looks cold. Today it is very confused, fairly large swells coming in from a dozen directions to pile up into steep pyramids which collapse as patches of white foam."

sailing ships. He analyzed and proved by excerpts from numerous logs the winds around a low pressure area are circular in shape, a coiling around a center, and so suggested as a name *"Cyclone,* which signifies, amongst other things, the coils of a snake." Unfortunately, as it is a term applied both to the savage hurricanes of the tropics and to the mildest of atmospheric depressions of the temperate zones, the name *cyclone* is a cause of some confusion; it should be understood to describe a type of circulation rather than a velocity of wind.

In the northern hemisphere, cyclones always revolve opposite to the movement of the hands of a watch; they are invariably "counterclockwise." By the same token, over the half of the world south of the equator, they revolve in the same direction as the hands of a watch; they are "clockwise." To add to the apparent confusion, but basically a simple concept, high-pressure areas are called *anticyclones,* because wind flows outward and away from the center, and in exactly the opposite direction from the rotation of cyclones on either side of the equator.

The life cycle of a typical extra-tropical cyclone, the most characteristic manifestation of weather in the temperate zone, might begin with the collision of two air masses, one composed of moist tropical air flowing northeastward and the other of cold polar air flowing southwestward. The junction could take place at any point over the earth's surface; such cyclones may and do form over the continents, but more have their origin over the oceans.

On meeting, each mass behaves in accordance with its nature: the cold air, being heavier, slides in under the warmer air in a long thin wedge. A cold front comes into being on the left of the line of meeting, a warm front on the right. Where they collide, generally a comparatively narrow zone less than 100 miles in width, the barometric pressure is lowered and the air begins a counterclockwise circulation. At the rear of the cold front a high-pressure area develops.

As the warm moist air is lifted its temperature lowers; clouds form and rain or snow falls. Progressively, as the system matures, the low pressure deepens and the winds increase. The frontal line of demarcation between the two air masses usually bends into the shape of a "V" as the whole system drifts along to the east; sometimes the cold front moves faster than the warm and completely encircles the warm air at the tongue of the front, so the center of low pressure is completely surrounded at ground level by cold air. At this stage the cyclone is *occluded,* and has reached its maximum intensity. Thereafter the low gradually fills up and disappears, or is absorbed by a newer and more vigorous cyclone which has developed at some other point on the front.

Such extra-tropical cyclones can range from the mild summer thundershowers which are followed by clear cool weather to the raging winter gales which lash shipping on the North Atlantic. Generally speaking, in winter two of these systems occur each week over the United States, and move eastward at a velocity of some 700 miles a day. They are less frequent and less severe in summer, and average only about 500 miles a day. But despite the rate of travel of the system as a whole, cyclones can cover enormous areas and take days to pass any one place. Most of our temperate zone changes in weather—cloud cover, temperature, wind velocity and direction—come from the progressive forward movement of the various characteristic parts of these fronts.

Of all the visible symbols of weather, none have affected and intrigued men as have clouds. Yet strangely no system of classification came into being until fairly recently. Even the Greeks, so close to nature and so apt in assigning names, completely failed in distinguishing between various types. It remained for an obscure London chemist by the name of Luke Howard to see the essential differences between the varieties of clouds, and to devise a simple but effective method of describing them.

High thin wisps of vapor, delicate and fragile, reminded Howard of a "lock of hair." These he called *cirrus,* the Latin word for hair. Others, spreading over the sky like a sheet, he called *stratus.*

Those which gathered into a turret, a heap, became *cumulus;* and the dark and threatening masses from which fell rain or snow he dubbed *nimbus,* which simply means "cloud." During the past century nothing better has been devised, and the ten major cloud classifications of modern meteorology are only various combinations of Luke Howard's lock of hair, sheet, heap, and plain cloud. So stripped of its Latin trimmings "cirro-stratus" is a sheet of delicate filmy cloud, the veil which does not completely hide the sun or moon but gives the sky a faintly milky look, and produces halos; "cumulo-nimbus" is a heavy mass of threatening black cloud, heaped high into the atmosphere, the familiar thunder-cloud of summer squalls.

As important to any study of weather is a system of determining and recording the velocity of the wind, and this too is a fairly recent development. The universally accepted scale of wind forces was devised by Rear Admiral Sir Francis Beaufort of the Royal Navy in 1805. His original scale did not tabulate velocity in terms of wind speed, but only in relation to the amount of sail a ship of the line could carry. Beginning at zero, a flat calm with "no headway," he went on up the scale to Force 12, a hurricane, where "no canvas can stand." As the ships changed, the first definitions lost their meaning: "A strong breeze" stood at Force 6 on the Beaufort Scale as "that to which a well-found ship could just carry in chase full-and-by royals and top-gallant-sails"; and Force 10, "A whole gale," was that in which "she could scarcely bear lower main topsail and reefed foresail." But even when the phraseology lost its meaning the divisions remained valid, and later generations modified the definitions to cover vessels or circumstances within their experience. Now all versions of the Beaufort Scale assign definite velocities to each division. Force 6 is still defined as "a strong breeze" but is listed as from 25 to 31 statute miles an hour, or from 22 to 27 knots; to help landsmen determine Force 6, it is noted on land "Large branches begin to move; telephone wires whistle; umbrellas are used with difficulty." To aid modern seamen, who would not have the faintest idea what sails a ship of the line "in chase" might carry, the definition is in terms of the appearance of the surface of the sea: "Large waves begin to form; white foam crests are more extensive everywhere; there may be some spray."

While most printed versions of the Beaufort Scale omit entirely any reference to the behavior of vessels and the sail they can carry through the various forces, the most recent Bowditch still lists a "Mode of estimating for average sized sailing trawler." At Force 6 "Smacks double-reef mainsail." At Force 7, they "remain in harbor, and those at sea lie-to." At Force 8, "Smacks take shelter if possible." Beyond Force 8—through Force 9, a "Strong gale"; Force 10, a "Whole gale"; Force 11, "Storm"; and Force 12, "Hurricane"—Bowditch is silent. Only rows of dots run across the columns, mute symbols of the hazard of the sea, of the eternal struggle: tiny oilskinned figures clawing at flogging canvas as sullen crests smash savagely out of the rain and spindrift, lonely men battling for their lives against an elemental and pitiless foe, their chances of survival summed up by a row of dots across a page.

For despite his knowledge of the laws of nature, of his high-sounding terms and definitions, his neat maps of highs and lows and wind directions and velocities, man has not conquered the heavens. Those of us who venture forth must be ready for whatever might be our lot, from a stagnant high hanging motionless off the coast of Labrador to a hurricane whirling up from the West Indies.

Thus the men of the past, thus we on *Caribbee*.

15th Day

~~~~~~

51° 08′ N.
31° 09′ W.
Run: noon to noon: 183 miles
Average speed: 7.62 knots
Total run to date: 1898 miles

Thursday, July 17. 4:00 a.m.: My day began an hour ago with
the pleasant task of calling the spinnaker. Now I sit in the cockpit and write by flashlight. The wind holds; if anything, it is
fresher than when we turned in. There still is no reason for it to
be blowing, so far as sky or barometer are concerned. Nothing
is essentially changed from the conditions of the past week. While
I cannot explain it, the glorious fact remains—we have wind.
And are properly appreciative.

A dying crescent of moon shows over the bow, beckoning us on
our way. Overhead, stars show intermittently through breaks in
the low scud, yet clouds have taken form around the horizon, and
the sea is distinct. It is that moment of transition between night
and day, when the first rays of the sun have stolen imperceptibly
over the horizon and objects begin to take form without your
realizing they are visible. Now I am aware I can distinguish the
reef points along the main, and the leading edge of the spinnaker,
and details of the mizzen rigging. But still the helmsman could
not see the compass card without the binnacle light, nor could
I write by the sky.

It seems impossible we could move so fast with so gentle a
breeze. The needle of the Kenyon hangs constantly at 8.2, and
occasionally creeps up to 8.5. Yet on the water off to windward

not a streak of foam is to be seen: just those "small, short wave-lets" of "glassy appearance" associated with Force 2 on the Beaufort Scale. But it must be a trick of the lighting or perhaps some unusual condition of the surface of the sea, as we agree the true wind is about south at 10 knots, enough to form whitecaps.

The spinnaker pole is well forward because our course and speed puts the wind on the beam. It is surprisingly warm; this air is coming to us from those sunny blue reaches toward the equator, the breeze we have been expecting. The sea has not yet built, and at this speed our old enemy, the underlying swell, is helpless. So we streak along toward England, wistfully regretful it could not have been like this sooner, and only fearful that the breeze might vanish back into the thin air.

6:00 a.m.: I write this sitting in the companionway, protected from a fine misting rain by the canvas dodger. It is colder than it was two hours ago, but not unpleasant.

Since dawn we have been able to see we were ringed by thick black clouds, a solid mass all around the horizon. For days clouds have been just more of those empty bottles, but at sea it never pays to be overly sure. So I sat on the after deckhouse, watching, trying to decide whether the squalls might carry a wallop of wind, or were only heavy with rain. Suddenly it occurred to me how down the centuries skippers have been doing just that: studying the windward sky, every sense alive to determine possible danger to ship and crew. The watch on deck waiting for a word, the watch below confidently asleep. Clouds towering higher, becoming blacker; wind increasing, sea building; ship beginning to stagger under the weight of canvas. Yet the breeze is fair; each moment furthers the passage . . . And the master stays by the wheel, watchful, or leans against the rigging and studies the masts above, and looks beyond to the heavens, sensitive to each play of force and each change in the sky.

As I scanned the clouds and thought my thoughts, I felt somehow close to being able to express the endless fascination of the sea, and the hold it may have on a man. For the constant challenge of the ocean is never matched on land; the moment-to-moment changes, the necessity for watchfulness and decision. Any other life becomes dull and routine.

Now we sail under the biggest and blackest cloud in sight. My earliest guess seems to have been right: more rain than wind. The donning of oilskins was more important than the clearing of the spinnaker halyard for instant running, but it could have been the other way around. *Caribbee* heels to a slight increase in breeze. Frank calls from the wheel we touch nine. Rain works its way down the back of my neck, for I am not wearing a sou'-wester. We move, we move.

England suddenly seems close.

1:10 p.m.: From 7:35, five minutes after I got up from the breakfast table, until 12:25, five minutes before I sat down to lunch, I slept as happily and peacefully as a babe in a cradle. For a moment before dropping off I luxuriated in the purely sensual satisfaction of a soft warm bunk, twisting and turning to work my way well down in the blankets, and enjoying the music of water rippling past the hull. And somehow during the time I slept I must have known that conditions were not changing, because Henry said when he awakened me I was grinning all the way 'round to the back of my head.

I am still grinning. A few minutes ago Frank posted our day's run as 183 miles, only slightly less than three times as much as we made the preceding 24 hours. And things still hold the same—improving, if anything. Now the barograph is catching up to the action of the wind, showing a gradual but steady descent. It stands at 30.35. At 10:00 Dick logged the breeze at south-southwest 15 knots; at noon southwest by south 18 knots; and at the moment we call it southwest 18 knots. So for the first time we have the wind we should have enjoyed ever since crossing 40° north latitude: Force 5, southwest.

This is close to our fastest and most satisfactory point of sailing. Every reaching sail is hard at work: parachute spinnaker, balloon forestaysail, main, mizzen staysail, mizzen—everything on board is flying except Henry's tablecloth, and as soon as the port watch can be persuaded to stop eating, we'll hang it up, too. The sea is beginning to build: the wave forms have lengthened and are well sprinkled with the white foam of breaking white-caps. But steering is still easy, so we tear along reeling off the miles with no effort at all. For once the wind does the work, and we poor slaves do nothing but ride along.

It is clear, warm, and sparkling. The sun shines brightly most of the time, but occasionally ducks under small cumulus clouds, the fat puffy clouds I always associate with fair weather. Oddly, however, even during the brightest periods the sea is never really blue; it has a cold grayish tone, a steely metallic quality, some-how carrying a feeling of the lonely expanses to the north.

At lunch Bobby bet me Frank's tomorrow's dinner dessert we would top 200 miles in the next 24 hours, and I came back by betting him Jack's dessert we would break 210. We are very sporting and wager their desserts on the slightest provocation, which shows what good-natured watchmates they are, but I am afraid it would take a riot squad to enable either of us to collect our winnings. So far neither has tried. But our bet was the first time any of us had dared assume out loud this wind would hold; that it is not another of those streaks which start by looking like a super-highway and end as a blind alley. To use an old Baha-mian expression, until now all of us have been "afraid to put mouth on it" for fear the wind would vanish.

Little wayfaring Chicken, little blue eyes, don't leave us now!

3:05 p.m.: The sleighride continues. Now we are logging the wind at 22 knots, while the direction remains southwest. There has been no change in sails, and only slight modifications in trim, during the last 2 hours.

But everything else has changed, a most astonishing demonstration of how swiftly things can alter at sea. This has become a real gray North Atlantic day. The sun is completely hidden by a solid blanket of low stratus, ragged at the bottom. A fine drizzling rain falls, barely heavier than thick mist, yet raw and penetrating. The wind has a new edge of chill. Astern the seas roll up longer and higher, and breaking crests are frequent; when one slaps aboard it seems to have more weight, just as this colder air seems to have more drive against the sails.

Square pole, ease sheet; let pole forward, trim sheet: the spinnaker rides high and round, head nearly lost in the mist above. Seas running up under counter, lifting stern; a momentary hang and shoot; seas passing forward with a roar under the bow. Roll and go: 9 knots, 9½, 10 knots. This is it: again this is what we came for.

Occasionally the main boom dips deeply into a passing crest, throwing a wide fan of spray. I remember when bathing in the lee scuppers it was impossible to hold a leg out rigidly against the rush of water, and suddenly have some comprehension of the strains involved: in the mast and halyard carrying the spinnaker, in the sheets and guys taking the thrust of the wind, in the preventers holding the main boom, in the rudder, in the steering-gear fittings. And am thankful for the engineering that computed the strains, and the honest craftsmanship that fashioned the materials to withstand them. As civilization advances, man is increasingly dependent upon the integrity and ability of his fellows: driving an automobile, traveling in a train, flying an airplane. And especially sailing a boat across the Atlantic.

5:10 p.m.: My last wheel trick was something of a workout. The sea is now large and long enough to make *Caribbee* sheer as the stern rises and the bow buries. And again there is no such thing as a satisfactory combination of clothes. Oilskins out here are like the ancient crack about women: you can't live with them, and you can't live without them. If you're dressed warmly enough to be comfortable on deck, after 15 minutes of wrestling with the helm you're steaming, and at the end of a half-hour trick are thoroughly parboiled.

But we're not complaining. During the last hour we averaged 9.2 knots, and on shoots down unusually big waves the Kenyon needle climbs to 10.5 and above. As Frank noted in the log at 5:00: "Going well—downhill, and less than a thousand to go." It is odd, but we almost have the feeling of being in coastal waters. Yet at the moment we are about the greatest distance from land of any part of the passage—Newfoundland, Greenland, Iceland, Azores, and British Isles. We really are in the middle of the deep blue sea in a very literal sense.

As I wrote that, the spinnaker broke. I heard Frank call urgently from the bow: "Curling, curling! Go down! Go down!" Then on a lower note: "It's broken." I look up and see the leading edge folded in against the rest of the sail; the huge expanse of nylon is aback, pressed against the headstay. At the wheel Jack grinds as hard as he can, while amidships Bobby heaves on the jerking line. The rudder takes effect. *Caribbee* swings sharply to port and we come almost before the wind. The sensation of rushing speed vanishes. It seems as though the wind has died, and the sea magically smoothed. Then the spinnaker fills with a crash, a sudden lift of hundreds upon hundreds of square feet of sail that shakes the whole boat. We come back up to course. Again the wind is heavy; *Caribbee* heels and water begins to rush past to leeward.

7:50 p.m.: My watchmates have already turned in. I sit alone in the cabin, feeling under me the alternating lift and fall of a boat being driven hard before a gradually freshening wind and rising sea. Along the hull is the swish of water, a sound not unlike the babbling of a brook running swiftly between narrow banks. It is a good sound. I hear calls from deck, the occasional thump of a block, the slap of breaking crests. To use another simile, a somewhat hackneyed one because it is so perfectly descriptive as to be inescapable, the hum of wind in the rigging makes *Caribbee* reverberate like a huge violin, a resonant and vibrant song of many pitches, as many notes as there are lengths of wire and rope aloft. It too is a good sound, for in it there is no note of malice, none of the deep-throated roar of the gale, the demoniac shriek of the squall.

It is raining. Visibility is poor. We now average 9.5 knots and shoot the seas at eleven. The wind has gone a fraction west of southwest, and has freshened to 25 knots—a good solid Force 6 on the Beaufort Scale, where according to Bowditch "Smacks double-reef gaff mainsail." Yet while fishing vessels larger and far more heavily constructed than *Caribbee* would theoretically shorten sail, we carry everything that can be hung from the masts. In harbor, fishermen from those same trawlers, lying alongside, would probably study the weight of our gear, our comparative lack of freeboard, our towering masts and gossamer rigging, and consider *Caribbee* a very pretty toy; they would most likely think her slippery, handy for afternoon sailing, but for the open sea—no. I can almost picture a grizzled old character spitting in the water as he shakes his head.

Which again makes me consider the somewhat fantastic nature of ocean racing. Here we are, nine men, driving a fragile complex of wood, metal, and cloth through driving rain and building sea, a thousand miles from the nearest harbor; no one to see or admire or applaud; no one to help if our temerity ends in disaster. We exceed the bounds of discretion, even go beyond what we know is good seamanship—those basic lessons passed down through generations of men who have fought the oceans. In us all there is a devotion to the somewhat formless and unspoken ideal of simply keeping the boat going at her maximum speed, a dedication which carries us beyond considerations of personal comfort and even safety.

Our attitude is not even wholly based on the competitive aspect of racing. It is that we all feel there is just one way to do things, one standard, one code, and we live up to it for our own satisfaction. We are driven by our own compulsions, each personal and secret, so nebulous we probably could not express them to our mates if we tried. But in our own way we are about as dedicated as it is possible for men to be.

16th Day

51° 06′ N.
25° 29′ W.
Run: noon to noon: 212 miles
Average speed: 8.83 knots
Total run to date: 2110 miles

Friday, July 18. 2:45 a.m.: During the night wind and sea moderated, and we are back to a comfortable but satisfying 8 to 8.5 on the Kenyon. The wind also shifted slightly. It is now about south-southwest at 12 to 15 knots. We reel off the miles. As Bunny Rigg might say if he were aboard: "Those Plymouth girls have us by a nylon towrope!"

I write this in the cockpit by flashlight. Beside my notebook lies the chronometer-watch we use on deck, and the navigator's notebook. I wait to take time when Frank can shoot the stars. He stands by the mizzen rigging, watching, occasionally squinting through the sextant to see if the horizon is yet well enough defined for a sight.

To the north more than to the east there is the first paling of the sky. While we slept the overcast cleared away, but scattered clouds lie ahead, in the east, and another mass is clustered to the southward. Directly above the sky is clear and the stars are brilliant. Nearer the horizon they are less distinct, as though a thin haze might be forming.

The ritual of morning stars is one of the most beautiful moments of the day: the navigator standing ready, at first a barely discernible silhouette as he identifies his prey by altitude and azimuth. Then an almost imperceptible glow begins to dissolve the weld of sea and sky, and gradually the line of the horizon becomes distinct. The day grows lighter, and the dimmer stars fade. The sky goes from black to gray, and slowly assumes delicate shadings of yellow and pink. Patches of foam from breaking crests appear pale gray against the darker gray of the sea, as though the water is loath to give up the stored blackness of the night.

"Stand by!" suddenly calls the navigator. "Stand by!" you repeat, mumbling seconds as the hand of the watch scurries around the dial . . . "Mark!" There is urgency in the command, the sense of communication of a precise instant in the eternity of time . . . You record hour, minute, and second, and the altitude, and the musical names assigned the stars by the ancients: Vega, Kochab, Altair, Capella, Jupiter, Dubhe, Aldebaran . . . Somehow it is a wonderful way to begin a day, a combining of old mysteries and modern precision. And you always feel grateful that again you are fixed on the earth's surface in relation to all other objects: to the islands, to the continents, to the reefs. Somehow you feel less alone.

9:25 a.m.: Around the horizon is a collection of clouds that prior to this passage would have had me standing at the weather rail. Now I sit in the companionway and watch them with a somewhat jaundiced and dispassionate eye. Since Bermuda too many have cried "wolf" for us to get excited by anything not equipped with neon lights, cowcatcher, and siren. Also large red crosses painted on sides and bottom.

North Atlantic clouds come in assorted sizes, shapes, and colors, and the showcase is usually full. At the moment I have only to raise my head to see tufted silver ones ahead, ragged gray ones to starboard, funereal black ones astern, and an odd bank of purplish-blue ones to port. Meanwhile nothing special happens. The track of the barograph remains comparatively level, the breeze blows at about the same velocity from the south-southwest, and we scoot along under the same combination of sails.

After awhile you seem to get used to living with any sort of threat on a companionably relaxed basis—even a volcano or the atom bomb.

Going along so comfortably, our only worry is chafe. It is really amazing how quickly any two surfaces in intermittent contact can show signs of wear. The problem usually greatest when carrying a spinnaker with the wind well forward, the working of the after guy against the main shrouds, we have solved by use of a wire guy and large rollers—exactly like spools for thread, but about 5 inches in diameter—bound to the shrouds. Elsewhere we are festooned with lengths of split hose, wrappings of canvas, and just plain tape. Miles and miles of each, it seems. Every adjustment of the sheets means endless shifting of bits and pieces of chafing gear. But the funniest chafe of all is along the luff of the mizzen staysail, where a procession of overfed types from cockpit to galley to cockpit has worn away the cloth where they squeeze past. Either we have to go on shorter rations or sew leather along the luff at tummy height! Add a new chapter to hazards of the sea.

11:35 a.m.: After a half-hour at the helm I am willing to admit we are overcanvased. My arms feel as though I have been trying to lift an elevator to the top of the Empire State Building with a hand crank. The breeze is back into the twenties and the sea is causing us to sheer. Yet we are going so well and there are so many minor variations of force and direction even within this consistent breeze I hate to change to a genoa. If it would blow 5 miles harder, or the breeze would go another point ahead, there would be no question. But each time I get ready to suggest the shift, the wind moderates a hair, or swings a little farther aft. So as a compromise have dropped the mizzen to ease the helm. It has helped: we still show over 9 knots and Bobby reports the wheel better.

This is glorious going. The sun is breaking through the current overhead assortment of clouds, small flannelly jobs with a warp and woof crosshatch of blue sky between, and it is almost warm. Occasionally a little crest slaps aboard forward, a tiny spatter of sparkling drops, just enough to keep the foredeck wet; and occasionally a sea races under the quarter wave to curl over the counter and run forward along the lee waterway. The spinnaker sheet fore guy is rigid enough to use as a chinning bar, you can jump up and down on the sheet, and we run down the miles for England. As Jack said a moment ago: "We don't even have a Bermuda Race-and-a-half left to go." I cautioned him against such comparisons later for fear of hurting the feelings of sensitive types, but it is true: the remaining distance seems like nothing. If this wind holds.

A trio of whales is off to leeward pacing us. They seem to be puffing mightily in an effort to keep up, but are not quite making it on a boat-for-boat basis. However, as they appear to be strictly Class B whales in over-all length I suppose we have to give them time. Which reminds me: where is *Samuel Pepys,* and what the hell is she doing?

7:40 p.m.: At 5:00 this afternoon, while I slept peacefully, *Caribbee* ran out from under a cover of clouds into brilliant sunshine. When Dick called me at 6:00 the after stateroom was brighter than it had been for days. For a few moments I lay in my bunk and looked across the cabin and through the porthole over the opposite bunk. I could tell we had been freed by the position of the main boom, and because we were standing up straighter while the water went past just as fast. As *Caribbee* rolled I would see only white rushing foam, a few feet beyond the port; then she would lift, and I would see the green-gray North Atlantic seas; and she would roll still farther and I would be looking up at a blue ellipse of cloudless sky. There would be a moment's pause as she poised on a crest, then she would shoot ahead, rolling, and the whole cycle would begin again.

The sunshine held during the cockpit cocktail session, adding a second reason for the gathering being the most noisy and cheer-

"*The saddest sight is the character at the wheel, completely useless yet unceasingly hopeful. No creature ashore or afloat is a more woeful spectacle than a racing helmsman without wind, all ready to go some place but nothing to go with, while the sails droop in folds.*"

"We have sighted a shark, a school of blackfish, the masts of a steamer hull down over the horizon, and a small southbound whale cutting across our bow. This part of the ocean is positively crowded."

ful in days. Gone with the calm are the long faces and quiet voices; when water bubbles under the counter, our spirits bubble in time. Now we bubble 9 knots worth—a lot of bubbling. Both for *Caribbee* and for us.

But as our watch was finishing dinner before taking over, Dick came below and said: "There's a black cloud bank coming up from astern. I can't tell what it means but you'd better bring oilies." And when I stuck my head through the companionway slide, there it was: from horizon to horizon it stretched, flat on top, dark and ominous, extending down to the water as a solid curtain. It lacked the neon lights and the red crosses, but everything else seemed to be present.

I stood by the weather backstay and watched. It gained fast. All afternoon there had been a pronounced swell from the north-west, persistent and heavy enough to buck the waves kicked up by our present southwest breeze, and this looked as though it might be the force behind those outriders. This is it, I kept think-ing; this has to be it, the northwest gale so long overdue. A boat can't cross the ocean and not take a beating somewhere; we can't go on talking about the Great Atlantic Calm of '52 and making derisive noises without Father Neptune doing something about it . . . Now we're going to get it, we puny mortals who have been wanting wind!

Wispy clouds raced overhead, low enough to rip their bellies on the mainmast, with the denser mass close behind—and we saw we had been fooled by the low sun: the clouds were not heavy and ominous at all, but only our traveling companion of the last 2 days, the flannel sky, temporarily left behind and hurrying to catch up. Now, as I write this, its leading edge is well ahead, al-though I can still see a narrow band of blue at the horizon, and we are all happy: the cloud, *Caribbee,* and us, because under the flannel cloud is just the wind we want: not too little, not too much, so we continue at 9 knots as peacefully as babes riding a carriage in the park.

10:35 p.m.: I am finally convinced the true southwesterly of the middle latitudes has come in. On going over the log, I find it was at 8:10 Wednesday night I noted: "Breeze hauling. On spinnaker." Now it has been aloft for 50-odd hours. There have been only minor variations in the strength and direction of the wind during that period, and we have run down a degree of longitude every five hours or less. Up here at latitude 51 degrees, a degree of longitude is only 37.9 nautical miles in length. We have thus taken a great leap forward on the track chart.

So at last we have the winds we expected to ride all the way across, those "prevailing westerlies" of the pilot charts. Having had a little leisure during this watch, I studied the log and found some interesting things. Beginning at noon of Friday, July 4, we sailed 635 miles, the distance of the course from Newport to Bermuda, in 72 hours 53 minutes. That figure represents an average speed over the bottom of 8.72 knots. The Cruising Club of America yearbook lists the Bermuda Race record for the present course as 75 hours 32 minutes, set by *Bolero* in 1950. So far good enough. But then beginning at 8:00 a.m., July 8, it took us 196 hours to sail the next 635 miles, a heart-breaking average of 3.24 knots. And in the 1946 Bermuda Race, the slowest since the war, the *last* boat in the fleet whose time was recorded made it to the finish line in 178 hours! Thus in two successive stretches across the Atlantic, *Caribbee* exceeded two records for another similar stretch: the fastest and the slowest. Now, if the wind holds, we will probably better our earlier pace.

So it has been a period of mad weather, when nature sharply reminds man his attempts to catalog her are futile. We had fresh breezes where the books said we might expect the light variables of the horse latitudes, and light variables from the east when we arrived in the charted area of the prevailing westerlies. Meanwhile the radio brings reports of record heat waves around the rim of the Atlantic, both in North America and in Europe.

Also in my study of the log I was reminded of something else:

how terrible was the period of aimless slatting and fruitless beating which reached its nadir on the morning of the sixteenth. Sails up, sails down, tacking endlessly on headers, getting nowhere, until Frank looked up from the chart in disgust and said: "We're going back and forth on the same damned line. It's just getting blacker and blacker from the pencil marks." Only the arrival of the first stages of this breeze in the morning kept us from a run that might have averaged less than a knot for 24 hours—1 mile per hour for working continuously, changing sails, calling them, tacking endlessly. Believe me: I have learned record passages are the pleasant ones!

As the winds have fluctuated, so have our moods. I know these notes reveal me as a person of "ups-ies" and "downs-ies." It is a characteristic for which I do not apologize; it appears even in the writings of the most outwardly stoic of the old adventurers. But this afternoon Bobby passed along a remark by Dick which shed some light on the curious rise or fall in the spirits of sailors on long passages as the speed goes up or down: you always think of the passage as continuing at the rate you are moving at the moment. It seems to be a universal failing. If you're enjoying a fair breeze and making 8 knots, you calculate how long it will take to cover the remaining miles at 8 knots, completely forgetting wind is the most fickle and undependable of commodities. You rub your hands and say gleefully "We'll be in next Tuesday." Everyone is elated. But then the breeze dies, or goes ahead, and the speed drops. You're making 2 knots. Immediately there is a new calculation and faces grow long. Someone growls: "Hell, we won't get there before Christmas." You feel cheated, and vow you'll never let your hopes soar again. And you don't, until the next fair slant.

✩ ✩
✩

OF ALL the manifestations of nature, a mighty storm at sea can be the most awesome. Through the centuries it has been a terrifying and deadly hazard, and untold are the bones of men and ships which lie on the floors of the oceans, and the bodies that have been cast upon the fringing shores.

Landsmen have little comprehension of this part of a sailor's world. Storms lose severity upon encountering large masses of land, and the very stability of the earth robs them of much of their terror: there may be a similar destructive force in the wind, but there is not the insane cauldron of the sea to deaden the senses and quench hope of survival. Only occasionally does a storm-driven sea invade the land to bring home some of the terror of turbulent waters, as in the Hooghly River disaster of 1737, when 300,000 people perished as the Bay of Bengal lifted 40 feet; or more recently when in September of 1900 more than 6000 were drowned at Galveston by a similar but smaller rise in the Gulf of Mexico.

It is impossible for anyone who has not experienced that most savage of storms, the hurricane, to comprehend its power. Wind ceases to be wind, and becomes a solid. It tears at every crevice, shakes the stoutest structure. Exposed to its full fury, a human finds it impossible to crawl, or even breathe. It lashes as it batters, carrying all before it: solid sheets of water, sand, trees, houses, spars.

Through the years seamen have recorded the power of great winds, attempting by mere words to convey a comprehension of nature amuck. "The severity of the wind is beyond description," recorded Captain Doutty of the ship *Runnymede*, England to Calcutta, Sunday, 10 November 1844. "There is nothing to compare to it, for unless present, no one could conceive the destructive power and weight of wind crushing everything before it, as if it were a metallic body . . ." "The hurricane was now, beyond description, dreadful," wrote the mate of a frigate caught at anchor on the southwest coast of Jamaica. "Its action was like that of fire: everything disappeared that opposed it: notwithstanding the size and solidity of the masts, powerfully supported by the shrouds, they were no longer able to resist its unremitting fury; the mizen-mast went first; in about three minutes after, the main-mast followed; and, instantly after, went the fore-mast and bow-sprit. Terror and astonishment, for a moment, occupied every mind. . . ."

The same story is told in the yellowed pages of countless logs, and undoubtedly exists in as many more lying at the bottom of the sea—logs whose final entry on the storm was never made. And in each is the groping for words to express the fury of wind and wave, their capacity for destruction. Even modern meteorologists cannot be definite: "It is very difficult to determine, even approximately, the velocity of hurricane winds," writes Ivan Tannehill of the U. S. Weather Bureau in his authoritative book *Hurricanes*. "In many violent hurricanes the wind instruments have been damaged or blown away before the highest storm winds were experienced." In some instances steel towers supporting the anemometers were wrecked; in other cases the buildings under them have been unroofed or destroyed. But, he continues: "Instrumental records indicate that the winds of the hurricane are sometimes sustained for intervals of five minutes at an average rate of more than 150 miles an hour. There is good reason to believe that the gusts . . . represent air movements for brief intervals that may reach as high as 250 miles an hour in the most violent storms." The highest velocity actually recorded by anemometer was a sustained blast of 188 miles an hour, beginning at 12:25 P.M. of April 12, 1934, at the U. S. Signal Service meteorological station on Mount Washington, New Hampshire; and at 12:31 a gust attained 231 miles an hour. The chief observer decided later the only thing which enabled the observatory building to withstand the impact was a heavy deposit of rough frost.

Despite the mass of data which has accumulated through the

years, meteorologists are not fully in agreement on the inception of these storms. Even the term "hurricane" is dubious in origin, although in general it is accepted as being a corruption of the Carib Indian name for "big wind." In early journals, it appears in many forms: "urican," "aracan," and "horacano" among them. Nor is *hurricane* used universally. Storms of the same general type are called *typhoons* in the North Pacific, *cyclones* in the Indian Ocean, *willy-willies* in Australia, and *baguios* in the Philippines. Further, there is a confusion in definition, as *hurricane* is used both to describe circular progressive storms originating in the Tropics, even though their velocity might not attain Force 12 on the Beaufort Scale; and the winds of all storms, regardless of nature or origin, whose speeds do reach or exceed Force 12, or 75 miles an hour.

Most hurricanes originate in the doldrums, that belt of super-heated, moisture-laden air lying along the equator. One school of thought maintains that as this air rises and is replaced by cooler air—the trade winds—atmospheric pressure is lowered. Rotation of the earth causes a deflection of the incoming air and a cyclone system is formed, a whirling of winds around the area of lowest pressure.

The other main theory is that tropical cyclones, like the milder extra-tropical cyclones of the temperate zones, are formed by the collision of masses of air of different type and temperature— in this case, along the front between the trade winds and the doldrums. Waves form at the point of collision, a central low-pressure area develops, and the storm begins. According to both theories, only a combination of favorable circumstances is needed to begin the rotation, after which the atmospheric pressure of the center progressively lowers with a consequent increase in the violence of the winds blowing into it.

Regardless of formation, hurricanes once begun follow a fairly regular pattern of development and progress. They have the form of a huge horizontal buzz-saw, whirling around a low-pres-

sure hub called the *eye,* and proceed from the tropics into the
temperate zones on a curved path known as the *track.* The outside diameter can vary greatly, although Bowditch gives the
"average area in which winds of gale force prevail" as some 300
miles, with a much smaller area near the center of true hurricane-
force winds, and the calm eye of from 7 to 20 miles across. The
forward rate of progress of the whole system along its track varies
from 5 to 20 miles an hour in the tropics to as much as 50 miles
an hour in the higher reaches of the North Atlantic.

The average tracks of hurricanes originating in the doldrums
lead westward and poleward in a parabolic curve until in middle
latitudes, when they *recurve* eastward. Most West Indian hurricanes blow themselves out at sea. But the track they may follow
depends on many things, including the placement and progress
of high- and low-pressure areas lying ahead in the temperate
zone. They may plow straight across the Caribbean to strike the
coast of Mexico; or may bend enough northward to sweep across
Florida, or Long Island, or Connecticut; or may swing out across
the Grand Banks of Newfoundland or any other part of the North
Atlantic to devastate shipping; or may even arrive at the coast of
Europe itself. And, while hurricanes do occur most frequently in
August, September, and October, they have been recorded in
every month of the year except January, as they have been recorded on every ocean except the South Atlantic.

Thus sailors have encountered hurricanes ever since ships have
ventured forth upon the sea. Columbus, on his return from the
First Voyage, encountered one off the Azores when the spirits of
his men were lifted by the hope of sighting familiar land. So imminent appeared their destruction the entire company vowed to
make a pilgrimage on their return to Spain, if they were spared,
and only good seamanship and perhaps Divine protection allowed them to proclaim their discovery of a New World. Although Columbus did not realize the storm which almost swallowed his ship was circular in nature, and did not record it as a

hurricane, it has come down that after a furious gale from the north there was a lull, and the wind returned with redoubled fury from the south. Had chance decreed this hurricane to be more severe, history might have been different.

It remained for later men to analyze the meaning of the shift Columbus and other captains experienced, and the explanation came surprisingly early. Piddington credited Captain Langford, author of *Philosophical Transactions*, published in 1698, with defining tropical cyclones as "whirlwinds." But Ivan Tannehill states a German geographer advanced the same theory a half-century earlier. As winds to a single observer always appear to be blowing in a straight line, and a circular movement in a whole system can only be detected by comparing a number of observations made at approximately the same time, it is somewhat amazing the discovery should have so far predated our modern synoptic weather maps, daily based on reports flashed from all parts of the world by telegraph and wireless.

But it is one thing for philosophers to understand the theory behind something as vast and nebulous as a system of winds, another for the poor sailor to be able to use it. So until Henry Piddington compiled *The Sailor's Horn-Book for the Law of Storms* in the middle of the nineteenth century, mariners blindly stood on toward their destruction, when they might have escaped. In his "Design of the Work" Piddington declared his intention was to show seamen—"from the Admiral of a great fleet down to the humble Master of a West India or Mediterranean trader . . . how to *avoid* Storms; how best to *manage in Storms* when they cannot be avoided; and how to *profit by Storms*." Although the latter point was debatable, the first two were not, and a "Horn-Card" became part of the equipment of every sailing ship. And nothing better has been devised to this day.

The Horn-Card was transparent; on its face concentric circles were printed to represent wind direction in relation to the eye of the storm, and oriented to the compass points. In use, the card was laid over a chart at the ship's position and rotated until the direction of the wind arrows coincided with the observed wind at the ship. The position of the ship in relation to the center of the storm was then immediately apparent, with each later shift or change in the barometric pressure serving as a check.

In the "Laws" Piddington stated methods of determining the probable future course of the storm; he defined the "dangerous" and "navigable" semicircles, giving rules for heaving to on the tack which would take a ship clear of the worst; and outlined the accompanying dangers, including the sea. "It is the sea, however, which is most to be dreaded in rotating gales. It is . . . a tremendous, cross, confused, outrageous sea, raised in pyramidal heaps by the wind from every point of the compass, and has been compared to surf breaking on a reef of rocks. In fact it is 'such a sea as gave a ship no chance.' Near the center of the hurricane a ship is always unmanageable, even if she has not lost masts or rudder; the lulls and terrific gusts, which follow one another in quick succession, are alone sufficient for this, but when we take into consideration the fierce conflict of raging waters, it is only wonderful how a vessel can live through such an encounter."

But even with the experience of bygone mariners to help him, the sailor whom fate has put directly in the path of an advancing tropical storm is in a desperate plight. At a distance of hundreds of miles huge swells radiating outward from the center make escape difficult, even if the warning signs are read and interpreted correctly, and long before the wind rises to full hurricane fury a small sailing vessel is hove to, helpless. Then if chance ordains the hurricane to be a severe one, survival becomes equally a matter of chance. Courage, seamanship, and endurance in the crew resolve simply into how much the ship can stand, and how furious wind and sea become. Yet despite this ancient knowledge men still sail the oceans of the world: to this extent are all sailors fatalists.

17th Day

50° 56′ N.
19° 59′ W.
Run: noon to noon: 207 miles
Average speed: 8.62 knots
Total run to date: 2317 miles

Saturday, July 19. 6:45 a.m.: The midnight log entry opens with the notation: "This day commences with pleasant westerly. Carrying spinnaker, balloon forestaysail, main, mizzen staysail, and mizzen." Yet for me this past 4-hour watch, now almost ended, has been one of the most tense and wearing ones of the passage. While dressing, after being routed out of my snug bunk at 2:45, I could tell things were rugged on deck. From my difficulty in maintaining balance against the lurch and roll I knew steering would be hard, and that the wind had freshened and the sea built. There was a roaring of water along the lee deck, a feeling of burying that indicated we might be on the verge of carrying too much sail.

Deck wasn't cheering: there was a slight glimmer of light in the east, but the whole sky was leaden and gray. A fine misting rain fell, and visibility was bad. The wind had backed still farther into the south, so we were carrying the spinnaker pole as far forward as it would go, right against the headstay. The sail was constantly on edge, even so. Even in the poor light I could see it curl.

I confess my inclination was to shift to a genoa while both watches were together. But then I thought perhaps things looked worse than they really were, as is always the case when first coming into a nasty night from a deep sleep, and did not want to give way to that first-awake letdown, the old pre-dawn loss of courage, when the tides in men are at their lowest ebb. And we would be comfortable again if only the wind would veer a couple of points to the west. Dick settled my doubts by telling me the wind had freed in the last half-hour, and showed signs of continuing around.

So we set ourselves at our stations and the port watch disappeared down the companionway sack-wards faster than any gophers ever popped into holes. I watched them with envy. But not for long, as there was plenty to keep us busy. Steering was particularly hard. The northwest swell still rolled in under the wind waves of our sou'wester, the same as yesterday, but both much bigger: the result was a nasty bucking sea, occasionally combining to make *Caribbee* take a violent sheer. With each sheer the spinnaker would curl deeply, and the man forward would call frantically: "Go down! Go down!" Sometimes the rudder would take effect; at other times the spinnaker would break and refill with a resounding crash. But we carried on, reluctant to do anything which might slow us, although we did strike the mizzen and mizzen staysail to ease steering.

And then we got it. We were asking for it, and we got it. I was at the wheel when suddenly there was a *ping!* from aloft, a sound like a breaking ukulele string magnified a few hundred times. The whole boat gave a jump, as though Father Neptune had given us a good swift boot in the stern. The spinnaker sagged, but then held and filled again.

At the moment of the ping I began bearing away as fast as I could grind the wheel, and as soon as we came off before the wind yelled: "What the hell happened?" For a moment no one knew, despite a cluster forward looking up the mast. Then Frank spotted the trouble: one spinnaker halyard had let go, cause for the moment unknown, and the sail had been caught by the other one. I have noted that for this race we installed twin halyards, so one backs up the other. Fortunately, it turns out.

It was a very minor accident compared to what might have happened, so we took the hint and switched to a genoa. Immediately there was an amazing change in conditions—in apparent conditions, that is. What a moment before had been a wild dawn—the break occurred at 4:50—became merely unpleasant: a fresh southerly wind thick with fine rain setting up a bobble of a sea, neither particularly vicious. Good seamanship and good sense dictated a switch. But ocean racing? We have dropped a knot on the Kenyon, and wait impatiently for more light so a man can go aloft to find what happened, and make repairs.

8:50 a.m.: After breakfast both watches assembled on deck. It was still blowing well over twenty, and the wind had moved even more to the south, putting it forward of the beam. The conflicting seas seemed more pronounced than ever, so it was almost impossible to walk along the deck without holding onto the liferail or some other stable object. Yet we rigged the bosun's chair and tied Frank in securely and up he went: up some 75 feet into the cold raw wind, the chill spitting rain. Around us the sea and the sky were gray and lonely. No gallery to applaud, no one to know or care except the knot of oilskinned shipmates hauling on the halyard; just one more unseen vignette of the countless thousands that have occurred on the empty ocean.

From amidships I watched him trace wild arcs as *Caribbee* plunged along at better than 8 knots: he would work awhile, hold on awhile as a particularly bad combination of seas made the motion worse, and lean to leeward for awhile. It took me a little time to figure the latter gesture was for the better downwind distribution of his breakfast pancakes. But finally he signaled to come down, and was lowered away, and we found what had happened: the strain on the halyard aloft had pulled out a splice in the strap that held the block. The ends of the wire looked like steel spaghetti. Frank had transferred the block to a spare strap at the masthead, and we were back in business. But it is not altogether pleasant to contemplate what might have happened if the second halyard had not been in place, and held: a huge nylon bag suddenly collapsing under our bows, fast to the ship by 150 feet of wire halyard, a wire foreguy, and two heavy linen sheets.

As amazed as I was at the news a splice had pulled, I was even more amazed by Frank's color when he reached the deck. On starting up, he had blended with his shipmates; on coming down he was exactly the color of pea soup—a rich green. He drank a cup of hot tea, to which I added a good slug of rum, and now sleeps. Just before dropping off he assured Henry that he was indeed the finest of cooks: the pancakes tasted as good coming up as they had going down.

10:00 a.m.: Now I have finally gotten to my bunk I am not sleepy, although while sitting on deck in the rain I could hardly wait, and a silly paraphrase from *Alice in Wonderland* kept running through my head in tuneless and monotonous repetition: "Sack of the evening, beautiful sack." As for the first time everything below is wet and clammy, perhaps I am staying awake to savor a little longer the sheer animal satisfaction of being dry and warm. Oilskins and sweaters hang throughout the cabin in odd places. Damp socks are jammed behind light bulbs and in the front of the bookcase. There isn't much difference in temperature between cockpit and main cabin, and unless the rain stops and we get some drying weather we will have to dig deep into our stock of spare gear.

Fuel is the only miscalculation we made in our advance planning. We could carry only a small supply of briquettes for the main cabin fireplace, to heat and dry the living quarters in case of necessity, but have a fair amount left despite keeping a fire going a couple of days on the Grand Banks. I will have Henry stoke up the grate before lunch. Our real shortage is in alcohol for the cooking stove. Neither Henry nor I took into consideration that on a long passage there would be more baking and midnight snacking. Or perhaps I should be more honest and say we didn't realize as a crew we would be capable of eating 24 hours a day, less only time for sleep and a few deck chores. We began the voyage by each watch putting on a kettle of water about a half-hour before calling the other, at night; after dressing, you could struggle to the galley for a mug-up of coffee, tea, soup, or cocoa. This noble practice degenerated into a kettle bubbling almost constantly, especially during the waking hours of those supermen, the port watch. So a couple of days ago, to the great sorrow of all hands, I had to decree rationing: stove on at night only at the three o'clock change in watches, a cold lunch, and no more baking. Really rugged! Shades of Thomas James and the other old searchers for the Northwest Passage! No more hot cornbread, no more apple pie! Survival does indeed become a matter of chance, and from now on *Caribbee* will be sailed with the desperation of men willing to risk all in a desperate gamble—no Plymouth, no pie. . . . But seriously, if I were ever again making a long passage in the higher latitudes I would allow double the usual consumption of cooking fuel for shorter trips in warmer climes, and add a little bit more as a reserve.

Otherwise we are in fine shape. Our planning for food was on the basis of a 3-week passage, with another 2 weeks of emergency food in reserve—real "iron rations," Coast Guard-approved survival food for use in lifeboats, the daily supply per man having less bulk than a package of cigarettes. What a comedown that would be! But Henry assures me we are in no danger of descending to such levels. While our consumption has been as great as is humanly possible there is still an ample reserve. One reason for this was the food already on the boat when the Trans-Atlantic stores came aboard in Bermuda: our planning had been done on a "bare boat" basis, so the 21-day supply was entirely in addition to canned goods left over from the Bermuda Race, and the "just in case" extras hidden deep in lockers and bilge.

I marvel at how well we have eaten. Italian spaghetti and meat balls; German sauerkraut and wieners; Chinese chop suey and chow mein; New England codfish balls and mashed potatoes;

New Orleans crawfish bisque and shrimp jambalaya; Boston baked beans; Mexican chili and tamales; Scotch kippers and Dutch ham and Alaskan salmon—our menu is cosmopolitan and varied. There seems to be nothing which cannot be found in canned form, even bread. On previous passages bread has been a real problem, for there are times when even the hardiest cook cannot bake in a small boat's oven; now bread comes in neat tins, and after weeks at sea tastes almost as good as the spanking-fresh product of the corner bakery. Rye, white, or whole wheat, take your choice. And I do not believe it is only our seagoing appetites that make everything so palatable: canned food when prepared with care and imagination can compare favorably with fresh, especially when enough thought goes into planning menus so there is no feeling of repetition. *Henri du Caribbee* has done well on all counts. One hazard I did not anticipate on this passage was having to turn sideways to get up the companionway.

Dick just came down to get the balloon jib. As he stood talking water collected in a puddle at his feet. It still rains, and the wind remains too far forward to carry a spinnaker. Hence the ballooner, in hopes of coaxing the speed back to 9 knots.

Seeing Dick cold and dripping made me feel even more snug, and suddenly sleepy. Lights out. Let her howl for somebody else —for the next 2 hours, anyway.

4:45 p.m.: We continue to be gluttons for punishment and work, but it is a form of gluttony that eats up the miles.

On deck at 1:00 to the same leaden sky and splitting rain, but found the wind trending slightly more towards the west. So all hands kept close watch on the masthead fly. By 2:00 the apparent breeze was a bit forward of the beam, by 2:30 it had come abeam, and by 2:45 the spinnaker was set and drawing. As it is now. And the wind has continued on around until we log it as a true southwester. Again the Kenyon has climbed to 9. The sea followed the wind aft, and steering is not too bad, although occasionally a big one will rise above the level of the taffrail to shoulder the stern high, bury the bow, and cause *Caribbee* to slice across the sea ahead. But this wind lacks the weight to make the process vicious.

Two hundred seven miles today, 212 yesterday. We're in the groove, really rolling. Now have less than one Bermuda Race left to go—about a Miami-Nassau plus a St. Pete-Havana. With continuing luck we could make the finish in another 3 days. "Continuing luck" of course means continuing wind and no major catastrophes to gear; by the law of averages we should get the first, and I'm not too concerned about the second.

Thinking back, I believe we have consistently gotten the maximum speed possible in the conditions we encountered. There were times when we went mighty slow—when we didn't go at all —but we can have the satisfaction of knowing we did everything possible with what we had. It is customary for a skipper to pay tribute to his crew, but in this case I feel every page of these notes tells a story that could not be summed up by any amount of flowery compliments. I can only add I do not believe there was ever a keener or more efficient crew, which let down less or remained as cheerful under trying conditions. And nothing could be more difficult than the old nightmare sensation of running like hell but staying in the same place, while in your imagination the goblins pursue like Olympic hurdlers.

7:15 p.m.: It is strange but I feel in the last few days we all have a different attitude about this race. At first there was constant speculation about the other boats, their qualities and potentials, and how they would be sailed. In a sense, for the first few days we were sailing hard because we were racing the others, a purely competitive sensation. But now I believe our concentration is solely on *Caribbee*. It has become a fetish to keep her moving as fast as possible; it has also become our greatest pleasure. She seems to us so wonderful, this supposedly inanimate object, we can do nothing else. She has carried us almost across an ocean, kept us safe and comfortable, responded to our every demand, forgiven our excesses. In return, we have learned her whims and desires, and are willing slaves to both.

"A real working morning . . . the first drying day since coming on the Banks . . .
Frank spent two hours aloft checking. . . . I sent up my Contax camera with an
ultra-wide-angle lens fitted and gave a photography lesson from the deck."

"*There is no more vital member of a crew than the man who can go aloft in weather fair or foul, and whose knowledge of rigging keeps all in order against the hours of test.*"

It would not be accurate if I said we do not frequently speculate on the other boats—sometimes pessimistically, feeling they might have skirted the calm while we lay helpless; sometimes optimistically, thinking the light weather must have been widespread enough to trap them, too. But now such speculation is more objective and fatalistic. The race is less important than the personal fact we have made this passage, have shared this experience. If some super-radar could suddenly show us the others either fantastically ahead or behind, so our efforts from here to the finish would make no difference to the outcome of the race, I am sure we would sail exactly the same way as we do now—as hard and well as we can.

This passage has clarified my perspective, as well as taught me more of the sea than I could have learned in another lifetime of coastal cruising. And I know, even as I calculate the miles to the finish, I would somehow be happier if it was 6000 instead of 600 miles. I know I shall be excited and delighted when we sail into Plymouth—yet sad. Even now I can remember vividly the moment almost exactly 20 years ago when the battered old ketch *Temptress* crawled into Ft. Pierce inlet ahead of an unseasonal tropical storm, 17 days out of the Chesapeake, the three of us aboard exhausted from being buffeted by a succession of gales off Cape Hatteras. It was my first passage on the open ocean. I had been frightened, I can say honestly: the deep roar of wind in the rigging, the heavy slam of seas rolling out of the night, the sheer insensitiveness and pitilessness of the ocean, not willing to quit when man had enough and begged for mercy. . . . Yet when we gained calm water beyond the roaring hell of the inlet, breaking heavily from the first swells of the advancing hurricane, I was sad. I knew something had ended that could never be had again, not in exactly the same way. And after a time even the fear and the exhaustion were part of the perfection of the memory.

As the most important memories of this crossing will remain not as a race but as a passage.

18th Day

50° 38′ N.
15° 07′ W.
Run: noon to noon: 187 miles
Average speed: 7.79 knots
Total run to date: 2504 miles

Sunday, July 20. 2:35 a.m.: It is hard to recall a more pleasant watch during the whole voyage—and I seem to remember beginning yesterday's entry in exactly the opposite mood. All a matter of outlook, circumstances, and a few miles an hour of wind velocity. And maybe how dinner digested. But this has been one to remember: one of the good ones that compensate for any number of the bad.

Yet, trying to analyze it, nothing special has happened, nor is it even a very beautiful night. The breeze holds in the southwest at about 15 knots. The rain has ended, but it is still overcast. There is much phosphorescence in the water. Porpoises hurtle through like gleaming missiles, criss-crossing under our keel, diving deep at the bow, leaving sparkling wakes—the only chilling thought, making me remember how 10 years ago in the same waters men watched the same show with terror, for a torpedo leaves the same track. Perhaps peace and thankfulness are the reasons for this pleasant mood: the spinnaker stays full, the needle of the Kenyon is steady at 8.5, and all seems right with the world. There is only the lift of the bow, the rush of water, the sound of the breeze, the loom of the sails, the slow weave back and forth of the masthead against the sky, the streak of the wave astern, the dim burst of whitecaps off to windward.

We discuss landfalls now. There is a slight feeling of unreality in talking of the Scilly Isles, Wolf Rock, Lizard Head, and the other goals of the early navigators. Even after months of preparation, and weeks—almost literally—of sailing, it doesn't seem real. And somehow, romantic that I am about all concerning the sea, this landfall is to me the most fitting a sailor could make. For down the centuries no spot on the globe has drawn the bows of so many ships: the Scilly Isles, gateway to the English Channel, to the North Sea, to the Baltic itself; the goal on the return voyages of Cabot and James and Raleigh and Drake and Anson and Nelson and all the others of that shadowy company who sailed wooden ships to the corners of the earth, yet somehow found themselves homeward bound. The keels that have graven this same water through which we sail! And the men who stood on the decks, or climbed the rigging, hungry for a sight of land in a way no man can understand today. . . . And we follow in their wakes, having gained at least a little comprehension of the magnitude of their achievements.

8:45 a.m.: This, the morning of our eighteenth day at sea, finds us under spinnaker, balloon forestaysail, main, mizzen staysail, and mizzen. I enumerate them to fix the picture in my own mind as I visualize the little ships that have passed along this track in earlier centuries. Our pale-blue nylon parachute is a far cry from the spritsail the *Golden Hind* would have been carrying as she rolled her way up from the south after the first English circumnavigation of the globe. Yet, in the direct evolution that can be traced in almost everything about ships and the lore of the sea, the tiny sail she set under the bowsprit is the direct ancestor of this enormous parachute.

We are having what I imagine is a typical day for these parts when not being lashed by gales. The wind is southwest at Force 4. There is some sea, raised not only by this present breeze, but a restless heaving and tumbling caused by winds far away, swells rolling in from several directions to run under each other, and the present wind waves. It is overcast; although there is a streak of blue sky astern, there are heavy clouds to windward, and we wear oilskins from the last rain. It fell from a black squall cloud now drifting off to leeward.

I never tire of watching the sea. I try to read its messages: those swells rolling in from the nor'west probably originated in a gale blowing off ice fields above the polar circle; those running in under them from the sou'west perhaps come from a disturbance off the Azores, a warm wind lashing warm blue water. Those gulls circling off to starboard probably hover over a school of fish, waiting for bigger fish to begin feeding so they can feed on the scraps. Closer two porpoises roll, lifting their heads to breathe before plunging back into the depths, and earlier we sighted a small whale.

To one who loves it, nothing is so varied as the sea. It can frighten you, tire you, madden you—but bore you? Never. Yet that is the question I am most often asked by landsmen, and more frequently by landswomen: "What do you do when you're off on a boat? Don't you get bored? Nothing but all that sea. . . ." If these notes have a motivation beyond a personal desire to some-day recapture the feeling of these hours and days, it might be to express why sailors are not bored at sea, and why they can never break its spell.

And the overwhelming fascination of the sea is its impersonality, alien to the comprehension of the landsman. The rainsquall which sprinkled our deck, the gale surging the pack ice off Spitzbergen, the calm in which we wallowed off the Grand Banks—all are completely impersonal, ordained in mysterious ways which have nothing to do with the desires of man, despite the incantations of holy men down the centuries. It is this impersonal quality which makes the sea frightening, yet endlessly fascinating: if you should lie becalmed until your water and food are exhausted, and die slowly and horribly as thousands of sailors have, the winds will not come because of your prayers; or if your ship is being slowly pounded to pieces by a gale and you collapse exhausted at the pump while water creeps up the bulkheads, your curses will not abate the fury of wind and wave. Men tire, ships tire—the sea, never. Thus it is the most elemental challenge to which men can respond: for man and the sea are each in their own way the most complex of nature's mysteries.

12:45 p.m.: Basil came up for a look before lunch and told the story of a Bahamian working for his father. The Negro was sitting forward when asked from the cockpit how the boat was doing. He called back: "Boss, don't know what de stern doin' but de bow goin' like hell!"

And now not only the bow of *Caribbee* is going like hell but the stern, too. We continue at close to 8 knots. After early rain the sky cleared, so the sun shines brightly—brilliantly, in fact, by comparison to so many days of overcast. The sea actually looks blue: not a Gulf Stream blue, but at least a cheerful simulation thereof. We enjoy sparkling whitecaps, blue sky, and a broad wake creaming astern. The day's run was down to 187 miles, as the breeze dropped when the rainsqualls were playing around and has not returned with quite the same punch. As I write, a new squall that has been gathering off to windward moves in, but we'll leave it to the port watch.

Turned my high boots inside out this morning and found them soaked. Can't remember a sea running into them, so it must be an accumulation of me. Am not surprised as I have worn them every watch for days, and this is the first drying weather. Now that I mention it, last night I discovered myself somewhat gamey. So will bathe on deck after lunch if the sun stays out.

9:10 p.m.: Dick noted in the log at 1500: "Skipper and port watch officer bathed in futile attempt to set proper example to balance of ship's company." It wasn't as heroic a deed as his entry makes it sound: rather a wonderful sensation, in fact, after the first shock wore off. But I must admit it was damned cold standing naked in the breeze while dipping up and pouring over buck-

ets of North Atlantic water. I seem to remember a crack about
there being times when cleanliness was not next to godliness, but
next to impossible. And we're only a few degrees away from the
latter.

I have just come below after a turn at watching the spinnaker.
Things are about the same on deck; same southwest breeze, although even lighter than this afternoon, and we slow progressively. Now down around 6 knots.

Occasionally it is possible to see familiar things with new eyes,
and as I descended the companionway this time the cabin looked
unbelievably snug and pleasant. I write at the swing table by the
light of the oil lamp on the bookcase forward. Frank is at the
navigator's desk, fussing with the radio direction-finder to make
sure it is working if we close the English coast in thick weather.
The whole cabin is suffused with a soft glow: the oil lamp, the dial
light of the direction-finder, the reflected light from the charts.
Around me the mahogany paneling gleams rich and mellow; a
few clothes are wedged around the fireplace, curtains are drawn
across the bunks, the clock and barometer glint over the door to
the after stateroom. Once again I feel nothing on earth can be so
snug and pleasant as the cabin of a small ship, a world of gentle
escape, where the wanderer can live as much at home as a turtle
in its shell.

11:00 p.m.: "Effed" again—"f" for frustrated. I was interrupted in the last entry by a sudden breaking loose of my most
dreaded hell, that Chinese water torture—slatting. Rudely torn
from my dreamy state of peaceful contemplation of the cabin,
and perhaps some philosophical comment of undying merit, I
scurried on deck to find the spinnaker had died and embraced
the port spreaders in its last agonies. Fortunately rigor mortis had
not set in and we were able to get it clear before anything serious
occurred. But then it draped itself in somber folds from masthead
to deck and refused to show any further sign of life.

Although during the afternoon the breeze had gradually

dropped we were not prepared for its total collapse, despite our old anathema, a slowly rising barometer. For an hour we lay motionless while the reef points beat their ghastly tattoo. Really grim. But then as despair mounted an entirely new breeze came in from due south, light but enough to fill the sails and get us moving. At this precise moment—2312 Zone Plus 2 Sunday 20 July 1952—we again move toward England. Decorously, it is true, at a pace around 4 knots, but something is better than nothing.

It is a completely dark night: no moon, no stars, no phosphorescence. The hidden depths below are no blacker than the sky above. We steal silently over the abyss.

☆ ☆
☆

No ASPECT of the sailor's world is more mysterious to the landsman than the practice of navigation. To find a precise point in a trackless waste seems neither art nor science, but magic. Yet in no other sphere of progress has the continuity of development been so clearly based on the heritage of the past, nor has the accumulated knowledge been so universally shared by men of all races, creeds, and nations.

The word *navigation* stems from the marriage of a Latin noun and verb: *navis,* a ship, and *agere,* to move or direct. Its progress has been essential to the development of every maritime civilization. In Europe, the first glimmerings of scientific navigation began with the introduction of the compass, although men had already made long voyages without its aid. There is considerable evidence that an expedition of Phoenicians circumnavigated Africa 600 years before the birth of Christ. There is also evidence the Greek Pythias of Marseilles reached Iceland and beyond 200 years later. Meanwhile the Polynesians found their way from island to island in the vast reaches of the Pacific by crude but accurate diagrams of the stars, and Norsemen regularly traded across the breadth of the North Atlantic by computing latitude from the length of the sun shadow cast along an oarsman's thwart by the gunwale of the ship.

There is much mystery surrounding the origin of the compass. It was long believed to have been invented in China and brought to Europe by Marco Polo about 1260; other theories credited it to the Chinese, but held it was the Arab pilots of the Mediterranean who introduced it to Italy. Yet evidence seems to indicate the compass might be a European development. The Greek philosopher Thales is reputed to have been familiar with the magnetic properties of iron ore, and known that particles orient themselves along a north-south line. According to Charles L. Petze, Jr., in *The Evolution of Celestial Navigation*, the Norwegians were using this principle aboard ship to establish direction in the eleventh century A.D., and about 1200 "the poet Guyot de Provins described a compass used by mariners in place of the Pole Star when the latter was obscured by storm or fog. Hugo de Bercy, in 1248, wrote that the construction of the compass had been changed, the needle 'now being' supported on two floats in a glass cup." In 1269 appeared a description of a pivoted compass complete with lubber's line, a circle divided into four quadrants of 90 degrees, and a form of pelorus for taking bearings—all common to the most modern instruments.

Equally obscure is the origin of those other adjuncts of basic navigation, the lead and the log, the first to tell men how much water lay under the keel, the second how fast and how far the ship had traveled. The "lead" might well have been the first aid man ever developed in his questing across the surface of the sea. In its earliest form it must have been a rock at the end of a twisted vine, lowered over the side of Neolithic rafts when drifting toward an unfamiliar shore. As metals were discovered, they replaced the stone, until finally lead was available, and used so universally its name became synonymous with the ancient device.

The development of the "log" was more complicated, being based on accurate units of time and distance. The navigators of the Middle Ages estimated progress by eye, watching bubbles and weed drift past. Later, bits of wood were thrown over from the bow and timed by sandglass as they passed two observers on deck; the interval required to pass indicated the speed of the vessels. Beginning in the sixteenth century a line was attached to the bit of wood, and it was timed as it floated astern: the origin of the "chip log," standard aboard sailing ships for the next three centuries. The "chip" was a wooden triangle weighted at the bottom to keep it upright in the water. It was attached to a bridle, in turn attached to a length of line knotted every 47 feet 3 inches. The chip was lowered over the taffrail. Floating vertically, it remained relatively motionless while the ship moved ahead. A sailor stood by with a 28-second sandglass. When the last grain ran through the line was stopped and the knots counted, the theory being that the proportion of 47 feet 3 inches is to 28 seconds as a sea mile of 6080 feet is to 1 hour. Thus if a ship ran out 7 knots in the line in 28 seconds she was covering 7 miles in an hour, so the term "knot" came into universal use as a definition of speed: one nautical mile per hour. Even after the modern rotating log was generally adopted—a dial aboard ship which recorded distance by counting the revolutions of a spinner towed astern, utilizing the same principle as the automobile speedometer—the term "knot" remained. Yet curiously although the phrase "knots per hour" was used regularly in the old journals by the finest sailors the world has ever known, today it is considered by some a landlubber's expression.

Thus the simplest implements of voyaging are compass, lead, and log. With these men still find their way for long distances in many parts of the world, practicing a type of navigation more art than science, "dead reckoning." "Dead" is a contraction and corruption of "deduced," where the ship's position is a matter of deduction after consideration of all possible variables—compass error, current, leeway, and even the human fallibilities of the helmsmen.

But even as sailors groped along by dead reckoning, gradually accumulating the knowledge that resulted in charts so others following might have some idea of what lay ahead, learned men were working to transform navigation into a science. Hipparchus in 130 B.C. had prepared a calendar and tables of astronomical phenomena, but these were forgotten during the Dark Ages. Of direct interest to medieval navigators, the *Toledan Tables* of Arzachel appeared in 1080 and the *Alfonsine Tables* in 1252, while Roger Bacon added his *Opus Majus* in 1267, first using the term *almanac* to describe tables giving data on the apparent motions of heavenly bodies. After 1500, books of tables and manuals of navigation appeared with increasing frequency, spurred by the invention of the printing press.

Concurrently ran the development of instruments for measuring the altitudes of the heavenly bodies: sun and stars, moon and planets. The earliest appears to have been the astrolabe, a circular disk marked in degrees and equipped with a suspension ring and movable sighting vane. In use, the instrument was held by the ring and allowed to swing free like a plumb bob. The vane was then moved until it pointed directly at the body being observed, and the altitude read off the scale. The astrolabe was known to astronomers long before the beginning of the Christian era, but was never satisfactory at sea. Still, it was used by Columbus and Vasco de Gama to determine latitude on their voyages of discovery, two of the most important in history.

In more general vogue were the cross-staff and quadrant, the latter the direct ancestor of the sextant. The former consisted of a wooden staff along which vertical crosspieces could slide; altitude was determined by sliding the crosspiece until the observer could see the heavenly body on the line of the upper arm, and the horizon on the lower. The angle was then shown on a scale along the central staff. This too was unsatisfactory as it required simultaneous judgment of two widely separated objects. The quadrant was simply an arc marked in degrees, with a movable arm to point at the sun or star while holding the base level with the horizon.

The sextant, although not unlike some forms of quadrants in appearance, was the first device that permitted the heavenly body being observed to be "brought down" to the horizon by a system of reflecting mirrors. This eliminated the need for guesswork, and permitted a degree of accuracy impossible with any previous instrument. Oddly, the sextant was invented at practically the same time on both sides of the Atlantic: by Thomas Godfrey, a Philadelphia glazier, in 1730, and by John Hadley, an English scientist, in 1731. Unable to decide who was first, the Royal Society made equal awards to both.

During the same fateful years the other requirement for scientific navigation was being fashioned by an obscure Yorkshire carpenter, John Harrison. In 1714 the British Parliament had passed an act offering a reward of "10,000 pounds for a method that would give the longitude with an accuracy of one degree on a voyage to any of the West Indian islands and return, 15,000 pounds for an accuracy of 40 minutes of longitude in arc, and 20,000 pounds for an accuracy of 30 minutes." Man had long been able to determine with fair accuracy his latitude, the distance north or south of the equator, but had no satisfactory method of calculating longitude, the distance east or west of a given point. But if the exact altitude of sun or star could be made with the knowledge of the exact time at some given point on the earth's surface, such as the Royal Observatory at Greenwich, a simple calculation would show the difference in time—readily converted into distance—between the two places. Harrison's invention, the

chronometer, was the answer. In 1736 his first version, an un-
wieldy mechanism weighing 65 pounds, was carefully laid on
pillows in the great cabin of H.M.S. *Centurion* for a voyage to
Lisbon. Its error was only 3 minutes of longitude. Harrison was
awarded 500 pounds and retired to perfect a smaller and more
rugged version. After much difficulty, including the opposition of
the Astronomer Royal, his "Harrison Number 4" finally proved
itself beyond any question. Taken from England to Barbados
and return in 1764 on a voyage lasting 154 days, the timekeeper
gained only 54 seconds over its rate, an error equal to 13.5 minutes of longitude.

Within four years the modern age of navigation had begun. In
1768 Captain James Cook left Plymouth for the Pacific in the
Endeavour to observe a predicted transit of the planet Venus, in
order to secure data to calculate more precisely the distance from
the earth to the sun. Aboard were not only the compass, lead, and
log of previous voyagers, but chronometer, sextant, and even a
Nautical Almanac from the Royal Observatory which had been
established at Greenwich. During his voyage the observations
made and recorded daily in the ship's log read like those of any
modern ship not equipped with the electronic inventions of the
last two decades.

Landsmen probably do not realize that for smaller vessels there
has been no basic advance in navigation since that first voyage of
Cook, with the possible exception of radio reception as a check
on the timekeeper, and establishment of lines of position. Loran,
radar, automatic position-computers, and all the other gadgets are
for large steamers and ships of war, not anachronistic little vessels
of wood and canvas. Instruments have been improved, tables
have been made more complete and simpler to use, yet the tools
and techniques are essentially those of two centuries ago. And let
fog or storm hide the sun and stars, and even sextant and chronometer become useless, forcing the sailor still farther back down

the ladder of centuries. Navigation is then no longer a science, but an art, and a prayerful one at that.

Thus still, for the small-boat sailor, a landfall at the end of a long passage has a quality of suspense, of thanksgiving, and will continue to so long as little ships sail the seas.

19th Day

50° 36′ N.
11° 20′ W.
Run: noon to noon: 143 miles
Average speed: 5.95 knots
Total run to date: 2647 miles

Monday, July 21. 6:15 a.m.: Between midnight and 5:30 a series of entries by various hands in the "Remarks" column of the ship's log tells the same dismal story: "0000—Day commences under spinnaker, main and mizzen staysail. 0100—Headed and practically becalmed. Shifted to ballooner. No log-reading at 0100 as busy changing sails. 0200—Practically becalmed since 0100. 0300–0530—Some days you can't make a nickel, not even a plugged devalued ha'penny. Took over with bare steerageway, ballooner set, squalls around. Began to shift to genoa, wind freed so set spinnaker instead. Now close-hauled barely laying course as other squalls prepare other shifts. Nuts!"

I must admit it was particularly hard to turn out at 2:45. Perhaps on a long race like this you tire cumulatively without realizing it; even when you eat and sleep well, and think you are relaxed, there is an underlying strain which comes from maintaining racing tension and alertness for many days in succession. Or perhaps it was because I was aware of the sound of slatting even before I was fully awake, or maybe it was the two huge obelisks of peanut butter and strawberry jam consumed before going below. Anyway, at 3:00 the leaden skies and drizzle seemed more unpleasant than usual, and the immediate question for decision—whether to continue under drifter, some 12° below course, or change to genoa, and lay course but at a slight sacrifice in speed—seemed distasteful and unimportant. Thus do skippers have their periods of letdown. But nevertheless gritted the teeth and girded the loins, or whatever you do under oilskins, and joined in dragging the genoa on deck. At the moment we were doing all of 2 knots in a direction vaguely towards Ireland. As we hanked the genoa on the stay we sensed the wind had shifted; the helmsman followed, keeping the ballooner full, all the way around the compass from 080 to 180 degrees. So we went onto the course, now 112 degrees, slacked sheets, and got out and set the spinnaker. Before it was even drawing properly the wind veered to the east of south, making it impossible to lay course, and finally headed us up to 050 degrees. At which point we set the genoa. We carry it as I write this; a puff is shoving us along at 8.6 knots, close-hauled but laying course. The sea is smooth, knocked flat by a hard shower.

Now that we move again guess I won't give up sailboating after all, especially as I look below and see the port watch eating grits and kippers, and our turn is next.

9:10 a.m.: It has turned into a sunny day, warm and sparkling. After the succession of dawn squalls a breeze came in from southwest at about 10 knots. Immediately went back to spinnaker and everything else that could be set. We move along at a comfortable 7 knots, our bow pointing directly for the Scilly Isles, now only a scant 200 miles beyond the horizon. As usual, our spirits keep time with *Caribbee,* and joy reigns.

A steamer angles across our bow, probably heading for the coast of France, or one of the Spanish ports. It is a rusty little tramp with a high skinny funnel and flat sheer, part of the company which roams the seas of the world unheralded and unloved, yet forms the true backbone of commerce. The pilot chart indicates separate lanes for "low-powered steamers" to keep the draft horses from under the feet of the greyhounds, to use a somewhat scrambled metaphor. Ever since we sighted our first we have had a fiendish desire to sail past, leaving it puffing along hopelessly in our wake. But unfortunately on the few occasions we have met a "low-powered steamer" the wind has given us even less power, and we have had to concede the advantage of good hard coal over the fickle commodity of the sky. As have windjamming sailors for the last hundred years. Think how it must have hurt the captain of a proud clipper of the '70's to watch an early paddle-wheeler go past in a calm, belching smoke and cinders, crew derisively waving ropes in the mockery of a tow! His reply must have been hotter than the steam in the wheezing boilers.

When the tramp first broke the line of the horizon I was in the midst of breakfast, plate piled high with "Georgia ice cream" and kippers. Somebody on deck shouted "Sail-ho! Pass up the binoculars!" I knew they were joking yet somehow got a terrific twinge. This suspense has really built up—has been building ever since the wind flopped on the Grand Banks and we lowered our sails.

Not only what the hell has happened to *Janabel, Samuel Pepys,* and company, but what about those eggs?

12:45 p.m.: We have finally attained a European coastal chart—Hydrographic Office No. 4431, *The English Channel.* Frank laid down our noon position as a running fix putting us on the margin: 50° 36′ north latitude, 11° 20′ west longitude. As the chart extends westward to exactly 11° 20′, we are barely on, but eat our way farther in at a present rate of 5 knots. Slow, but we hope sure.

Our pencilled position lies almost over a sounding of 586 fathoms—3516 feet, a little more than a half-mile. Not far astern are depths of 1300 fathoms, 2000 fathoms. Close ahead the bottom rises rapidly. Before midnight we should cross the 100-fathom curve and be in true coastal waters. Thus we have left astern the Abyss, are on the Slope, and within hours will be over the Shelf. In a sense, our ocean voyage is over.

I have been studying the coast we approach. It is rugged and formidable, a graveyard of ships through the centuries. Some 60

"I seem to remember a crack about there being times when cleanliness was not next to godliness, but next to impossible. And we're only a few degrees away from the latter."

"The main problems of shipkeeping on a passage of this sort are mildew and chafe
... they can be kept under control by constant vigilance; we make hourly inspections for chafe ... and of course sun damp sails on deck whenever conditions
permit."

miles to the north stretches the coast of Ireland, long narrow fingers of land thrusting out to sea, deep bays between. Off them lie detached shoals with beautiful names, but none the less dangerous for that: Fastnet Rock, Great Skellig, Inishtearaght, Inishtooskert, Inishvickillane. Still farther north, and farther offshore, lonely Rockall lies in wait.

Ahead are the Scilly Isles, a collection of small islands and rocks lifting abruptly from depths of 60 fathoms. They lie about 30 miles off Land's End, and are the real guardians of England and the Channel. Before a lighthouse was established on Bishop Rock—one of the world's great feats of construction—they were murderously fatal to ships groping homeward through thick weather, and beyond count were the returning sailors whose last view of their native land was a rock in the boiling surf.

Somewhat over a degree to the south of Land's End the shoulder of France protrudes to divide the Channel from the Bay of Biscay. Off this coast extend other dangers, culminating in Île d'Ouessant—Ushant—and smaller islands and rocks behind and to the south. Here are some of the most terrific tides on this planet: a daily rise and fall of over 30 feet, and currents up to 10 knots in velocity.

None of this coast is to be feared in good weather, especially when approaching with the navigational precision made possible by modern instruments. But it has not been much more than a century since men lacked the equipment to make accurate landfalls after long passages. A degree in longitude was a relatively minor error, although a mistake of a few miles might put a ship in danger.

Yet in bad weather many modern aids are useless to the navigator of a small vessel. If he cannot see the sun or stars because of overcast, sextant and chronometer and precisely calculated tables are useless; if fog is thick, lighthouses remain invisible, buoys cannot be found. Current is a force defying absolutely accurate assessment despite neat diagrams of arrows showing average strength and direction of flow. Large steamers have little difficulty because the beams of radar and loran cut through any murk, but even they at times change arrival or departure schedules because of forces still beyond the control of man.

And here bad weather can mean more than blinding fog. This coast is literally the leeward side of the Atlantic. Nearly every storm which develops over the North American continent, or in the West Indies, or in the wastes of the Atlantic itself, moves eastward to spend its force on the land mass of Europe. Land's End, the southernmost tip of England, lies almost exactly on the fiftieth parallel of latitude. On the western side of the ocean the same parallel cuts across the upper part of Newfoundland and just misses Hudson Bay. Consequently these are northern waters, subject to violent gales originating when the warm westerlies collide with air masses chilled by polar ice. Except in the northern reaches of Canada, and off the coast of Labrador, our side of the ocean does not experience extra-tropical cyclones of such intensity—and even there the sea is not comparable as the waves have not had the fetch to attain full development.

Since wind systems travel from west to east, and the prevailing winds are westerly, the British Isles and adjacent coasts are at the leeward end of a 3000-mile sweep of ocean; and when long deep-water waves come on soundings and encounter strong tides, very fancy and unpleasant things can happen. Such as breakers forming at the mouth of the English Channel in 100 fathoms of water, a roaring maelstrom not wholly comprehensible to anyone who has not experienced it.

But these gloomy aspects have little bearing on the present case. There is every indication this good weather will hold—in fact, judging by the barometer, there is more danger of calm than gale. Since noon yesterday we have towed a spinner log, more accurate than the Kenyon, in case we can get no sights as we close the coast.

So, as has been true for nineteen days, our only worry is the wind—and our competitors.

4:25 p.m.: I hardly know how to begin this one. My last sentence must have been premonitory. I no sooner closed my notebook than the breeze died. In the 3 hours since I do not believe we have covered 3 miles. All the calms that have gone before are as nothing: there is not a breath of wind, not the faintest stirring of air. Smoke blown aloft merely vanishes: it does not move away.

Around *Caribbee* the water lies flat. Directly under us it has a color of its own, blue, but elsewhere it takes on the color of the sky. Even at this unhappy moment I must admire the scene: I have never seen such magnificent clouds, and each is faithfully reproduced in the sea. There are fluffy white cumulus overhead, extending off to the northwest layer on layer, each whiter and rounder than the other; to the northeast there is a flat bank of stratus with grayish overtones and a darker streak in the middle; to the southeast another bank which is somehow silver and blue; and astern, to the southwest, the sun shining on and through rippled cirrus formations makes them a brilliant white, almost incandescent.

But if I seem to like the situation, I don't. I simply can't do justice to how I feel. Here we are, smelling the carrot, not getting any closer. Seventy miles away lies Fastnet Rock, that horrendous symbol of tempest and raging sea, and here we sit, contemplating our luncheon garbage.

A British Broadcasting Corporation weather forecast has done nothing to cheer us: fresh northwest winds in the areas to the north of our position, fresh southwest winds in the areas to the south, and—buck up, old boy!—"light variables for the Fastnet area."

Fickle fate, withdraw that finger!

5:45 p.m.: Spirits on this vessel are more attuned to wind than the most sensitive thermometer to temperature or barometer to pressure: with the first few minutes of a faint southwest breeze we show signs of life. Spinnaker up and drawing. Three-point-five knots on the Kenyon.

8:10 p.m.: Red sunset. Beautiful. But not this sailor's delight. Tomorrow will probably be another lousy lovely day.

20th Day

50° 11′ N.
  9° 00′ W.
Run: noon to noon: 93 miles
Average speed: 3.87 knots
Total run to date: 2740 miles

Tuesday, July 22. 2:45 a.m.: At eleven this watch began as badly as any. Beautiful clear night, sea calm. And ditto the sky: calm as calm can be. Spinnaker in limp folds. Stars reflecting.

But at 0050 a mild zephyr arrived from the north to lift the spinnaker and send us on our way. From forward came the chuckle of a bow wave, and the wheel developed a function other than support for the helmsman's elbows. Speed went up above 6 knots; we changed to a heavier spinnaker sheet.

Now I go below with some feeling of relaxation. Am thoroughly bushed. I have willed *Caribbee* ahead so hard during these past hours I couldn't be more tired if I had swum ahead and towed her.

A magnificent dawn is shaping up. Frank has already gotten star sights.

8:15 a.m.: I never thought I would look on blue skies with aversion. Yet within the last half-hour the cloud bank overhead since midnight lifted, and it is warm and sunny. I hasten to add my feeling is not based on any loss of love for the sparkling day: it is only that after midnight we enjoyed a very pleasant little breeze from the north—not a slashing blustering sort of northerly wind, but one robust enough to send us on our way at 7 knots on the port tack. Lately we have found in these latitudes the wind dwells exclusively within and under clouds; it is a shy and retiring phenomenon, needing shelter and companionship, and when the clouds go away and leave you the wind goes too. We have grown to fear clearing skies and a rising barometer. Now we have both.

It suddenly occurs in our entire passage east we have had very little of this type of sailing: a moderate breeze where we log a comfortable average speed. Either it has blown quite hard, so we lugged what we carried, or we have had no wind at all. That has been true all the way from Newport, for the race to Bermuda was the same. At the moment we might be stealing along the western shore of the Chesapeake or having a Sunday afternoon spin on Long Island Sound. Since we are on soundings and under the lee of Ireland with a new and moderate breeze there is no sea except the tiniest of whitecaps. There is no underlying swell whatever; if we should go flat I am sure the masthead would not weave at all.

Everything combines to give me the feeling we approach land: the mildness of the day, the smoothness of the sea, a certain indefinable gaiety among the shipmates. As the old-timers would have said, we are "smelling the shore."

10:10 a.m.: We have our first tangible sign of nearing the finish. A Royal Air Force Coastal Command patrol plane has been circling for the past 20 minutes. Now it is disappearing into the west. Frank watches through binoculars to see if it circles again, which might indicate it is over another boat.

From the moment it came close I tried to signal with the Aldis lamp. The first series of dots and dashes that flashed from an open hatch aft we read without difficulty: "Welcome." I signalled "Thanks," and added the question uppermost in all minds: "Any others sighted?" Then our ability to read International Morse broke down entirely. A long series of dots and dashes blinked as the big flying boat circled. We could read just enough to be maddening, scribbling down letters and blanks. Now we can put together a great variety of phrases, ranging from "*Janabel* finished yesterday" to "You are first congratulations."

Frank has announced the plane disappeared over the horizon in a straight line, which would indicate no other boat is close astern. A new and intense wave of speculation has broken out about our competitors. Everyone is talking at once, and there are as many theories as there are talkers. Opinions vary as greatly as our interpretations of the plane's message: all the way from the wildest optimism to the most abject pessimism. One feels the whole fleet must have been trapped in the calm together, and *Caribbee* because of her higher rig and larger fore-triangle would have moved best through the light variables; another says none of the others would have gone so far north, so consequently never stopped at all and are now sipping Plymouth gin in the bar of the Hoe House. For once I keep quiet. Just for this moment I really don't care too much. It has been such a wonderful experience and I have enjoyed it so much despite the low moments that I am satisfied, regardless of the other boats.

But I know damned well that mood won't last long.

11:30 a.m.: Feel as restless as a cat on a hot stove. We are doing a consistent 7 to 7.5 knots but it is like being tied to a dock. During the last hour the wind went farther into the east so we shifted from spinnaker to balloon jib, without any particular loss of speed.

For once a clearing sky did not kill the breeze. We go beautifully. Everything sparkles—the water, the sky, even the air. As I sit in the lee side of the cockpit and look ahead I am reminded of a similar day and circumstance; the recollection is so vivid if I could not place it exactly it would worry me until I did. For in '49 we had precisely similar conditions when *Caribbee* left Kalmar, Sweden, for the tiny Danish island of Christiansö. We came out into the Baltic from behind Öland Island carrying this same balloon jib, sheeted the same way, and the glint of sun across the water was the same, the curl of the bow wave and the toss of white foam off to leeward was the same, and so was the look of the sky and the feel of the air and the heft of the breeze. And we reached down the sunlit Baltic then as we are now reaching across the approaches to the English Channel, with the same feeling of unreality that goes with making dreams come true. Life can offer no more.

2:30 p.m.: Have just finished a super-lunch. On our twentieth day at sea Henry fed us a real smörgåsbord, in perfect harmony with my recollection of this morning: herring, two kinds of cheese, sardines, cold ham, chicken and tongue—only the snaaps and beer missing, and we'll be having them soon.

The northerly wind holds, blowing fresh and cold from a cloudless sky of deep blue. It has somewhat the feel of coming directly off ice. Out of the sun several sweaters and a windbreaker are necessary, yet the sun is bright enough for warmth if one is sheltered. The port watch has been able to add fore and mizzen staysails, and our speed is up to eight.

Frank announces we have been pushed 10 miles to the southward of our course. He has been studying a tremendous document entitled *Atlas of Tides and Tidal Currents in the British Isles and Adjacent Waters,* and blames the set on a current flowing out of the Irish Sea. Even so we are still to the northward of the Scilly Isles, although the usual approach is from the south. Before leaving Bermuda Alf Loomis suggested we hold up toward Fastnet Rock, off the southern coast of Ireland, because in other races some boats have been headed as they neared the Channel, and it would give us a better slant for the windward work. We have followed his advice, although we were 60 rather than the recommended 40 miles south of the Fastnet when it was abeam.

What might be called the "navigator's moment" is near at hand. Day after day Frank has been squinting at the sun and stars, calling *"Mark!"* as he brought them to the horizon, and disappearing down the companionway to cover large sheets of paper with the mystic symbols of his craft. Each noon he has added a dot and a line to the chart on the cabin bulkhead, announced the distance we covered in the preceding 24 hours, and answered questions relating to our exact location on the terrestrial sphere with casual aplomb. He tells us how far south we pass an unseen rock, and mumbles about a current taking us 10 miles from where we should be, and we have had to take his word. One piece of water looks amazingly like another, and it is hard to argue. But now Frank has to put up. He says the Scilly Isles lie ahead. We are steering the course he directs. If he is right, we meet: the real "navigator's moment" comes when a ship has run her distance and all hands begin scanning the horizon for what they have been told they should see. Generations of navigators have perspired untold buckets of blood when the line of sea and sky remained unbroken.

But our trusty navigator shows no sign of strain, or that anything the least bit out of the ordinary is about to happen. Today, as usual, he used his navigator's prerogative of being below at noon to lunch with both watches. Our landfall is assured.

8:20 p.m.: There may have been lovelier sunsets in my experience, but I cannot remember any. But I can recall one exactly the same, and that, curiously enough, was on the evening of the day I was reminded of this afternoon—the day we sailed from Kalmar. Then, as now, there was not a cloud and the entire sky was a deep and unbelievable Kodachrome blue; the sun set behind a distant haze so it was a brilliant red, but not bright enough to hurt the eyes, while the sky took on wonderful soft shades of rose as the sun dipped below the horizon. Almost imperceptibly the tint changed to the palest of lavender, then an even deeper blue, and it was night.

Late this afternoon the RAF plane came back, and the port watch deciphered its message as "None in sight." So between the beauty of the night, the steadiness of the breeze, the message, and our current progress, *Caribbee* is a happy ship. Exciting things are afoot: there is even talk of Basil shaving and Henry hints of a landfall pie.

At the moment the only active person aboard is our navigator, and he is busier than a whole litter of poodle puppies. Since dawn he has been stalking stars and sun with the sextant, not leaving anything to chance. A few minutes ago I went over his plot with him. We are now on a larger scale chart bearing the impressive title *South Coast of Ireland to Land's End Including Approaches to the Irish Sea and Bristol Channel.* Our course is penciled in as a bold black line angling down to clear Round Island, at the north end of the Scilly Isles, and it is closely intersected with lines of positions and running fixes. Round Island shows as a light flashing red every 30 seconds, having a visibility of 19 miles. Bishop Rock, 8 miles south-southwest of Round Island, is group flashing, two every 15 seconds, and has a visibility of 18 miles. And here our navigator gets himself well out on a limb: he predicts that because of the angle at which we approach the Scilly Isles, and the clarity of the night, we will sight both lights at the same time, the red flash of Round Island almost over the bow, the twin white flashes of Bishop Rock off to starboard. And even adds a time—before we go off watch at 11:00, if the breeze stays the same.

So now we rush toward our landfall at almost 8 knots. This dry cold wind holds steady from the north. The evening BBC weather forecast predicted "fresh to occasionally strong north to northeast winds" for the Plymouth area, so perhaps coming in north of the Scillies will make us a few minutes, after all. We are carrying balloon jib and mizzen staysail in addition to main and mizzen. All sheets are started. If the forecast is correct we should be able to continue like this right to the Lizard: Round Island to starboard, Seven Stones Lightship to port, Wolf Rock to starboard, Lizard Head close to port. Then, if the wind goes northeast, we will only have to beat up the Channel from the Lizard to Plymouth. A mere nothing.

It suddenly occurs what a wonderful way this is to end an open-water passage, driving along for a landfall on a clear night at 8 knots, decks dry except for spray forward, sails patterned against the stars, a wide path of foam under the counter. No other sensation could match it. This is why we can never stop, we who once know the lure of the sea.

10:40 p.m.: Taking time off deck to record one of the big moments of my life. Five minutes ago the forward lookout picked up Round Island and Bishop Rock lights, the red flash over the bow, the twin white flashes off to starboard, exactly as Frank predicted.

So we have sailed across the Atlantic, *Caribbee* and those aboard: the light on Block Island fading astern on the evening of June 21, the lights of the Scilly Isles rising out of the sea July 22. Virtually a month, except for a few days in Bermuda, to cross an ocean other men fly across in hours.

But I might note Father Neptune gave me the gentlest of hints as I went forward to have a better look. I had almost reached the bow pulpit when a small sea slapped aboard, drenching me thoroughly. The North Atlantic is still cold and solid. I could almost hear the old boy growling through the seaweed in his beard: "You got off light, son. Don't go around acting like a salty character."

OK, pop.

☆ ☆
☆

BELOW the surface of the sea lies a world of filtered sunshine paling into impenetrable darkness, of deadening cold and intolerable pressure, of vast areas and utter silence. Mountains far more majestic than the Andes or Himalayas rise mile after mile to terminate in peaks under the keels of passing ships; gorges infinitely greater than the Grand Canyon groove the rocky floor. Through the mountains and the valleys and "the dark unfathomed caves" move types of life inconceivably more numerous and varied in form than the denizens of the land, engaged in a struggle for existence incomparably more fierce.

For centuries men sailed the oceans with no comprehension of what lay beyond the coastal shallows, their probing limited to depths which could be reached by weights attached to a few hundred feet of rope. Gradually knowledge accumulated, but even today the ocean abyss is the earth's last frontier, likely to remain inviolate in the foreseeable future. "Could the waters of the Atlantic be drawn off so as to expose to view this great sea-gash which separates continents, and extends from the Arctic to the Antarctic, it would present a scene the most rugged, grand, and imposing," wrote Matthew Maury. "The very ribs of the solid earth, with the foundations of the sea, would be brought to light, and we should have presented to us in one view, in the empty cradle of the ocean, 'a thousand fearful wrecks,' with that array of dead men's skulls, great anchors, heaps of pearl and inestimable stones, which, in the poet's eye, lie scattered on the bottom of the sea, making it hideous with sights of ugly death."

But despite fluctuations of the ocean's level—from 600 feet above its present height during the Ordovician period, 350,000,-000 years ago, when the North American continent was reduced to a group of scattered islands, to recessions when trees grew on the floor of the Baltic and a land bridge extended from Alaska to Siberia—it is doubtful if the waters of the Atlantic or any other ocean will be "drawn off." Thus man will never see a panorama as rugged and fantastic as could exist on any dead world in the far reaches of the universe.

Yet modern oceanography is making possible some idea of the vastness of the ocean in relation to the land, and glimmerings of the hidden contours lying between the continents. First, it is necessary to understand that 70 per cent of the surface of planet Earth is covered by water, making it more properly planet Ocean, as has been suggested. This vast sheet of water has been calculated as having a volume of some 300,000,000 cubic miles. And while the mean depth of the oceans of the world is about 13,000 feet, the average height of the land is only about 2800 feet. Thus if a celestial bulldozer could shove all the land into the water, and somehow complete the job of spreading the earth evenly into the crevices until the central core was a perfectly smooth ball, an ocean 8000 feet deep would roll unbroken around this planet.

Like so many other steps in man's technical progress, the means of determining the depths of the ocean came as a result of trying to achieve something else. In the early days of navigation measuring the water under the keel of a ship was a laborious process of lowering weights attached to ropes. The difficulties can be imagined. During an Antarctic expedition in 1839 Sir James Clark Ross pieced together a line of 3600 fathoms and made the first successful sounding of the ocean abyss, reaching bottom at 2425 fathoms. Yet by 1854, when Maury brought together all known records, there were only 180 soundings of the Atlantic depths. Maury was responsible for many more, substituting strong twine for rope, and in 1870 Lord Kelvin introduced his deep-sea sounding machine of wire on a geared drum. Until World War I when the submarine menace forced development of underwater listening devices, no better way of finding depth was invented. But antisubmarine research resulted in "sonic sounding," a method of transmitting a sound from the ship and measuring the time of the echo from the bottom in terms of the velocity of sound through sea water, some 4800 feet a second. Continuous soundings could thus be recorded on lengths of graph paper, accurately depicting every hill and valley of the sea floor below. For the first time man could have some understanding of the hidden depths.

The first surprise was the unevenness of the ocean bottom. It had long been envisioned as an almost level plain, a characterless expanse covered by mud and sediment. Immediately the fallacy of this concept became apparent as soundings accumulated in the hydrographic offices of the world faster than they could be recorded on charts. Then swiftly followed comprehension of how much greater were the variations than comparable ones on land: the mountains higher, the valleys deeper, the escarpments steeper, the canyons more complex. Vast ranges of mountains appeared, mountains which if bathed in sunshine and capped by snow would surpass anything visible in majesty and beauty— yet their slopes were wrapped in eternal darkness and quiet, and subjected to pressure sufficient to crush any terrestrial life. . . . And systems of rivers as defined and complicated as the Mississippi Basin, buried far beneath any explicable rise of the bottom, or fall of the sea. . . . And trenches so deep Mount Everest, symbol to man of virtually unconquerable height, could be dropped in and still be buried by a mile of water.

With the knowledge came a new concept of the hidden world of the sea, a division into three major classifications: the *Shelf,* the *Slope,* and the *Abyss.* To put it another way: the continental shallows, the pillars supporting the land masses, and the floor of the sea itself, the basalt crust over the flaming core of planet Earth. Of the flooded areas of the world, 7 per cent is Shelf, 15 per cent Slope, and 78 per cent Abyss.

Of these it is easiest to visualize the Shelf, the gently sloping shoulders of continents and islands, presently drowned extensions of land which have alternately been flooded and exposed during past geological ages. Generally speaking, the characteristics of a coast below water are similar to the visible part coming down to the tide line. This is understandable when it is remembered our present shores are being swallowed by the rising level of the sea at a rate of 8 inches per century, as glaciers and the polar ice pack melt in the current warm cycle of the earth. In ages to come, it is predicted, the level of the ocean will rise from 100 to 200 feet, transforming much of our present coastal countryside into Shelf, and completely altering the maps of the world.

In all oceans the average Shelf width is 30 miles, and its outer depth 72 fathoms, giving it a gradient of 15 feet in a mile, an incline barely perceptible to the eye. Here live almost all the plants and animals of the sea which humans know or use for food. For as plant life is unable to survive in the rarefied atmosphere of higher altitudes, so it cannot live in the depths of the sea. Below 200 feet plant life is scarce, although in some areas of exceptionally clear water plants find enough sunlight to manufacture food in depths of 600 feet.

At a usual depth of between 360 and 480 feet begins the Slope, the suddenly steepening descent of the bottom toward the floor of the sea. The average Slope extends down to some 12,000 feet, but can drop as deeply as 30,000 feet. Thus the Slope is a series of terrific escarpments, towering pillars of rock buttressing the islands and the continents. These vast cliffs are deeply grooved by canyons and gorges far greater than anything above the surface of the sea, just as the escarpments themselves dwarf anything beheld by the eyes of men. For the Slope marks the part of this planet which does not belong to man, an alien and eerie void of eternal darkness, pressures up to 7 tons per square inch, and animals that feed only on other animals.

At the base of the Slope the floor of the sea becomes less steep. Beyond extends the Abyss, the very name a frightening symbol of the unknown, the "bottomless gulph" of the ancient cosmogonies. In the vastness and the silence and the stillness—far below the reach of the most savage waves which lash the surface—dwell creatures strange and terrible, moving blindly across canyons of the greatest magnificence, their being only suspected by men above. Here for hundreds of miles may extend a range of mountains, there a drowned river system, here strange isolated peaks with flattened tops, there a gorge gaping even deeper into

the core of the earth, here a level plain. . . . All hidden by utter
and complete darkness, dead and soundless in a living world, part
of the immutable secret of the universe. . . .

Strangely, the greatest depths of the ocean do not lie far from
shore, but at the bases of some of the most precipitous mountain
ranges which thrust above the surface. The deepest discovered
chasm is the trench which winds across the Pacific past the Mari-
anas, the Bonin Islands, and along the steep shore of Japan, an
awesome abyss attaining 35,640 feet. In the Atlantic the greatest
depth is close to the north shore of Puerto Rico and the Virgin
Islands, where the Brownson Deep descends to 30,250 feet. It is
thought by many geologists these depths are part of nature's universal scheme of compensation: that at the bases of great mountains there is a fault in the earth's crust to balance the height
above.

Another feature of the Abyss is the sediment, the gradual accumulation of erosion and decay through the eons. There are
places where it is many miles in depth, others where submarine
currents have swept the rock bare, but seismic echo-soundings
show that in general several thousand feet of sediment cover the
floor of the ocean. Yet some scientists estimate as little as 1 inch
might accumulate in 2500 years, a process so leisurely as to further remind man of his status on even his own planet, that minute
speck in space.

On *Caribbee* we had one knowledge not shared by the sailors
of old: a comprehension of the nature of the Abyss, of the dimension below the surface. Bermuda itself we could visualize as
the only exposed peak of a mighty system of mountains thrusting
up from the floor of the Western Atlantic Basin. As we sailed
north and east, we moved over lesser peaks dropping down to
hills and valleys, then reached the Slope off Newfoundland, a
fantastic escarpment towering out of the Abyss. As we won-
dered what the weather gods above might have in store, below
the depths were rising from 2247 fathoms to 1565 to 1291 to 1008.

"It was almost impossible to walk along the deck without holding to the liferail or some other stable object. Yet we rigged the bos'n's chair and tied Frank in securely, and up he went: up some 75 feet into the cold raw wind, the chill spitting rain."

"A boat is more complex than any house: we are driven across the sea by our sails, which in turn depend upon an intricate web of steel, wood and linen. To keep all in order, we must not only have the skills to use the tools, but must be steeplejacks and tightrope walkers."

"The port watch finally decided the time had come for a bath, regardless of temperature and consequences.... Basil was chosen as the first victim, and as he carefully inserted a toe Dick poured in an extra bucket of water. There was a scream that must have scared bonefish off the flats in Middle Bight."

"Ahead a long low band of dark cloud extends all the way across the sky, black and somehow ominous. . . . Our bow points at the center of it, and each minute it looks blacker and solider. . . . We crawl towards it, watchful."

Then suddenly, in the space of a few miles, came the gigantic lift: 1000 fathoms rising to 500, to 200, to less than 100, and we were over the Grand Banks, part of the Continental Shelf, a vast drowned plateau spreading like a fan under the sea, one of the widest Shelf areas of the world.

And beyond the Banks to the east Flemish Cap, a flattish hillock, separated by a valley nearly 100 miles wide, but not very deep as submarine valleys go. Then another Slope, the final plunge into the Abyss separating the continents of North America and Europe. Far from traveling over a level and featureless plain, then, we were crossing some of the most awesome geological heritages of the genesis of planet Earth: a vast river system, not unlike the Mississippi, extending south from Greenland and deeply etching the floor of the sea with canyons and gorges and the arms of many tributaries; and beyond, the Mid-Atlantic Ridge—the greatest mountain range of this world, a complex of peaks and valleys winding down the center of the ocean from Iceland to Antarctica, 10,000 miles long and 500 miles wide, mostly lying 9000 feet deep, but with one of its visible manifestations, Mount Pico in the Azores, towering 7613 feet above the surface and plunging 20,000 feet below.

And beyond the sheer rock cliffs of the Ridge the lesser peaks diminish into hills, gradually merging into one of the rare plains of the ocean, the Eastern Atlantic Basin, a fairly level floor covered deeply with sediment, its vast expanse broken only by small knolls believed to be volcanic in origin. Then again the rise of the Slope, this one supporting the Isles of Britain, the Shelf beyond dipping down into the shallow sluice called the English Channel, and rising again to the continent of Europe itself.

So man has added a new dimension to his knowledge: the dimension of depth. To the ancients the sea itself was the limiting boundary. The Greeks called it *Oceanos Potamos*, the Ocean River, conceiving it as a stream flowing endlessly around the rim of the world. Any human who attempted to penetrate its mysteries would pass into darkness and finally plunge into the abyss, from which there could be no return. To the real hazards of the sea were added the terrors of the imagination.

Yet men quested. Today the Abyss is a definable scientific term. Perhaps in some future age, when sails and their use are as forgotten as the ox cart, humans will roam the floor of the sea. Only then will man's conquest of his planet be complete. Thus the ocean is the ultimate challenge, as it was the first.

21st Day

50° 02′ N.
 4° 44′ W.
Run: noon to noon: 183 miles
Average speed: 7.62 knots
Total run to date: 2923 miles

Wednesday, July 23. 6:35 a.m.: I start this day with a very red face. Last night when turning in at 11:00 I was at first too keyed up to sleep; then finally went off so heavily I did not awaken when Bill Sherar came down and switched on the light over my bunk. Every other time I have come instantly awake—or at least conscious—so it did not occur to him to shake me. This time nothing happened. I slept on peacefully while the rest of the starboard watch dressed and went on deck. It was only when I did not appear in the cockpit that Dick began to wonder what had happened: he came down to find me dead to the world. Thus for the first time on the passage I was late for watch—and on what might be the last call.

For we rush along the Cornwall coast at 8.5 knots and better. A little before 1:30 Round Island was abeam to starboard, at 2:30 Seven Stones Lightship was abeam to port, a run of over 9 miles. Now we approach Lizard Head. At this rate, we could cross the finish line around noon.

When I came on deck it was still black dark. Off the starboard quarter Peninnis Head light blinked every 15 seconds, marking the eastern extremity of the Scilly Isles. On the port quarter Seven Stones Lightship added its group flash, guarding a nasty collection of rocks lying only slightly north of a direct course from Round Island to Lizard Head. The chart was heavily cross-hatched with fixes to make sure we kept clear of Pollard Rock and South Stone, both barely above the surface, and hardly the welcome we wanted. And almost abeam to port flashed Long-ships Light, and beyond that Pendeen Watch-House, on the coast of England itself; and off to starboard Wolf Rock. Quite a collection of lights, symbolizing the importance and the potential dangers of the shore we close so easily.

The sun came up flat and very red behind a thin haze, not threateningly, but with the look of a hot summer day at home. By its light we could see Wolf Rock was a lone finger thrusting from the sea, while the Longships rose above a rocky base in the form of a flat pyramid. Beyond towered the Cornwall coast; bold cliffs lifting abruptly from the water, with smooth green table lands above, and houses breaking the line of the sky. Nothing ever looked lovelier, or more inviting. We could smell the land as plainly as we could see it: earth and grass, and even a touch of barnyard.

Before us lies Lizard Head, a long flat point pushing out beyond the cliffs, the southernmost tip of England. The ships which have sailed 'round the Lizard through the years! Here has passed the whole cavalcade of history, from the first Phoenicians through the Vikings and Romans to the Spanish Armada, and the ships that carried the Union Jack to every corner of the world—for "Never the isle so little, never the sea so lone, but over the palm and the scud, the British flag has flown." And here have passed the ships of many wars, from an early struggle in which a mother attempted to dominate a growing child, to the most recent one, where the child grown to manhood returned to help its mother. No waters could have a greater story for one who loves the sea.

So we begin our last lap, the dangers of the open ocean and the hazards of the landfall behind. Beyond Lizard Head we follow the coast approximately 45 miles to the finish line off Plymouth Breakwater. At 5:00, when we were in the lee of

Land's End, the wind lightened and went ahead, so we struck the staysails. Crossing Mounts Bay it came back, slightly east of north. We now log it as 15 knots, and show 7.9 on the Kenyon. To avoid being blanketed by Lizard Head, as the breeze will be directly off the shore and we would be close under the cliffs, we have altered course somewhat to the southward, and steer 109 degrees. Also since 0400 we have carried a fair tide of 1.1 knots, which is supposed to increase to around 2 knots when we are off the Lizard. So everything is perfect, even the weather forecast: the morning BBC broadcast said there is a ridge of high pressure over the British Isles, and predicts a continuance of "good weather" and moderate northerly winds for the Plymouth area.

Our watch is almost over, probably the last of the passage, for if the wind holds we should be inside Plymouth harbor by 1:00, sails down and furled, gin—and I hope a bit of ice—firmly in hand. As I sit here on deck I can look down into the cabin: the port watch breakfasts in a very festive mood. There is talk of shaving and packing, and Basil and Bobby wonder how to get to Helsinki in time to sail a couple of races, for the Olympic Games were proceeding while *Caribbee* wasn't.

Henry hands up a cup of coffee. I abandon writing for other pleasures—there is no greater animal satisfaction than the first cup of coffee on deck on a warm sunny morning. And especially when contemplating the Cornwall coast with the whole Atlantic astern.

10:30 a.m.: Now it appears we are to get a final kick in the teeth—or elsewhere—from fate. For we are almost as thoroughly becalmed as we have been at any time during the passage.

When we brought Lizard Head abeam the wind dropped off to nothing, as sharply as if it had been cut with a knife. The ballooner went hard aback against the spreaders, and the only reason we didn't begin slatting was there was no swell. Everything just went limp, and stayed that way. We consoled ourselves with the thought the tide would carry us clear of the wind shadow from the high land, even if no puffs found their way through, and so it happened. We crept away from the cliffs and the breeze came back, lifting us from a drift to 5 knots. But after we stole out into the open Channel the breeze died again, and has stayed dead. We have the barest of steerageway. All hands are shaved, and *Caribbee* has been chammied and polished until she glistens and gleams, yet we get nowhere; astern the Lizard is still in sight, and barely over the curve of the horizon awaits the finish, and we cannot move.

"Effed" again—and I don't mean frustrated.

12:00 p.m.: For sale: one ocean racer damned cheap. Only ocean racer isn't the proper term. You can't race standing still. And that is what we're doing.

There is not an iota of wind, not the slightest vagrant breath. The English Channel lies as flat as I have ever seen any body of water, anywhere. There are no ripples, no bubbles.

Off to port some 8 miles is the coast of Cornwall. Over it tower masses of cumulous clouds, motionless. They are the typical clouds of a hot summer day. Under them the air must be stagnant and still. A mile or so to starboard a steamer is passing. Smoke bends back from her stack because of her forward speed, but then goes straight up.

A few minutes ago we shifted from genoa to drifter. For a brief period after passing the Lizard we had a light northeaster, and so made the previous change. But now the drifter is useless. No sail can work when even cigarette smoke will not eddy.

The BBC noon weather forecast continues to promise moderate north to northeast winds for this area. I am sure the old wind that carried us from the Scilly Isles to Land's End is still blowing, out clear of the coast. This condition must be purely local. The broadcast also said England was "enjoying fine summer weather, with temperatures well above normal." A bloody heat wave, in other words, with currents of warmed air rising over the land to block off the sea breeze. Maybe we'll get a squall later, or perhaps an afternoon wind will develop and blow in toward the shore. Meanwhile we are made doubly unhappy by the virtual certainty anyone astern is coming along at full speed, closing whatever gap there may be. Thus once again the hare takes an unintentional nap—and I have a premonition this is the one that puts him in the pot.

5:35 p.m.: Since coming on deck at one I have worked and schemed and fretted harder than ever before in a lifetime. The same goes for my watchmates, too. And we have gotten nowhere. Less than nowhere at times, in fact, as for short periods the tide has carried us sternwards toward the Lizard.

Yet we have not wholly lost steerageway during the watch. Always we have been creeping along, perhaps a knot, at times only a half-knot, with bare response from the helm, but always by dint of unremitting concentration we have managed to keep headed toward Plymouth and moving through the water. I have absolutely no idea how many times in the last 4 hours we have jibed spinnaker, main, and mizzen, and struck and reset the mizzen staysail. Frank, as always, has been tireless and is a real wind hawk, spotting the faintest tracery on the water so we are ready when it comes. I feel as though I am out on my feet, as punch-drunk as a fighter shuffling on his heels. Only a zephyr more true in strength and direction than any since noon is giving me this momentary respite.

All afternoon we have been having a very odd race—with an anchored bombing target. It shows prominently on chart 4449, *Lizard Head to Start Point.* Our noon position put us 1 mile due south of it, our 2:00 position 1.2 miles southeast of it, and our 3:30 position 3 miles northeast of it. Between 1:00 and 3:00 we gained when a puff lifted the spinnaker and sent bubbles astern, then it would creep up again as we went flat and the current inexorably took us astern. Only the change of the tide enabled us to drop it. As we struggled, a series of RAF planes made runs, dropping smoke bombs. Not only did we watch their marksmanship out of curiosity, but also to see if the rising smoke gave any indication of wind movement in the upper air. Nil.

Somehow this seems a hell of a way to end a 3000-mile race. But I suppose more than ever it should underline the vagaries of sailboating, and in those vagaries lies the fascination; for nothing is ever the same twice, and you can spend a lifetime studying the sea and the weather and the thousand other things which make a boat go safely and well, and still learn a new lesson on every afternoon sail. Today we work desperately and get nowhere. A competitor astern may be sliding along at close to hull speed while the crew chat in the cockpit. We know we are sailing our boat as well, for during the past 5 hours we have passed and dropped out of sight astern three small yachts. "Passed" is the word, despite our snail's pace: we are moving, and they aren't, and the tide does the rest. So to be momentarily philosophical, there are factors beyond anyone's control: the important thing from a racing point of view is to look back and know you have sailed your boat as hard as you possibly could in every condition fate sent your way; and from a sailor's point of view to know boat and crew measured up to the sea. I think we can honestly say both.

But to hell with the consolation. What we want is wind.

8:00 p.m.: Conditions unchanged. Channel absolutely still. Occasional cat's-paws keep us moving. Now the starboard watch struggles for steerageway: they have jibed again. Somehow this amazing new parachute spinnaker stays full when there is no discernible wind on the water, masthead fly, or cigarette at deck level.

Tonight the keeper of the Eddystone Light is on the job: it flashes brilliantly off to starboard. The sky is clear except for a heat haze lying over the land.

At 7:00 Frank estimated we had 13 miles to go. Basil is complaining. At this rate he will have to shave again.

"*What might be called the 'navigator's moment' is near at hand. Day after day Frank has been squinting at the sun and stars, calling 'Mark!'... But now he has to put up. He says the Scilly Isles lie ahead. We are steering the course he directs. If he is right, we meet....*"

"For sale: one ocean racer damned cheap. Only ocean racer isn't the proper term. You can't race standing still.... there is not an iota of wind, not the slightest vagrant breath. The English Channel lies flat...."

22nd Day

50° 20′ N.
 4° 10′ W.
Run: noon to 0019: 28 miles
Average speed: 2.27 knots
Total run to finish: 2951 miles

Thursday, July 24. 2:30 a.m.: Everything seems most unnaturally still. There is not a sound, not a motion. *Caribbee* is secured alongside a floating dock in the inner harbor of Plymouth. The welcoming committee has gone ashore, the bottles of whisky and gin are put away, the shipmates lie asleep. I write in my bunk, a towel tucked around the light to keep it from disturbing Frank.

Well, it's over. At 19 minutes 40 seconds past midnight, Greenwich time, we crossed the "extension of a line between Plymouth Breakwater Fort and the Breakwater Lighthouse, leaving the Breakwater Lighthouse to starboard," as required by the Race circular. There was a brilliant flash of light on our sails, and we had finished, 21 days 3 hours 19 minutes 40 seconds after the gun fired off St. David's Head.

I had finally gone to sleep about 9:00, completely worn out from work on deck and nervous tension. Perhaps I was able to drop off when I sensed *Caribbee* beginning to move, because it was about then Dick entered in the log: "Light evening breeze from west-northwest," and the speed went up from 2.1 to 5.3, and later to 6.0. The wind veered around into the east of north, so the port watch changed from spinnaker to genoa. This carried them up to Rame Head, breeze gradually dropping, and close under

233

Penlee Point, the actual entrance to Plymouth harbor. Then the breeze dropped entirely.

I awoke from a heavy sleep when we stopped. Coming on deck I had a hard time orienting myself. It was about 11:00 and lights were everywhere. The breakwater lay about a mile and a half ahead. We were on the port tack. A very light wind blew directly off the shore.

It was strange, but there was a sort of hush on deck. I was the last man up, and I felt it as soon as I appeared. No one was speaking and even the necessary deck jobs were being done without the usual bustle and dash. The spreader lights were on, and everyone looked tense, too.

The quiet was partially a matter of the tide. Frank was running a series of cross bearings to see if a current was carrying us astern. As Dick muttered: "Anchoring now would be the final cruelty." But instead the red and white flashes of the light on the end of the breakwater seemed to be getting closer, and the bearings verified a favoring drift. Then cigarette smoke began to curl off to the east and a faint air came in from the west, almost abeam. Within seconds the genoa was down and the balloon jib up. The breeze at first was too light to lift even so light a sail. Basil took off the wire sheet with its heavy shackle and put on the very light spinnaker sheet we had been using all afternoon, a flag halyard of nylon hardly thicker than a stout fishing line. The sail lifted and we began to move, Basil tending the sheet by hand.

Without anyone saying a word we closed the gap: one mile, a half mile, a quarter of a mile. The absolute silence of concentration on deck as we willed the breeze to hold; the absolute silence of a boat stealing along over still water with a barely perceptible breeze filling her sails . . . But about 100 yards from the finish the spell was abruptly broken: the wind suddenly freshened and shifted ahead, forcing us to the starboard tack. There was pandemonium on deck as suppressed energies were released: Basil ripped out a string of curses as the sheet bit deeply into his hands; there was a stampede roughly equivalent to a herd of buffalo as the foreguy was released, sheets put in place, winches manned . . . And no sooner had we gained steerageway on the new tack than another flaw put us aback again, and the whole sequence was repeated.

Somehow, just as we crabbed around on the other tack, there was that flash of light from the fort and we were across—after waiting for the moment for three weeks we were all too busy to know it had happened.

I stood up at the wheel and stared at the fort.

We were over, we had finished.

Retrospect

~~~~~~

Marabu finished at 5:12 A.M.

I peered out the companionway about 6:00 and astern her mast was silhouetted against the dawn sky. Somehow it was one of the most unreal moments of the entire passage: the thought she had been so close behind yet we had been so completely un-aware of each other, the rim of the horizon isolating us as effectively as if we had been sailing the oceans of separate planets.

Janabel finished at 6:44 in the evening.

Both told the same story: calms, smooth seas, and light head winds. But they had shared an unusual experience. Early in the morning of Monday, July 14, 1726 miles from Bermuda, each boat sighted a sail. As reported in the British publication *Yachts and Yachting*, "*Janabel's* crew guessed the other was *Marabu*, which proved to be right. *Marabu* was coming up on the opposite tack and stayed in sight all day, always behind. On July 15th *Marabu* was sighted again, but ahead about two miles this time. Then she tacked to windward and lost about a mile, and with *Janabel* averaging 3 to 5 knots. On July 16th, after a complete calm, a slight breeze came in from the north-northeast and *Marabu* was again sighted to windward, so *Janabel* decided to head up and come up to her lest she did to them what *Janabel* had done to *Marabu* the day before from their windward position. They ended about 200 yards apart with *Janabel* ahead and wished each other good morning.

"During the 17th *Janabel* again gained on *Marabu*, who had once again passed them in the night. On July 18th *Marabu* was still close behind and all day she tacked back and forth and by nightfall began to work away to windward.

"On the 19th *Marabu* was sighted to windward and *Janabel* headed up slightly to keep her in sight, making about 7 knots. On the 20th *Marabu* appeared to be a little ahead and on the 21st she came down again with the wind slightly further ahead. Just before 8 o'clock in the morning she came under *Janabel's* stern and started to work up to her. The calms came again and they covered only 15 miles.

"On the 22nd three tired Mother Carey's chickens came aboard to break the monotony and after a rest they flew off. *Marabu* had slipped away, holding a breeze which *Janabel* seemed to have lost. Depressed, her crew launched a dinghy to see what rowing felt like again, and even a row over to a French trawler was contemplated to buy some fish. That night the breeze freshened . . ."

Thus after leaving a tiny dot in the vast Atlantic, and steering what Bligh called "direct and contrary courses" for nearly two weeks, two evenly matched and rated boats came within each other's circle of visibility at a point some hundred miles north of the great-circle course from Bermuda to England; with all the ocean to choose from, their quest for wind had led them to the same spot. Then for nine days they waged an hour-to-hour duel, first one ahead, then the other, while tension mounted.

Curiously, when they came together on the 14th both were well ahead of *Caribbee*. A comparison of the track charts shows we had pulled away during the first 3 days at about the same rate we had dropped them astern off Bermuda. Our courses had virtually overlapped while all of us had held as close to the wind as possible. But by the 6th the result of our decision to go north of the great circle became apparent as the tracks angled apart; and by the 7th we were on the Grand Banks of Newfoundland while they were almost exactly back on the original great-circle route, some 300 miles to the south.

After the 7th, *Janabel* and *Marabu* continued close to the great circle, out of sight of each other but steering approximately parallel courses, until the 9th, when *Janabel* took a tack to the north. On the 11th, *Marabu* followed, coming toward her rival on the 12th, parallelling but closing the gap during the day and night of the 13th, to be within sight the next morning.

Both had found more breeze than *Caribbee* and had escaped the heavy fog and bitter cold. So on that fateful afternoon of the fourteenth—Bastille Day—when we raised our glasses over the starboard quarter as we drank a toast to *Janabel* and the spirit of La Belle France, we were facing in the wrong direction. We should have turned to the starboard bow. And also added a pink gin for *Marabu,* off in the same direction.

For our northern course had taken us smack into a stagnant high-pressure area, as we had feared at the time. Mr. R. E. Spencer, Acting Chief of the Climatological Services Department of the U. S. Weather Bureau, confirmed our suspicions in a post-race summary by stating the "July 1952 mean high-pressure measurements reveal in a striking manner the abnormal conditions you encountered. The daily weather charts show that a high pressure center was located a little over 1000 miles east of Bermuda on the day of your departure. During the next two days it moved westward as far as Longitude 50° West. It then curved sharply northward and then northeastward so as to reach Latitude 40° North and Longitude 40° West by July 7th. The weak frontal system that caused the weather you observed between July 7th and 10th drifted eastward thereafter but primarily it simply dissipated and you came under the influence of another high-pressure area that intensified well to the east of Newfoundland beginning on the 10th. This was the high center that was destined to dominate the weather along your course for the ensuing week. This broad and fairly strong high pressure area meandered considerably but most of the time it remained well within a radius of 500 miles to the south and east of Latitude 50° North, Longitude 35° West, until July 18th; hence the very light southeast winds you encountered. From July 18th on, the high pressure area remained south and east of Latitude 45° North, Longitude 30° West and generally drifted southward, allowing stronger winds with a westerly component to be observed during a portion of the remainder of your trip. This last week was also the first time since July 5th that the customary migrating low-pressure areas moving in a general northeastward direction toward Iceland showed a central pressure of less than 1005 millibars. There is no special significance to this or any other specific central pressure value but it does give an indication that the relatively weak intensity of the migratory low-pressure areas combined with the high center to establish pressure gradients that would not be associated with winds helpful to you"—the final sentence a fine piece of scientific understatement.

So we had shivered and flopped around in our private vacuum while *Marabu* and *Janabel* kept moving, slowly, it is true, but somewhat more surely, because it took us until noon of the 16th to arrive at a point almost exactly north of where they had been on the 14th. But then a breeze arrived to release us from bondage, and we rapidly narrowed their lead. After the next 24 hours we were only a little behind; by noon of the 18th we had gone ahead; and each succeeding day opened the gap wider—until the final day, when they closed with a rush while we lay dead in the glassy waters behind Lizard Head.

But when *Janabel* had not arrived after the combined crews of *Marabu* and *Caribbee* had finished lunch, we knew we were not only First to Finish but First in Class I. There remained only the smaller boats, *Joliette* and *Samuel Pepys*, and we would know the over-all winner of the best corrected time in fleet.

We spent the afternoon sampling the product of the Gin Factory—literally—in a wonderful old building which had housed the Pilgrim Fathers while they readied the *Mayflower* for sea; and then wandered through the streets of Plymouth, sadly scarred and pocked by bombing; and climbed to the Hoe, where Drake had paused in his bowling to look down on the Spanish Armada. Zib arrived from London that night and we had our first dinner ashore since Bermuda; the next morning we sailed for Cowes and spent that night anchored off The Castle of the Royal Yacht Squadron; and the next day drove up to London.

It was slightly unreal to remember at times while all this was going on we were still racing: that the race did not end until the last boat had crossed the line.

What of *Samuel Pepys,* that recurrent question during our passage east?

"*Caribbee's* plan, we felt sure, would favour the boldest course," afterward wrote Erroll Bruce in *Blackwood's Magazine.* "Driven northwards by the anti-cyclonic easterlies she would make for the Gulf Stream, whose warm current, besides helping her to the east, should upset the balance of the air and breed gales. Soon after that she would brave a thousand miles of ocean in which icebergs drift in mid-summer, having broken away from the Labrador coast in May. Within this thousand miles of anxiety she would cross the Grand Banks, the richest fishing ground in the world, which stretches a couple of hundred miles from Newfoundland's Cape Race. Here, in July, almost continual fog could be expected. Then on past the Flemish Cap into the mid-ocean wastes, far north of the main shipping routes, and an area where the chart legend states 'Winds usually westerly and often stormy.' This route would be considerably longer than the direct route on the Great Circle, and longer, too, than the rhumb line or straight route traced on the chart, which leads south of the Gulf Stream, clear of fog, ice, and areas of high gale expectations.

"The northern route would offer the minimum of comfort to the crew of any small sailing craft, while it was only a reasonable gamble that it would give a faster passage in the uncertainties of the Western Ocean. Yet the odds were in favour of this more difficult course, and since we felt certain that it would be taken by *Caribbee,* it must obviously be our plan as well. 'Know ye not,' wrote Saint Paul to the men of Corinth, 'that they which run in a race run all, but one receiveth the prize? So run that ye may win.'"

So *Samuel Pepys* slammed across the line with the set determination of sailing the northern route, properly analyzing our plan, undertaken in the hope of shaking loose from the *Pepys* and finding more wind. A few minutes before the start, unrecorded in my personal log but not forgotten by either boat, during a shouted exchange of farewells and good wishes I had bet the red socks I was wearing—mementos of a successful Southern Ocean Racing Circuit campaign the previous winter, beginning with the Ft. Lauderdale–Cat Cay Race—against a red stocking cap being worn by Ian Quarrie, one of the *Pepys* crew. And the *Pepys* was collectively after those socks with a fierce determination.

They had been uncomfortable during those first few days while we were enjoying a pleasant sail: such is the principal reward of waterline length. While we were airy and cool below and relatively dry on deck, they were battened down and oil-skinned as they drove hard in our wake. Yet this was precisely *Caribbee's* best going, and we literally ran away from the *Pepys* as shown by an analysis of the race prepared by Erroll Bruce to assist me in writing this "Retrospect." "For the first few days a high-pressure center to the east of Bermuda gave easterly winds that drove all the yachts on fast reaches to the northward, some swinging northeastward as the wind veered. After 5 days of this fast going the various race strategies were well established. *Caribbee* was clear away and up to the north on the Tail of the Grand Banks; the other two of her class were close to each other on the Great Circle; *Joliette* was also on the Great Circle some 200 miles behind them. *Samuel Pepys* was roughly in the track of *Caribbee*, although she was aiming further to the north, and was over 300 miles astern; up to that time *Samuel Pepys* had accumulated a handicap of 20 hours from *Caribbee*, and as no yacht in the race could sail 300 miles in 20 hours she was a long way behind.

"During the later part of this period a wave formed in the frontal system near *Samuel Pepys* causing a strong enough local gale to put her under bare poles for an hour or two. This wave might have developed into a depression and set off the normal sequence of low-pressure centers that would have given prevailing westerly winds for the rest of the race; however, the high-pressure system was too firmly established, so the wave dissipated and instead a weak frontal system drifted eastward for the next three days, giving all the yachts very light variable head winds and much fog. None covered much distance during these three days, but *Caribbee* more than held her own on the rest of her class; by then she owed *Samuel Pepys* some 30 hours of handicap and was better than 400 miles ahead.

"The 10th of July was the critical day of the race. A very high pressure center formed to the east of Newfoundland, and *Caribbee* was just about in its midst, so there was nothing she could possibly do to help her position. Aboard *Samuel Pepys* we made a good guess that this dead area was ahead and decided to turn 70 degrees to starboard pointing at Africa; we abandoned the northern route, and made for the Great Circle route 200 miles away to gain the benefit of the Gulf Stream current. I knew quite well that this would bring me hundreds of miles astern of those already on the Great Circle track, but the strategy was entirely based on beating *Caribbee*, and I reckoned to out-sail the others with still 2000 miles to go."

Part of Erroll Bruce's decision to turn to the southward was due to a dramatic occurrence, a one-in-ten million chance fate put in his way, and the crew of the *Pepys* rightly figured as an omen. As related in *Blackwood's Magazine:* "At noon I was still undecided which way to turn, when Larney reported the fog clear, with an aircraft circling many miles to the southeast. From the lower cross-trees the binoculars disclosed two masts of a ship, with between them two black shapes, made to look enormous by some mirage effect, signalling a ship not under command. We sailed off toward her with a quiet breeze coming up out of the east.

"It was three hours before we got close enough to distinguish all the details of a freighter of some five thousand tons, lying across the wind and sounding blasts of her siren as we were sighted. 'What are you going to do, Skipper,' asked the mate; 'take her in tow, or hoist her inboard?' It was hard to know what a tiny yacht, without even an auxiliary engine, could do for a ship a thousand times her size and many hundred miles from any land. Yet she was making every effort to attract attention. The question needed no answer when another ship was sighted coming up from the west. However, the incident had solved the previous problem of which route we should take. Having beaten twelve miles back to the southeast, it seemed an omen that we should abandon the northern route and make back for the Great Circle . . ."

So back went the *Pepys* while *Caribbee* "suffered many days of calm on the northern route, floating in a foggy sea right in the middle of the near-stationary anticyclone." As the analysis continued, "Until 16th July this high center kept station somewhere between the main truck and mizzen head of *Caribbee,* putting her way back a day and a half astern of her class mates, who were sailing in sight of each other. *Samuel Pepys* complained of light head winds, but since her drastic alteration of plan she had nearly held her own on the southern group without calling on handicap; she also shortened the lead of *Caribbee* to 320 miles while her handicap allowance had increased to 56 hours, so there was very little between them, although on 16th July *Samuel Pepys* just led on handicap.

"By this time *Caribbee* had at last outpaced the high center, which had drifted to the south towards the Azores, where it ought have been all along. This gave all the big-class yachts a good breeze abaft the beam; they had converged on each other, until on 17th July *Marabu* and *Janabel* in company were a hundred miles on the beam of *Caribbee,* to the south of her. At the same time the small class felt the wind, but being well to the westward, they had it before the beam to give a fast reach.

"With the high pressure center back near the Azores, the stage was cleared for the usual North Atlantic depressions to move along their northeasterly tracks toward Iceland and bring in some variety, besides more light patches. By the 22nd July, *Caribbee* had outsailed her class rivals and was nearly a hundred miles dead ahead of them; relative to *Samuel Pepys,* she was 460 miles ahead with about 90 hours to give away. As *Samuel Pepys* had averaged 5 knots over the course, the advantage probably lay with *Caribbee* after allowing for handicap, but it was a very close thing indeed.

"The Azores high was still determined to take a hand in the race, and pushed out a ridge that reached across the center of England, so *Caribbee* was cursed with an English Channel drift on her last day and took 17 hours to cover the last 45 miles from the Lizard to Plymouth; this affected all the yachts to varying degrees, and that day *Samuel Pepys,* 450 miles to the westward, only covered 45 miles in 24 hours. But under the Royal Ocean Racing Club rules calms benefit the low-rating yacht.

"During the next 4 days, *Samuel Pepys* was driven very hard, knowing to the minute what time she must finish to beat *Caribbee,* while the large class could do nothing but wait for the result. During three of these days the wind was brisk, and well exceeded the mean wind speed throughout the race."

Erroll Bruce and his mates, crouched in the tiny cabin of *Samuel Pepys,* had heard the report of our finish when they were nearly 500 miles off the coast of England. "About dawn I turned the radio to the first news broadcast we had heard since sailing," he wrote in *Blackwood's Magazine.* "Even the man just off duty from the middle watch woke with a start when a yacht's name was mentioned. *Caribbee* had finished the race a couple of hours before, while both other big yachts had been sighted in the English Channel. There was an impatient hush as I fumbled with slide-rule and handicap list, before announcing the situation. 'We must finish by 6:28 P.M. on Monday to beat *Caribbee*. That's four days and twelve hours, with four hundred and fifty-one miles to go.'

"An excited babble of conversation broke out at this good news. 'Only a hundred miles a day,' said Ian. 'We can't miss those red socks.' But I had previously heard the shipping weather forecast and broke up the dawn hilarity by snapping at the mate. That forecast was right. An hour later the wind failed, to leave the boat scarcely making headway, with a ten-foot-high swell running from the northwest. Never has a calm been more trying. For hour after hour she averaged less than two knots; sometimes she stopped altogether with the sea's glassy surface frosted by drizzle."

So the crew of the *Pepys* had their private hell of calm and slatting, too, but then a north-northeast breeze came fresh and cold from a clear sky, sending them boiling across the miles. "Hour by hour our chances improved, but we could still be becalmed or held by a foul tide in the Channel. With the sun scarcely obscured since dawn, and visibility at its clearest, navigation was no problem. Already we knew to within a few minutes when I could climb up on to the boom and see land. Yet that in no way lessened the thrill of the landfall on the twenty-sixth day since leaving land astern. It mattered not a jot then whether we were first or last in the race; we had crossed the Atlantic with our own efforts, and England was in sight."

The sea smoothed but the wind held; the tiny *Samuel Pepys* drove for the Lizard as the sun set and lights began to flash along the coast, as they have gleamed for other generations of Englishmen homeward-bound. "The coast of Cornwall grew closer in the darkness, until the sea was quite calm, but the cliffs of Mullion kept much of the wind, too. As she dropped back to four knots, and then to three, anxiety increased with only another hour before the tide turned against us at the Lizard. Minutes felt like hours, and I imagined her held in bond for another six hours until the tide turned again in our favor. . . . We might yet be becalmed, the wind was so light. But once clear of the cliffs the wind came again briskly. . . ."

Samuel Pepys finished at 9:35:05 in the morning of Monday, July 28th, 4 days 8 hours 15 minutes 25 seconds behind *Caribbee* on a boat-for-boat basis, but 6 hours 44 minutes 55 seconds ahead on corrected time. She had covered that last lap from Lizard Head to Plymouth Breakwater in 9 hours 15 minutes—with all the vicissitudes of 3000 miles of open Atlantic, the final 40-odd in sheltered water could be the margin of victory. Thus sailboat racing. The hare's final unintentional nap was indeed the one that put him in the pot.

In London on Monday after lunch I took a taxi to the club-house of the Royal Ocean Racing Club. Posted on the bulletin was the final score:

CLASS I

Yacht	*Finished*			*Elapsed Time*				*Corrected Time*			
	hr.	min.	sec.	day	hr.	min.	sec.	day	hr.	min.	sec.
Caribbee	01	19	40	21	03	19	40	17	11	48	49
	24 July										
Marabu	05	12	00	21	07	12	00	17	21	24	29
	24 July										
Janabel	18	44	10	21	20	44	10	17	23	10	32
	24 July										

CLASS III

Samuel Pepys	09	35	05	25	11	35	05	17	05	03	54
	28 July										
Joliette	22	11	20	25	00	11	20	17	22	34	32
	27 July										

After a look I sent Erroll Bruce and his crew a telegram at Plymouth. "Congratulations from all aboard *Caribbee*. Red socks being washed."

The Trans-Atlantic Race of 1952 was over.

Acknowledgments

I wish to thank the following authors and publishers for permission to quote or otherwise use material: Alfred F. Loomis and William Morrow and Company for extracts from *Ocean Racing;* Uffa Fox and Charles Scribner's Sons for material from *Sailing, Seamanship and Yacht Construction;* Ivan Tannehill and the Princeton University Press for quotations from *Hurricanes;* Charles L. Petze, Jr., and Motor Boating Publishing Company for quotations from *The Evolution of Celestial Navigation;* Bill Smart, editor of *Yachts and Yachting,* for extracts from the news columns of that magazine; Commander Erroll Bruce, Royal Navy, and *Blackwood's Magazine* for excerpts from the article *Trans-Atlantic* in the October 1952 issue and John S. Colman and W. W. Norton and Company, Inc., for background information from *The Sea and Its Mysteries.* In addition, those anonymous benefactors of mankind who compile the various government publications summarizing all that is known of the sailor's three-deck world: the surface of the sea, the ocean of atmosphere above, and the hidden depths.

Also, I wish to acknowledge the contribution of R. E. Spencer, Acting Chief, Climatological Services Division of the United States Department of Commerce Weather Bureau, in preparing a summary of weather over the North Atlantic during the period covered by this book; R. E. Lenozyk, Office of the Commander,

United States Coast Guard, International Ice Patrol, Woods Hole Oceanographic Institute, for a description of ice conditions for the same period, as well as background information on the Ice Patrol, and the usual behavior of drift ice; and Commander Erroll Bruce, Royal Navy, for an analysis of the race and over-all strategy from the viewpoint of *Samuel Pepys*.

The illustrations of *Caribbee* under sail are reproduced by courtesy of the following photographers: Facing page 16, the Bermuda News Bureau. Page 64, left, Beken and Son, Cowes; right, Vaudine Herbster, Annapolis. Page 65, right, Marion Warren, Annapolis. Also, photographs upper left page 32 and page 193 are by Frank MacLear.

And finally, I desire to thank Alfred F. Loomis and Henry K. Rigg for checking the manuscript prior to publication.

C. M.

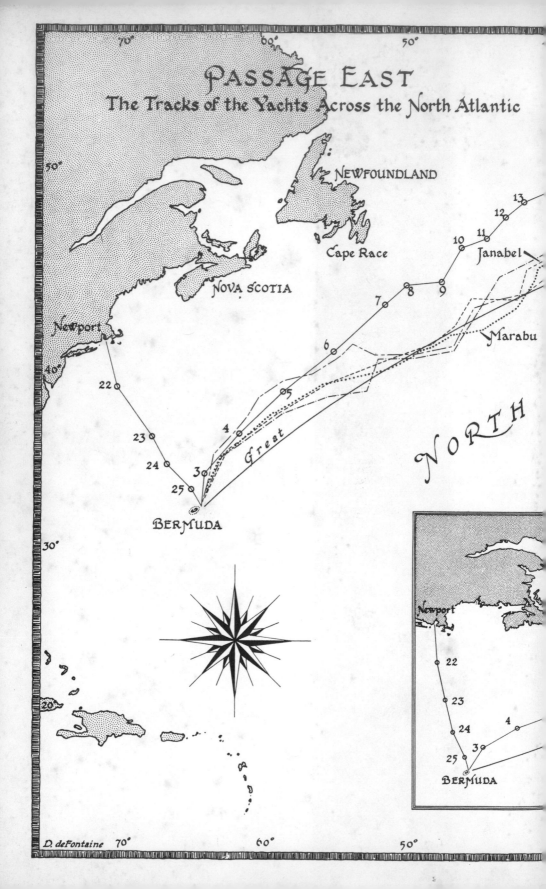

PASSAGE EAST
The Tracks of the Yachts Across the North Atlantic